WILDEBEEST
in a RAINSTORM

Also by Jon Bowermaster

Governor

Saving the Earth

Crossing Antarctica

The Adventures and Misadventures of Peter Beard in Africa

Birthplace of the Winds

Alone Against the Sea

Descending the Dragon

For Young Adults

Over the Top of the World

Aleutian Adventures

WILDEBEEST
in a RAINSTORM

Profiles of Our Most Intriguing Adventurers,
Conservationists, Shagbags and Wanderers

MENASHA RIDGE PRESS

JON BOWERMASTER

MENASHA RIDGE PRESS
www.menasharidge.com

Your Guide to the Outdoors Since 1982

First published in the United States of America in 2009 by Menasha Ridge Press.

MENASHA RIDGE PRESS

P.O. Box 43673
Birmingham, AL 35243
USA
www.menasharidge.com

Library of Congress Cataloguing-in-Publication Data:

Bowermaster, Jon, 1954– .

Wildebeest in a Rainstorm: Profiles of Our Most Intriguing Adventurers, Conservationists, Shagbags and Wanderers.

by Jon Bowermaster – 1st ed.
p. cm.

ISBN-13: 978-0-89732-689-6
ISBN-10: 0-89732-689-X

Environmentalists–Biography. 2. Adventure and adventurers–Biography. I. Title.
GE55.B69 2009
333.72092'2–dc22

2008052458

EDITOR: Jack Heffron
DESIGNER: Fiona Stewart
Printed in the United States of America
Distributed by Publishers Group West

FOR FIONA

INTRODUCTION

During the past twenty-plus years, I've been privileged to travel the world, often in the company of some of the most high-profile, committed, hell-bent, hot-headed, and more than occasionally wacky characters in the outdoor world: conservationists, adventurers and explorers, entrepreneurs, sportsmen, politicos, and scientists. Their unrelenting commitment to accomplishing big things is inspiring, but their eccentricities are electric, too—and, yes, they are all eccentrics. Think about it. Mike Fay walked across the Congo forest armed only with a machete. Will Steger dogsledded 3,741 miles across Antarctica. Doug Tompkins has bought 2.5 million acres of South American forest (and counting) in a struggle to preserve it. Renée Askins fought tooth and nail to bring wolves back to the American West, against armed and sexist opposition. Titouan Lamazou sailed around the world solo faster than anyone had before without stopping, carrying premade casts for his arms and legs so that if one were broken he wouldn't have to stop. These are big thinkers and big doers.

I have also witnessed less publicized but no less successful efforts. Winona LaDuke went back to her Minnesota reservation to try to buy back long-lost lands for her community. Wangari Maathai planted trees across Kenya to put women to work and preserve a fragile environment. Brady Watson plunged deep into Nicaraguan forests to talk war-ravaged settlers into leaving the equally ravaged trees alone. Claudio Cristino set Easter Island's *moai* back on their feet after they'd been knocked down by warring tribes and tsunami waves. Sir Richard Branson - the admitted heir to P. T. Barnum - has never hesitated at getting his own message heard.

All have paid a price for their commitment. David Brower was fired by every environmental group he started. Bobby Kennedy Jr. has won more environmental battles than he's lost, but despite his hard work and good name, has endured both psychic and physical scars. No one sacrificed more than Ned Gillette, who was shot to death at a time when he could have assumed his most risky adventures were behind him.

What binds these individuals is their willingness to keep pushing against often monstrous opposition. Perhaps my most intense reporting assignment came in 1991, when I spent several months in East Africa with photographer/conservationist/Tarzan-with-a-brain Peter Beard. We were working on a book; my mission was to travel back with him to some of the places he'd wandered and documented during his forty years in Kenya. Along the way he reunited us with the *crème de la crème* of African wildlife managers and conservationists; Peter has always had a way of befriending the very best of men and women.

He moved to Africa in the early 1960s because he loved the romance of the place, turned on as a teenager by Karen Blixen's *Out of Africa*. Over his several decades on the continent, he came to love the place itself, even as he was often disappointed by its people and their impact on it. Over the years, he'd been jailed by thug-politicians intent on forcing him out of his adopted home so that they could seize his valuable property and watched the once-rich game parks suffer from mismanagement, all the while photographing and filming what he profoundly dubbed *The End of the Game*. By the time I traveled Kenya with him, the rapid rise of the human population was threatening to destroy his version of paradise forever. We camped out at his Hog Ranch, which overlooks Karen Blixen's coffee farm. Local crime had forced him to employ round-the-clock armed watchmen. Several of his neighbors would be murdered in their suburban Nairobi homes. The most profound sound echoing through the valley at night was no longer the roar of lions but the howling of hundreds of roaming junkyard dogs.

One dusk, sitting by an open fire as Beard worked on his "life-thickening" diaries, I asked how he managed to stay optimistic about Kenya even as he watched it transform and suffer. His response was pure Beard: "I just hunker down like a wildebeest in a rainstorm. You just put your head down . . . and wait. When the rain stops, the sun invariably returns."

Like a wildebeest in a rainstorm. Each one of the characters profiled here has endured and grown and learned from their own passions and disillusionments. Yet each has pressed on, kept pessimism at bay, and ultimately accomplished what they set out to do.

"My biggest whine?" Beard continued as the sun set over the Masai Mara. "It's all gone by too fast."

—Jon Bowermaster, Stone Ridge, New York

ACKNOWLEDGMENTS

*None of these profiles would exist without the support
of a network of great editors, who over the years allowed
me to introduce the occasional odd character to their pages.
In no particular order, thank you to Deborah Kirk,
Klara Glowczewska, Ted Moncreiff, Bruce Weber,
Alex Ward, John Rasmus, Jann Wenner, Michael Robbins,
Roger Cohn, Graham Boynton, Tom Wallace, Chris Connelly,
Susan Lyne, and Mark Bryant. Thanks also to my agent
of twenty-plus years, Stuart Krichevsky and his officemates
Shana Cohen and Kathryne Wick, as well as the team at
Menasha Ridge Press, especially editor Jack Heffron.*

CONTENTS

THE CONSERVATIONISTS

Promises to Keep • *David Brower* *15*

Earth of a Nation • *Winona LaDuke* *25*

Endangered Species • *George Schaller* *35*

Mega-Paddle • *Michael Fay* *43*

Take This Park and Shove It • *Doug Tompkins* *53*

Cry Wolf • *Renée Askins* *66*

Great Expectations • *Robert F. Kennedy Jr.* *73*

Rumormongering Among the Insectheads • *Wangari Maathai* *92*

Is Carol Browner in Over Her Head? • *Carol Browner* *95*

Heaven Can Wait • *Brady Watson* *105*

After the Fall • *Claudio Cristino* *113*

THE ARTISTES

Wild Man in Africa • *Peter Beard* *127*

Rebuilding Peter Beard • *Peter Beard* *141*

Bad Blood • *George Butler* *149*

Bones of Contention • *Gillies Turle* *161*

THE SPORTSMEN

The Great Lamazou • *Titouan Lamazou* *171*

A Man for All Seasons • *Sir Richard Branson* *185*

Raising the Stakes • *Will Steger* *197*

Murder in the Karakoram • *Ned Gillette* *211*

Uphill Racer • *A. J. Kitt* *223*

Warren Miller Reels 'em In • *Warren Miller* *233*

Happiness Is Being Single! • *Jake Burton Carpenter* *244*

THE CONSERVATIONISTS

*"My credo? 'There is only one ocean, though its coves have
many names and a single sea of atmosphere with no coves at all.'
This is the only planet we have and we need a renewed stirring
of love for the Earth. Today we must have an ecological
conscience in every sphere of human activity. Every one.
There can't be any exceptions. We're all on this planet and we've
got to take care of it. That's what being an environmentalist is."*

—David Brower, *Promises to Keep*

PROMISES TO KEEP

David Brower

Destinations, 1995

On a warm fall night fifty friends of Friends of the Earth gather for a small reunion, to celebrate the twenty-fifth anniversary of the first office of the San Francisco-based environmental group. They mingle in the old firehouse on Pacific Street, toasting the past, railing about the present. FOE moved into this five-story building in 1969, at the invitation of a hip young ad agency called Freeman, Mander and Gossage. The combined talents of the virulent environmentalists and cutting-edge ad men proved effective and successful; within a decade Friends of the Earth would have offices in fifty-two countries.

This night, propped against the red brick walls of the entryway are blow-ups of full-page ads run in newspapers during the 1960s, 1970s, and 1980s. The ads are the trademark of Friends founder David Brower. They are smart, attention-getting, with bold headlines that made big pronouncements: "They're Killing Whales Again," "Ecology and War," "An Open Pit Big Enough to Be Seen From the Moon."

But the most evocative of all the ads is the most simple. Created in 1969, it reads: "David Brower Has Been Fired as Executive Director of the Sierra Club. To Protest, Sign Here."

It was in the unsettled days after his dismissal from the Sierra Club that Brower founded Friends of the Earth. Tonight the group's first employee, Tom Turner, remembers those good old days. From a perch on a circular staircase, he recalls the non-stop motion spurred on by the fermenting minds of ecology, protest, and publicity that always seemed to be dropping in, hanging out. "Ideas flowed, action followed, and nobody worked harder than Dave," says Turner, with a nod to the tall, snowy-haired man in the midst of the crowd. With little prodding, Dave Brower himself takes to the wrought-iron stairs. The eighty-two-year-old former climber hikes up the steps stiffly, due to a knee first strained in a 1936 skiing accident. Before dwelling on the past, he brings the crowd up to date on his activities of the past couple weeks. There were speeches at Rutgers and Oberlin ("I'm always impressed with what young people can do before older people tell them it's impossible"), followed by a trip to Ottawa where he is organizing an environmental "Council on the Americas." From there it was to Atlanta, where he was welcomed by Jimmy Carter (just returned from Haiti). The environmentalist was trying to woo the former president to sign on to his most recent undertaking, a group called simply CPR, for "Conservation, Preservation, Restoration." "I felt very privileged," says Brower, "to be meeting with the most important man on the planet on that day . . . because he helped avoid a war." An odd sentiment coming from a man who never stepped back from a good fight in defense of the wilderness.

Brower likes and respects Carter, and I understand why. Both are outsiders who have hardly faded away. Both are highly moral men who believe in doing things the right way—at least the right way as they see it. Both are principled, dogmatic, thus irritants to those who disagree with them. Both can come off as cantankerous, even contemptuous if those around them don't stand with their feet on the same moral high ground. After a couple one-liners ("Like George Burns says, 'If you're going to get old, get as old as you can get.'"), Brower recalls "many powerful and successful ideas were born here in this old firehouse." Then he turns up the oratory skills honed over years of speechmaking, fundraising, and testifying on behalf of wildness and wilderness. "I've had some successes, but no victories—just stays of execution," he suggests. "In my time all I've done is slow the rate of destruction down as things get steadily worse." Then he warns: "We don't have much more time, I don't think we have twenty years. Too many things are irrevocable. Ozone and global warming problems are just two things we still don't know enough about. We've got respected scientists saying we're in trouble, but Rush Limbaugh calms the masses by saying 'No problem, don't worry.'

"Still I remain an optimist. Everybody should be, because being a pessimist gives you no alternative except martinis."

He clambers down the stairs to warm applause and spends an hour signing copies of his autobiography. After a top-to-bottom tour of the five-story townhouse, he notes the irony that the onetime home to the seat-of-the-pants Friends office is now rented out to filmmakers and record companies for parties. It's also for sale, for a million bucks. "Oh what I would do with this building," says Brower wistfully. "I would turn it again into a place for ideas, not a disco."

It is hard to imagine anyone who has had a greater impact on the rise of environmental activism in this century than David Brower. Virtually everyone else has followed in his footsteps, followed his lead. Militant, effective, always controversial; though he was instrumental in saving the Grand Canyon, he was also fired twice as head of national environmental groups. "I am a radical by dictionary definition, but not the way the media uses the word. Radical should be regarded as good." Time and many, many battles have taken their toll. He jokes about Alzheimer's. "A long time ago I walked along the Croton aqueduct with Justice Douglas. We were trying to prove something, but I've forgotten now what it was."

The first executive director of the Sierra Club, founder of Friends of the Earth, the League of Conservation Voters, and Earth Island Institute, leader of successful campaigns to create or preserve ten national parks (including Redwoods, North Cascades, Point Reyes, and Kings Canyon), he helped stop dams across the Grand Canyon, helped to create the National Wilderness Preservation system, initiated the international Fate of the Earth Conferences and has been nominated twice for the Nobel Peace Prize. John McPhee wrote a book about Brower in the late 1960s, branding him with a moniker that has stuck—the Archdruid. Not everyone is a fan, of course—the Bureau of Reclamation called him the Antichrist. Others have described him variously as nature's own ad man, an ecological Isaiah, the sacramentarian of *ecologia americana*. In 1966 *Time* labeled him the "country's number one working conservationist." More recently, Brower acolyte and energy savant Amory Lovins calls him "our generation's Thoreau or Emerson." "Throughout his career he's kept ten years ahead of everyone else," says Lovins.

The morning after the Friends reunion, Brower is rummaging around his redwood house pitched on a hill overlooking Berkeley, San Francisco Bay, and the Golden Gate Bridge. The house—which he built in 1947—resembles the owner's mind: rambling, crowded with the detritus of a wildly interesting life. On a living room wall hang a color photograph of the Grand Canyon (which he helped save from damming) and a pair of Ansel Adams prints, "Tenaya Lake" and "Aspens, New Mexico." (The two met on a trail in the Sierras in the 1930s and became collaborators for life. It was Adams who recommended Brower for the job of Sierra Club executive director in 1952 . . . then seventeen years later led the move to have him fired.)

He has always called Berkeley, where he was born in 1912, home, though he figures he's been on the road half his adult life. This morning, Anne—his wife of forty-one years, mother of their four children—pads around in bathrobe and slippers. The Archdruid is dressed in early-fall California-wear: blue turtleneck, Patagonia climbing shorts, running shoes. Though he is 82.25 and walks rather stiffly, he still has the build of the athletic climber and long-distance hiker he was in his youth.

The living room feels truly lived in; every flat surface is covered with videos, books, boxes of papers, collected rocks, sticks, and gee-gaws picked up on trails around the globe. An issue of *Newsweek* boasting Jimmy Carter's smiling mug lies on the coffee table; so does a *National Geographic* all about the National Parks, featuring stunning pictures of a half-dozen places Brower is responsible for preserving.

As we talk the midday sun fills behind Brower's head, casting him in halo-ish soft light. It is a glow many environmentalists firmly believe he deserves. And he is a deity of sorts, though a cynical one: "Homo sapiens haven't done anything well for a thousand years except multiply," he preaches this day. And a little ego-driven: When asked to recommend good books about the environment, the first he suggests is the book about him. He is opinionated: he thinks Jimmy Carter is getting a bad post-Haiti rap. He can be surly: this morning he is still angry with Earth Island executive director John Knox for what he saw as an oversight, when the night before Knox didn't offer Earth Island president Carl Anthony an opportunity to address the crowd. "This is a very important man and I thought he slighted him." He's been known to be paranoid: to this day he is convinced that lobbying by Pacific Gas and Electric, which was trying to build Diablo Canyon, a nuclear facility on California's central coast, helped push him out of the Sierra Club. *Time* magazine reporters have interviewed him seven times in his life and yet his name has never appeared in those stories;

he's convinced it is due to his virulent anti-anti-corporation attitudes and the corporate ownership of the media, in this case Time-Life Inc. He can come off as egotistical: claiming, for example, that Al Gore's call for "a Marshall Plan for the environment" originated in a 1981 Brower stump speech. In his own defense, Brower admits he may have been tactless, disorganized, and "a bad correspondent" but blames his firing on the Sierra Club's having lost courage, engaging increasingly in twin tactics he views as debilitating the environmental movement—compromise and negotiation. "In my experience as executive director of the Sierra Club, every time we compromised, we lost; every time we didn't, we won. People need to compromise; it's reasonable in a pluralistic society where there are a great many interests. People don't agree on everything. But those compromises should not be made by advocates." A prolific and long-winded writer of letters, treatises, journey accounts, and polemics, he is the first to admit he can be "short on tact." As environmental issues have grown more complex, more "professionalized," Brower is still considered radical. Though a philosopher-king to some, he is a paranoid pain-in-the-ass to others. "After a while you just want to say, 'Dave, get real,'" says one Washington-based environmental leader.

Despite the bruises gathered from numerous intellectual battles, Brower is as in demand today as he was thirty years ago, his schedule jammed with speaking engagements, conferences, and awards banquets. "I was taught a lesson early in life," he says, "that if you hang tough, you can save things. I think I've proved that adage to be true.

"I think, if anything, that's what I've been guilty of—hanging in there. Building support, letting people know what the alternatives are, what you can do besides screw something else up. I think we've trashed enough."

To me, what makes Brower most interesting and relevant is that he truly knows and loves the places he has worked to protect. Far too many environmental pros that I know live lives that revolve around conference rooms, law offices, and cocktail fundraisers. Most have never made a stick stew while camping in the bush, or dangled precariously from a rock ledge or whitewater boulder. In his eighties, Brower gets as big a kick talking about his climbing days as he does any legal victory. "Very few of my contemporaries are still out there. A shocking thing. When I climbed Shiprock, there was a team of four; only two of us are still alive. Of the climb of Mt. Waddington, four out of eight are dead. That's pretty sad—to be missing so many people."

As a young man he established himself as a top climber, making first ascents of seventy summits. He entered college when he was sixteen, but dropped out during his second year, citing the Depression as "a convenient excuse." He still calls Yosemite "my Mecca"; McPhee claimed that if Brower were set down at night anywhere in the Sierra Nevada, with the coming of morning he would know just where he was. In 1939 Brower was the first man to reach the summit of New Mexico's spherical/mystical Shiprock. During World War II he served as an instructor for the U.S. 10th Mountain troops and saw action as a combat intelligence officer in the Italian Alps. After the war he worked as an editor at the University of California Press and volunteered as much as he could for the Sierra Club.

His initial ecological awareness began in the early 1920s, though he did not know the word ecology at the time. "We would pass through some very nice forests as we drove into the Sierras and I remember one particular spot where I went into this forest and discovered a spring.

"I came back a few years later and the place had been logged. There was no forest to speak of and there was no spring. I felt deprived and angered—who the hell did this to my forest? That was the first time I was annoyed. I was eight or nine." When Brower first joined the Sierra Club in 1933, it was primarily a loose organization of California outdoor enthusiasts who relished in taking hiking/climbing trips together into the Sierras—carrying on in the name of the founder, John Muir. It wasn't long before Brower developed a vision for the club as a potent force for what was then known as "conservation." Under his directorship—1952–1969—the club grew to seventy-seven thousand. He became expert at marshaling the club's collective influence behind many of the most important environmental causes, creating what fellow Californian Wallace Stegner dubbed "a chorus of voices for the wilderness."

"Initially we were trying to save it for the people who want to experience it. Now I'm very much concerned with saving it for the information it contains about the way the world works. Nature is the ultimate encyclopedia. It's in many languages. Some of the languages we haven't learned to read yet. The challenge is to find out how the world works—not only up in the atmosphere, but underneath. In the best of all worlds, Brower would like to see the world's population reduced and held at 5 billion; cut man's hunger for destroying natural resources; live more lightly on the planet and use technology to repair the things we've destroyed.

"Home sapiens have been around for just 300,000 years, which is a very short time. Yet we're about to wipe ourselves out, because we are so bright we're going to drown ourselves in our own cleverness. We can do it. We're well on our way."

Brower is not without regrets. While he managed to save the Grand Canyon, he did not save Glen Canyon, just upstream, which was flooded to create Lake Powell and to generate hydroelectricity. Today he still gets teary-eyed talking about that loss, which he regards the biggest of his career. "Give me back Glen Canyon and I'd leave the earth quietly."

It is perhaps Brower's use of words and pictures that is his greatest legacy. Following in the footsteps of painters like Albert Bierstadt, Charles Robinson, and Thomas Hill and writers like John Muir, Thomas Hutchings, and Wallace Stegner, he used words and images as preservation tools. Another role model was William Henry Jackson, whose late-nineteenth-century photographs of the immaculate West, carefully distributed to congressmen in Washington, helped Teddy Roosevelt create the National Park System. Brower's first "exhibit format" book was inspired by the Ansel Adams/Nancy Newhall photography exhibit "This Is the American Earth," which ran in Yosemite in 1955. The twenty-nine big picture books to follow (twenty with the Sierra Club, nine with Friends of the Earth) brought in many new members and as importantly brought the wilderness into people's homes. "In the late 1930s, when the Sierra Club was fighting to establish Kings Canyon National Park, I was twenty-six and it was really my first battle. I found two things that worked well: articles in the 'Sierra Club Bulletin' and a film. I made most of the film myself. It was just a silent color film, but it showed what the potential of Kings Canyon was, what the country was like, how it was enjoyed by Sierra Club trips, and what would happen if it wasn't saved. I toured the state and the country showing that film to as many audiences as possible. Ansel Adams put together a beautiful, large-format book too. The book had quite an effect, particularly on Franklin Roosevelt, Secretary of the Interior Harold Ickes.

We won that battle . . . it was that success that convinced me of the effectiveness of books and photographs."

Along the way, the Archdruid picked up enemies as well as accolades. By the time he was tossed from his job running the Sierra Club in 1969, he had earned the enmity of many, including some of his oldest friends. (Typical criticism: "As his success grew, he paid less and less attention to what people in the club were thinking and saying. I don't think the man changed so much as he developed. He began to think, 'I am the Sierra Club.'") His critics, concerned he would bankrupt the club, voted him out of the job; two and a half years later they made up by unanimously voting him honorary vice president. Today, Brower explains that dismissal—devastating at the time—this way: "A ship in harbor is safe," he likes to say, "but that is not what ships are built for."

As we talk, Brower delves into various piles and boxes of papers, searching for evidence to support his claims and theories. His collection of overflowing boxes of papers is currently being inventoried by the University of California-Berkeley's Bancroft Library. They estimate there are enough to fill a room eleven stories tall. We attempt to count just the groups Brower is credited with starting.

"It's hard, isn't it?" he ponders. "For example, I started Friends of the Earth, and it's now in fifty-two countries. Is that fifty-two groups I started? To be honest, I don't know the exact number: let's just say quite a few."

Friends of the Earth was begun a month after Brower was fired by the Sierra Club; its charge was to be more politically and legislatively active, involved in protest of nuclear power and to "charge ahead with publishing and damn the torpedoes." Built at first on the strength of his name and his connections, Friends grew rapidly and in what was becoming a pattern, he was forced from its board in 1979.

Rebounding from that dismissal, and borrowing from Margaret Mead's reference to "the island earth," in 1982 he founded the Earth Island Institute. Its stated goal was "to add ecological consciousness to all spheres of human activity." Today it supports a number of small but potent grass-roots campaigns, and is regarded one of the most successful extreme environmental groups in the country. Brower is the group's chairman and keeps an office at its San Francisco headquarters.

Never satisfied concentrating on just one thing, Brower's newest project, the one for which he was trying to enlist Jimmy Carter, is called Global CPR. He has enlisted a long list of international environmental heavies to lend their name to its masthead, and he is planning a "Restoration Fair" for the spring of 1995. That should correspond with publication of the third volume of his quasi-autobiography, this titled *Let the Mountains Speak and the Rivers Run.* "I'm most interested right now in restoration, trying to put back together as much as we can of the things we've carelessly torn apart in the industrial age," he says. "Science is not saving us at all; it's creating far more problems than it is solving. The handiest examples are two things they thought were totally benign—PCBs and CFCs. They claimed these were benign solutions.

"Now they're claiming that bio-engineering is benign; well, you just know they are going to come up with something really horrible that results from that."

He understands his role as a leader of the extreme, on hand to keep pushing the edges of the envelope. "If the Sierra Club isn't doing what I want, I start another organization. If Friends of the Earth isn't, I start another. To see if I can, by setting a new example, have some influence on what the Sierra Club does, or Friends of the Earth does. And to a certain extent, that has worked, and it needs to work right now, especially."

Though an honorary vice president of the Sierra Club, which required a unanimous vote, and back on its board of directors, he can still be critical of the group. "The club is so eager to appear reasonable that it goes soft, undercuts the strong grass-roots efforts of chapters, groups, and other organizations—as if the new professionalization and prioritization requires rampant tenderization." As the sun peaks, filling the room with midday light, Brower gets ready to head down the hill to do what he can in the minutes, days, months, years he's got left. Standing, he remembers the words of Nancy Newhall, whose text graced many of Ansel Adams's photo books: "Conservation is humanity caring for the future."

"My credo? 'There is only one ocean, though its coves have many names and a single sea of atmosphere with no coves at all.' This is the only planet we have and we need a renewed stirring of love for the Earth.

Today we must have an ecological conscience in every sphere of human activity. Every one. There can't be any exceptions. We're all on this planet and we've got to take care of it. That's what being an environmentalist is."

On that note, Brower is off to change into sport coat and slacks. Katie McGinty, environmental adviser to President Clinton, is visiting the Earth Island office this afternoon and he doesn't want to miss an opportunity to say hello, to offer some counsel to the counselor . . . to continue the conversation.

David Brower died of cancer in 2000, at his Berkeley home. He was 88. Today the Sierra Club has 675,000 members, Friends of the Earth one million members internationally. Russell Train, EPA Administrator under President Nixon, said at his death, "Thank God for Dave Brower; he makes it so easy for the rest of us to be reasonable."

EARTH OF A NATION
Winona LaDuke
Harper's, 1993

The sky is royal blue, the kind of blue only extreme cold can create. Deep snow crunches underfoot and the tall trees, mostly white birches and Norway pines, sway in the winds that sweep across northern Minnesota in the dead of winter. It is ten degrees below zero.

Winona LaDuke, wrapped warmly in white jeans, rubber boots, parka, and beaver-skin headband, stands in the middle of the snow and looks up at the tall trees bending. But for the wind, it is quiet all around. "Listen," she says softly. "Listen."

If there is a theme to the young life of Winona Helena Basha LaDuke, it is "listen." Listen to the experiences of your ancestors. Listen to your predecessors in the modern-day fight of Indians around the world trying to regain lost lands. Listen to the politicians and carpetbaggers, the white men and women, even the rednecks (including those who insist on referring to your people as "timber niggers"). Listen to the Ivy League academics, the environmentalists and human rights activists. Listen to them all, then act. If you've listened well, when you act, it will make a difference.

LaDuke's little red cabin sits on Round Lake, in the southeastern corner of the White Earth Indian Reservation. She is the only Indian living on the lake; most of her tribe of Ojibwe live nearby, on lands owned by the tribal council and managed by the federal government, in trailer homes or HUD-built, low-cost, low-quality housing. This is the first winter her cabin has been insulated.

Inside, the four-room house is marked by the clutter of a single parent trying to raise two small children (Wasayben, four, and Ajuuak, two). A children's-sized teepee sits in front of a television and VCR. The walls are decorated with Indian poster art, the bookshelves (boards on cinder blocks) overflow, with everything from Jerry Rubin's *Do It* to *Raising Small Livestock*. The wastebaskets are made of birch bark, the blankets a bright Navajo weave.

Part Ojibwe, part Russian Jew, Harvard-educated and grass roots trained, LaDuke is a leader in the loosely connected, emerging class of Indian women organizing to preserve Indian lands and culture. Ten years ago she returned to the reservation where her father was born, committed to helping her community escape the poverty and refugee status that is the accepted, if unfortunate, way of life for Indians on reservations across the country. Using skills and political instinct developed working on other reservations and in the halls of the Ivy League (her degree from Harvard is in economic development; she also attended MIT and has a master's degree in rural development from Antioch), her White Earth Land Recovery Project is a novel approach to reacquiring Indian land for Indians. Marrying processes refined by groups like the Nature Conservancy and various rainforest action groups, her goal is simple: to return land that once belonged to the Ojibwe, and simultaneously to help them develop a sustainable economy to pull them up from poverty.

She describes herself as simply "an organizer." (Louise Erdrich, her friend of a half dozen years, calls her a "true hero." Fellow indigenous organizer Tom Goldtooth calls Winona "our ambassador.")

This day, she appears to be wearing a dozen hats. She is scurrying more than usual because tomorrow she goes on the road with the Indigo Girls for a three-city "Honor the Earth" fundraiser organized by LaDuke to benefit the Indigenous Women's Network, of which she is president. She follows that up with one-day speaking commitments at the University of Illinois and University of Wisconsin, and then she is off to the University of Oregon for three months to teach a course on International Human Rights. She plans to be back on the reservation by the time the wild rice season begins in June. She is thin and olive-skinned, with deep-set eyes and an unexpected, deep-throated laugh. A colorful beaded pin holds up her jet-black hair. We talk over breakfast of bannock, locally produced maple syrup, chokecherries, and yogurt.

"Before us, most people felt there wasn't anything they could do to get their land back. They'd been told so many times that somebody else will take care of it for you, or don't even try, but we had quite a few hundred supporters. When you have five hundred Indians turn up at a council meeting, that's very substantial on a reservation.

"[We're] trying to preserve it because it is our culture. Our land, this land, reaffirms us, makes us who we are, and gives us the instructions that form our lives. If you lose control of your land, you become awash, you lose your essence."

The White Earth Reservation is 837,000 acres of pine, rolling hills, hardwoods, more than five hundred lakes, and prairie—thirty-six miles by thirty-six miles—1,300 square miles; only 6 percent, 53,100 acres, is owned by the tribe. About four thousand Ojibwe live on the reservation. The unemployment rate is about 80 percent; median income for Indians is $2,500. The res's number one product appears to be not timber or wild rice, but poverty.

It has long been regarded an unquantifiable mess, its land sold, stolen, or taken by non-Indians over the past ninety years, resulting in a patchwork where Indians and non-Indians live shoulder to shoulder in confusion and conflict.

The treaty between U.S. and Ojibwe established White Earth in 1867. Twenty years later settlers demanded it be opened to whites. In 1887 the General Allotment Act subdivided reservations into 80- and 160-acre tracts and allotted them to individuals or families. Within twenty years, the White Earth Reservation had largely been traded by threat, dupe, or drink for tin money, old horses, used pianos, and other worthless junk. In 1889, the Nelson Act called for Indians to give up reservations for their own safety and protection. From that point forward, the reservation as bastions for Indians was forever lost. Lumber companies, railroads, and myriad other carpetbaggers grabbed Indian lands, mostly by duping the uneducated Indians into turning over their land.

By 1904, 99 percent of the land had been divided into individual parcels. Within twenty years more than 700,000 acres had been "removed" from Indian ownership by a complex system of tax forfeitures, minor and full-blood sales, and numerous illegal transactions. Lumber companies moved in and cleared the pine forests; Indians who stayed were forced into poverty and disease. Economic ruin overtook the tribe that called itself "Anishinabe," the Original People. By 1934 only 7,890 acres remained in Indian hands.

By the 1930s over half of the tribe had been forced to flee the reservation, most to big cities, from Minneapolis to Los Angeles. Today, only four thousand of the twenty thousand enrolled tribal members still live on the reservation, surrounded by non-Indian landholders. Unemployment is high, and so are arrest records; education and life expectancy are low. Paupers on a rich land.

The modern-day fight to get the land back has pitted Indian against Indian, small farmers against bureaucrats, and politicians against their constituencies. No one argues that Indians were wrongfully deprived of their land, yet no one could agree on how to correct the injustice. Until LaDuke's White Earth Land Recovery Project.

The one constant is that the majority of Indians living on the reservation have maintained a relationship to the land. More than three-quarters hunt deer and many hunt ducks, geese, and small animals; over half harvest wild rice and maple syrup, fish, leeches, or pick berries and materials for baskets and handicrafts. But since they control so little of the land, they are often accused (or arrested for) trespassing on federal, state, county, or private lands.

LaDuke returned to the reservation in 1982 (to be, at twenty-three, a high school principal; the job lasted just six months; "I was still a kid, too," she laughs). She joined with traditionalists on the reservation bent on recovering land. In 1988, with a twenty-thousand-dollar Reebok Human Rights Award, she started the White Earth Land Recovery Project (WELRP), intent on suing, cajoling, and even paying cash to get back Indian land. One-third of the reservation was owned by the federal, county, and state governments. Another third was owned by big corporations, mostly lumber companies. The rest was in the hands of small farmers and resort home-owners from Fargo and the Twin Cities.

It was a novel approach, far different from the warrior-with-a-gun approach that is too often the image people have of Indians fighting for their land. She cites as her models the Nature Conservancy, the Rain-forest Action Network, and the Trust for Public Lands. "The goal is to develop an integrated program which will get them land back, provide resource for local economy, embark on educational programs for Indians and non-Indians alike, and to strengthen relationships with communities on reservations."

The long-term goal is recovery of one-third of the reservation in the next twenty years; LaDuke says 750 acres a year would be fine. Priorities are burial grounds or other areas of cultural importance, lands containing endangered species or medicinal plants, and lands that can be used for long-term, sustainable development.

"It is impossible to preserve and manage our natural resources with no control over our land base, and it is impossible to develop a comprehensive economic-development program without access to our full resources. We must consolidate our land base if we are to plan for the future of our community."

Today what started out as a land conservancy has turned into full-fledged economic and cultural development. While acquiring land is the first priority, it is followed closely by efforts to build an economy for the Indians. With LaDuke's encouragement, a wild rice cooperative was started. The same is planned for sugar bushing and leeching. They're looking at buying a berry farm to be worked by natives. In the winter most of the Indians on the reservation still hunt for food.

The WELRP has also started education programs and encouraged law school interns to come and research burial grounds, title issues, and policy options. Work with the Trust for Public Lands to develop a long-term acquisition campaign. Its nearly $200,000 annual budget comes from foundations, churches, and individuals. "I do a lot of begging," admits LaDuke. So far the project has reacquired just over one thousand acres, including a forty-acre burial site near the village of Pine Point, a 121-acre woodland on the northern edge of the res, and 715 acres of farmland and timber in Becker County. She has the mixed blessing of the reservation's tribal council, which has a penchant for controlling things on the reservation. She admits she works harder than most of her Harvard classmates for less money, but that she's happier.

"A lot of our work is about recovering the land itself, but it's also about recovering and preserving that relationship. Because colonialism, the church, development plans, and American notions of progress and of standards of living defined by income rather than quality of life are things that begin to permeate our value system."

Her father, Vincent LaDuke, was the son of an Ojibwe man and woman of German/Norwegian stock. Born in 1929 just south of Lengby, in Mahnomen County, north of the Wild Rice River, he attended LaDuke

School on the reservation. When he was fifteen, he appeared before the White Earth Tribal Council and tried to tell the members how to manage the tribe's resources better by encouraging self-sufficiency. When land was privately allotted, the LaDukes owned fifteen eighty-acre plots. Today they own one. Some was sold to timber barons, some was tricked out of them, and the rest lost to tax forfeiture. People were encouraged to move off the reservation to the big cities.

In Los Angeles and Reno, Vincent LaDuke worked with various Indian self-help groups to draw attention to the problems of Indians during Eisenhower's days. He hitchhiked to Washington DC wearing a war bonnet and carrying a sign saying, "Have Blanket, Will Travel." On this trip he met Betty Bernstein, daughter of a Russian Jew from New York, a painter who had lived and worked with Indians in Santa Fe, and whom he married on the White Earth Reservation in 1958. Winona was their only daughter and the trio lived off unemployment insurance when he wasn't falling off horses as a Hollywood extra. Her parents divorced when she was five.

After the divorce, Winona lived with her mother in Oregon and later was educated on the East Coast. Her experiences with the reservation were occasional childhood visits to her father's relatives. Though of mixed blood, the color of her skin indicated she was "different," and Winona remembers being beaten up, by words and small fists, as a schoolgirl.

She was always a smart kid: skipped third grade, spent a six-week summer workshop at Columbia University, worked in nursing homes, observed her parents' activist leanings. Her mother encouraged her to work on Indian issues.

"Harvard was more distasteful than racist. I was one of seven Indians there, and that made me novel. They thought there were no Indians left, so they treated you the same way kids perceive Indians to be. After all that I had gone through in school in Oregon, I felt like I was starting from scratch."

Faye Brown, an Indian activist from Boston and LaDuke's Cambridge roommate now lives in Minneapolis. "I think the further she got from her roots, the more she felt compelled to seek them. And you can't get much further from the reservation than Harvard."

"I 'returned' here in 1982. This is where my community is from, so it is my home," says LaDuke. "Three-quarters of our people are refugees, but they all call this home. I always knew when I was little that this was my home. My family talked about it that way."

Back on the reservation, after the principal's job fell through, with her last $750, she started the IKWE Marketing Collective to market rice and crafts.

It is greatly ironic that her father, who passed away in June, went on to become "Sun Bear," the popular New Age guru who guided dominions of Indian wannabes and was author of several pop-spiritual books, including *The Medicine Wheel* and *Sun Bear's Path to Progress*. Despite her love for her father, she has trouble with white people wanting to take on Indian ways.

She is suspect of whites too drawn to Native American ways and cultures, concerned that they are co-opting Indians but making the mistake that "being Indian" is transferable. In her mind "the essence" of one's being is found in the land and the blood. "That cannot be bought," she says. "People shouldn't donate money or land to us out of guilt, but because it's right."

At the WELRP office, Bob Shimek, one of five staffers, studies an "assignment" chart on the wall. One of his projects for coming months is to visit white farmers on the reservation tottery and drum up interest in non-pesticide agriculture. "Better get me a hard hat," he jokes. Born on the reservation, he has organized on behalf of Indians around the country. He returned to White Earth two years ago, to provide his sons with a "home." He has known Winona for a decade and calls her simply "unique." He also readily admits that he prefers, and even expects, to be led by women. "They're the force here, the mothers, the creators, the teachers. They should lead. They have the most responsibility for passing things along through our children. They deserve respect."

"There is a lot of respect for women, traditionally, in this community," Winona had explained earlier in the day, as we raced over snow-covered backloads in her Jeep (Cherokee, of course). "We have a lot of influence in traditional culture. What has happened to us in the last thirty or forty years has adversely affected the status of women in significant ways.

Values of the European value system have permeated our culture: often a woman organizer does encounter that. Most indigenous cultures view women with reverence and women in turn exercise influence and authority in their communities.

"In our culture men and women are viewed as having equal standing but different roles. As you get into the cash economy, women who have a central part in their economic system are put into a marginal part of the dominant society. And it's replicated on this reservation. Almost without exception, every decision maker in the tribal council structure is a man. All the service positions are women. And there's not a lot of encouragement of women to excel, unless perhaps in education or health care."

Tom Goldtooth is director of the Indigenous Environmental Network. He calls LaDuke "our ambassador, on a national and international level. With that Harvard education, she has the language that the non-Indian community can understand. And she has that connection to the grassroots community across the country. She is able to bring our issues to the national and international audience. That's how we obtain support. She is our most effective fundraiser for these initiatives. The bottom line is that we need a lot more Winonas."

"I learned my organizing skills between years at Harvard and working with Navajos fighting uranium mining," LaDuke says. "Most of my education [came from] . . . working with people engaged in this resistance. I've seen people organize, and I've seen people stop things. That is the greatest wealth that I have, much, much more important than the four-year college education I have.

"A lot of non-Indians find me acceptable, because I am college educated, because I've been [through] what they've been through, because I'm lighter and because I'm a woman. The guys I work with in my office are great big guys, great big Indians. I take them down to a meeting and a lot of times people are scared of them . . . all their worst, racist, illogical, deep-set, American-settler fears are all of a sudden right in their faces. So when I walk in, the reaction is relief. "

Despite the success she is having, there is still a lot of prejudice against Indians in the area. She and her kids are followed in stores in nearby Detroit Lakes, her kids admonished not to touch anything. They are hassled by cops. There is also a burgeoning anti-Indian movement, particularly among the 500,000 non-Indians who live on reservation lands, particularly strong in Wisconsin, South Dakota, Washington, Montana . . . and Minnesota. Everybody's competing for limited resources. "It's not easy being Indian in the nuclear age," LaDuke says.

There is also a lot of environmental racism targeting Native Americans. Uranium mining, hydropower, strip mining, oil exploitation, mercury contamination, emissions discharge frontier projects, toxic waste dumping, nuclear waste contamination, PCB contamination, acid rain, and nuclear bomb testing all happen on Indian reservations. "Indigenous people remain on the front lines of the struggle to protect our environment," says LaDuke. "It's like the holocaust of the Americas, unmatched on a world scale."

It is 6:30 in the morning. The cabin's living room is dark. It has snowed overnight and is not yet zero degrees. Outside the wind whistles, accompanying LaDuke as she rocks Ajuuak, gently cooing in Ojibwe and English (Ojibberish, she calls it). She is trying to wean him, and he squawks, half asleep. The smell in the dark cabin is of sage and fresh coffee.

I wonder how she maintains her obvious sense of optimism given the size of the battle she's engaged in. "I try to live by an ethical code," she explains, "called Minobimaatisiiwin. It means both the 'good life' and 'continuous rebirth' central to our value system. We honor one another, we honor our women as the givers of lives, we honor our old people and ancestors, and we honor ourselves as part of creation. Implicit in Minobimaatisiiwin is continuous habitation of place, an intimate understanding of the relationship between humans and the ecosystem and of the need to maintain this balance.

"Sometimes I get discouraged because you're fighting a big evil. Things that give me courage are when I see other people who are engaged in fighting even bigger fights with fewer resources.

"But compared to a lot of organizations, we have a lot of support. And we don't have a gun to our heads. Like the Cree in James Bay, threatened by hydropower dams threatening their lands and rivers. We have time to think, strategize. We have financial and political resources. Most of the resistance to us is in the community."

She says too she is hopeful because of the growing environmental consciousness across the country, crossed with the success of grass-roots groups nationwide.

"I think ours is more indicative of the majority of native struggles than the Russell Means, big warrior buck image. The media has been attracted to and fascinated by armed resistance. But the majority of resistance is not armed. The ways the media paints Indians today, there are those radicals then there are Indians with briefcases, with nothing in between. Our story is a story of the in between, of the people on the front line.

"But always remember, we are on the defense, not the offense."

Winona LaDuke remains executive director of White Earth Land Recovery Project, as well Honor the Earth. She was Ralph Nader's vice presidential running mate on the U.S. Green Party ticket in 1996 and 2000.

ENDANGERED SPECIES

George Schaller

Wildlife Conservation, 1994

The great naturalist writer Peter Mathiessen has known the great field biologist George Schaller for more than twenty years. They have traveled and worked together in some of the world's most wild places; each has won prizes for books on conservation. Schaller was in fact the conscience of Mathiessen's award-winning *The Snow Leopard,* an account of a 1970s trip the pair made through the Himalayas.

In his account of the trip, Mathiessen remembers one day in particular, one spent walking for ten hours. At the end of the day, he wrote, "My feet hurt from sharp rock shale; while taking rice supper in a local hut, GS investigates wetness in his sneaker and finds it full of his own blood." Mathiessen shouldn't have been surprised; in fact this was a condition Schaller—already being called "the finest field biologist working"—had known before. Before setting out with Schaller, Mathiessen had been warned by a mutual friend, "I look forward to learning what you and George see, hear, and accomplish in a march through Nepal. I should warn you, the last friend I had who went walking with George in Asia came back—or more properly, turned back—when his boots were full of blood. . . ." In Nepal, when Mathiessen asked Schaller if that anecdote were true, Schaller replied it was. "That chap was out of shape," he said.

In 1994, nearly twenty years later, the man Mathiessen described as "single-minded, not easy to know," lay flat on his back amidst nearly two thousand antelope in the Tibetan outback. He was only the second Westerner to have traveled to the desolate, twenty-thousand-foot Aru Range. As the antelope surrounded him—herd after herd after herd—Schaller gloried in the once-in-a-lifetime event. Standing in the sub-freezing cold, in the middle of one of the few undamaged ecosystems on the planet, Schaller was truly in his element.

Truth is, he is only truly happy in the bush, a suspicion confirmed by his wife of thirty-two years, Kay. She has been his constant companion in the field and readily admits it is rare for him to really be comfortable in their Connecticut two-story. "He has an itch for going," is how she puts it. "He needs to be where it is wild." (From Tibet, Schaller writes: "After about an hour's climb we reached the ridge. Here at ten thousand feet it was cold, but we were liberated from the valley, a horizon suddenly offering visual release. Mountains sparkled in air so clear that it seemed I could hurl a rock into the Pitiao River far below. On the other side of the Pitiao valley was a grass slope with only an upper fringe of trees of remembrance of forests past. Beyond, at over twenty thousand feet, the ice pyramid of Siguniang held itself aloof from the hills. . . . All day we followed the ridge as again and again it lunged upward. The forest was silent yet full of sound, with iced boughs tinkling like temple bells in gusts of wind.")

George Schaller's "office" is wherever he is at the moment. If it's the hills surrounding Nepal's Annapurna or Dhaulagiri, he'll hunker down to write his daily observations in a wood-heated hut crowded with Sherpa. If trekking through the Qian Tang region of northwest Tibet— a vast, bleak territory of sparsely grassed plains broken by hills, valleys, lakes, and snowy peaks, populated by wild yaks and asses, lyre-horned Tibetan antelopes, gazelles, and blue sheep—his constant, essential note taking may take place inside a cold tent. ("Once when walking far north of the Aru basin, we met a lynx in a desolate place where the plains are as gray and corrugated as a yak chip. The land was empty, with little grass and few animals; an occasional gray-rumped Tibetan woolly hare— a species unique to the plateau—huddled in a shallow scrape. No humans came to this isolated spot. But the lynx had settled here. At rest on a cliff, he apparently thought us inconsequential; there was not even fire in his eyes as he gazed in our direction. . . .")

He is as comfortable studying an animal from behind a six-foot-tall anthill as most are gossiping around the office water cooler. Whether he's spent the day observing the mating rituals of antelopes, sifting through the dung heaps left behind by lionesses, counting gnawed bamboo shoots, or smelling tree trunks for panda markings, Schaller insists his best work is done in the world's most remote wilds; even at the risk of pain and suffering, as he discloses one particular day spent observing antelope in the freezing Tibetan plains. ("I marveled at their stamina at these altitudes. And I also noted that my eyeballs were freezing.")

Tall and lean, the sixty-year-old scientist's appearance smacks of "professor." "Rugged" and "adventuresome" are not terms you would choose—upon first impression—to describe Schaller. Yet rugged and adventuresome he and his life certainly have been. Officially dubbed "the most famous field biologist in the world" by the *New York Times*, his boss calls him "one of the most caring men in the world." William Conway, director of the New York Zoological Society, has known Schaller for twenty-five years. He insists, "What keeps George going is that he cares so much about the places he visits, the people he finds there, and the animals he studies. He is like no other biologist I've met." Cohorts and competitors alike (yes, even the field of biology can be cutthroat) see Schaller as unique as the varied landscapes where he's spent his life. Put under the microscope, he is observed to be stern, pragmatic, and even cold; only a few who have worked with him regard Schaller as warm and convivial. (He told Mathiessen, "Once the data start coming, I don't care about much else" and "the fewer people, the better.")

Yet for all his Germanic stiffness, the very same peers and protégés continue to seek him out for confirmation and attention. If there is a guru of field biology, George Schaller is it. Nature writer Geoffrey Ward claims, "No scientist is better at letting the rest of us in on just how the natural world works; no poet sees that world with greater clarity or writes about it with more grace." His fame has even made it to the big screen. Early in the movie *Gorillas in the Mist*, Sigourney Weaver, as the naturalist Dian Fossey, flees headlong down a mountain slope, pursued by a roaring male gorilla. "What does Schaller's book say when a gorilla charges?" her tracker asks moments later as she recovers in safety. "It says, 'Never run,'" replies Fossey, yet another of Schaller's followers and admirers.

The author of ten critically acclaimed books, Schaller calls the wild places where he works "sacred spaces." He seeks out wilderness where nature exists in its original state, largely preserved from man's intrusion. Along the way he has confronted lions in Africa's Serengeti Plain, tigers in India, wild sheep and goats in Nepal and Pakistan, and jaguar in Brazil.

His pioneering study of the mountain gorilla was the first to discover that the species was in danger of extinction, setting the stage for Fossey and others that followed. Since 1985 he has focused on studying the snow leopards of Tibet and the Gobi Desert and the great pandas of China. It is the beauty and unknown of these special places that keeps Schaller going back out.

The person who knows him best, wife Kay, has observed her husband in virtually every situation, yet prefers not to label him. Those who know the couple best insist it is she who allows her well-known husband to stay focused, aiding all of his projects by accompanying him into the bush, keeping track of animals, analyzing data, typing his manuscripts (some suggest she even lends a certain grace to his writing with her "editing"). "As always, she made a home for us in the wilderness, a place of human warmth in a bitter environment," Schaller writes of Kay, in the preface to his most recent book, the National Book Award–winning *The Last Panda*. Later he would recall a night they spent in a tent far from civilization, reliving their adventuresome life, regretting only the changes that have ruined many of the "sacred places" they have seen. ("We talked of our years in the Serengeti, of driving into the golden dawn and finding a group of tawny lions beneath an umbrella acacia. And we talked of tigers in India. And of Brazil and Pakistan. . . . We were spoiled, and this sometimes made it difficult for us to adapt continually to society. . . .")

Schaller's priority these days is organizing wildlife reserves—what he calls "living museums"—to preserve both the natural systems and biodiversity he cares so much about. Like sound ecotourism, this also involves including the local people. "Unless you deal with the local people that surround these reserves in ever greater densities, you're going to lose it. The challenge, and here I think ecotourism is very important, is to find innovative ways to deal with the local people so they will not destroy it. That requires that some money goes to them." The lack of sincerity of the big international conservation groups is a major theme of *The Last Panda*. In it he chastises zoos, governments, and international conservation groups for sanctimoniously swearing fealty to the ideal of saving species—specifically the endangered pandas—and charges that stupidity, greed, and indifference are causing mankind to hasten the loss of the world's wildlife. The book has been a critical and popular success, spawning a new look at how zoos and conservation groups try and "save" animals. Already Schaller is on to new places, new beasts. Specifically he is working with governments and conservationists in Laos and Zaire to set up reserves.

But it is perhaps his work over the past four years in the Qian Tang region of northwest Tibet that may prove his greatest effort ever, an effort to create a wildlife reserve in a place where he was the first Western biologist to work. He walked or traveled by horse or camel or yak across most of the region, cataloging animals, surveying populations, and observing migrations.

The "stern pragmatist" of Mathiessen's *Snow Leopard* continues to insist, "You can only make intimate contact with an area on foot, roofless, exposed to the raw bite of wind." (He remembers one raw Tibet morning: ". . . the plain stretched into the sun's blinding light to a horizon of white hills aloof in their barrenness. A herdsman's tent huddled in the fold of the hills. A wolf strolled along a distant cutback, and a flock of horned larks twittered by. And all around, the antelope danced on the tawny grass in their ancient ritual. . . .")

Back in civilization, his office is a narrow slot in the basement of a brick building in the heart of the Bronx Zoo. I find him there between trips, looking more than a bit out of place. Newly renovated, the space is bare but for a wooden desk and several framed prints—of pandas—leaned against the wall. A telephone is the only hint of modernity. Though his title is director for science of Wildlife Conservation International, Schaller doesn't demand fancy appointments. After all, this is a guy who is perfectly comfortable using a dung heap for a desk.

Born in Berlin in 1933, son of a German diplomat, Schaller still speaks with a strong accent. He lived across Europe before moving to the States, with his mother, in 1947. As a boy he collected birds' eggs, kept a mini-zoo of salamanders, snakes, opossums, and other creatures. It wasn't until his undergraduate years at the University of Alaska that he realized he could extend his boyhood passion for the natural world into a livelihood. "I've never been interested in anything but the outdoors," he confesses. Today he insists his primary goal is to help alert the public's attention to a global "century of destruction" in which he believes that humans are destroying natural resources, particularly plants and animals, at such a rate that mankind will ultimately be threatened. Though hardly a typical tourist, Schaller believes the current boom in ecotourism—if done properly, by skilled and committed companies—is one avenue for preserving both wilds and wildlife. "The greatest irony of my life is that I don't really enjoy traveling," he laughs. "I enjoy being somewhere, but not the getting there." In fact he insists he's worked hard all his life "to go to places that people generally have not reached."

Recently that place has been Tibet, particularly a region that had been essentially closed to outsiders since 1908. Few tourists have been allowed inside the border, but Schaller thinks they should be, as a way to ensure the region's survival. He says the Chinese government is considering allowing a few high-priced tours. "But they must be strictly controlled," says Schaller, "because it's an area about the size of California with no human population. You can't just have people roaming around. It would be a little awkward for everyone involved if tourists disappeared. "This is where ecotour companies come in," he suggests. "Governments will never have enough money to protect areas like this. It is going to be up to tour companies— either individually or together—to try to help protect certain of the remaining wilderness areas where they enjoy taking tourists.

"For many areas of the world good tourism—which means limited numbers of strictly controlled people that are aware of the environment, that are knowledgeable about what they are up to, that don't litter, that don't disturb the animals, that treat the local people with respect—can have a real benefit. Otherwise such regions might just disappear. If an area has foreigners coming and looking and the money from their visit stays there, local people are more likely to protect it. If nobody ever visits, say the rainforest, the more likely it will be logged."

Schaller though questions the sincerity of many tour operators who advertise ecotours. "With rare exception, tour companies go into an area, enjoy it, and leave. I think tour companies have to sit down with the local village or group of villages and say, 'Hey, this is a nice forest and the only place in the region where you can see 234 species of birds in two days. We'd love to come in here to watch birds. How can we help protect this? What will prevent you from shooting the wildlife or cutting down critical trees? Do you want a school and a teacher? If we provide that, will you do this in return? Do you need a medical clinic? Do you need help in planting a eucalyptus plantation to provide some fuel wood instead of cutting out this area of brush because that's a great nesting area for this species?'"

He worries, as do many in the tourist and conservation industries, that ecotourism has become a buzzword, a gimmick, a sales pitch with little more meaning than "New" or "Improved" printed on a box of soap flakes. "Most ecotourism has never really helped local people," says Schaller, "because they make very little money. It's the middlemen and the politicians who make the money; very little trickles down. Until there is a code of conduct, guidelines for companies that they have to meet before they're allowed to call themselves ecotourism, it will not truly help." He remains a constant critic of many wildlife policymakers because he truly cares about not only the animals but also the places that have been his focus, his life's work.

He also contends that companies billing themselves as ecotours must be accredited and must police themselves. "So that if somebody writes in, 'This tour guide paid a local chap to permit me to touch the gorillas, which is against regulations,' that the tour company is somehow punished. I've seen it repeatedly with tourists, where they are in effect paying to do something wrong that they know is wrong. For example, in Cana Park in central India, where people are taken out on elephant back to look at tigers. It's a tremendous experience, and on the whole very well run. But if you pay off the mahout, the guy who guides the elephant, he will linger behind after the others leave and then chase the tiger. Because people want to see the tiger run, which they don't like to do in the midday heat. That's the kind of thing good ecotours simply would not permit." He insists part of the success of ecotourism falls on the shoulders of the traveler. "People ought to do more than just cover miles and then kill time. If you're going to go spend six thousand dollars to go to the Antarctic, for example, you ought to read up on the exploration history of the continent, about the penguins and krill." He suggests too that guides on ecotours should meet certain standards, even be accredited. "Far too often tour guides are picked simply because they're available, not because of any special knowledge."

When asked to assess his own place in the world, Schaller sounds poetic. "The more rare and remote a species, the greater the challenge to become a chronicler of its life," he says. "I view myself basically as a nineteenth century wanderer with a scientific bent on an intangible and elusive search. There is an atavistic pleasure in crossing the Tibetan plateau, our camel caravan lonely and lost between earth and sky, or trailing a string of porters through the mysterious silence of a rainforest. At times I have been labeled misanthropic because I usually avoid the conviviality of a scientific team on such ventures. Aside from my wife, Kay, and my sons, I prefer my own kind in small doses. Author Peter Fleming noted some years ago that 'the trouble about journeys nowadays is that they are easy to make but difficult to justify.' Conservation now offers ample justification."

On this warm spring day in the middle of the Bronx his agenda is more bureaucratic than adventuresome. Loping jacketless through the zoo, a sheaf of papers in his hand, I test his reaction to being labeled "the most famous field biologist in the world."

"They have to call you something, I guess," is his muted response. "Think of it this way. I've been fortunate in having studied a number of spectacular animals. If scientifically I had done just as good a job, if not a better job, studying various rodents around the world, nobody would ever have heard of me."

George Schaller, 79, is still vice president of the Science and Exploration Program at the Bronx Zoo-based Wildlife Conservation Society. In 2007 he worked with Pakistan, Afghanistan, Tajikistan, and China to develop a new Peace Park to protect 20,000 square miles of habitat for the largest wild sheep species, the Marco Polo sheep.

MEGA-PADDLE

Michael Fay

Condé Nast Traveler, 2006

I t had been a long, hot day paddling sea kayaks on the Atlantic Ocean, paralleling the coast of the small West African nation of Gabon, smack on the equator. Eight hours on a hard plastic seat, sometimes as much as three miles offshore, on rolling, mostly calm seas. We were looking forward to surfing the heavily loaded plastic boats into shore, to stretch legs and every other imaginable body part.

Yet at day's end we found ourselves happily sitting in the surf zone, back paddling against big rolling waves attempting to push us toward the white sand beach known as Petit Loango. What kept us at sea? A Noah's Ark of big animals emerging from the forest onto the shore right in front of us. As sizable tarpons exposed silver underbellies next to us, big, brown forest elephants emerged to munch on the sandy grass. A family of buffaloes ruminated not far from where dwarf crocodiles sunned themselves in the nearby lagoon. And then the Holy Grail—surfing hippos—emerged, a trio of them, readying for an end-of-the-afternoon swim. Our welcoming party!

It was difficult to make a move toward shore for fear we'd spook the big beasts. "I've never seen anything like this from the seat of a kayak," says my partner in this adventure, Michael Fay. That's saying a lot, since a few years back the American biologist and environmental activist walked 456 straight days across the Congo forest to document its biodiversity and draw attention to its vulnerability, ending his journey near this very beach.

We tread water for an hour before surfing into the wide beach. While we linger in the setting sun, I ask Fay if this spot has a name. "Well, sometimes we call it Hippo Camp, for the big guys who surf here. Or Croc Camp, nothing formal. Why, do you have an idea?" I kind of prefer Baobab Camp, since we are standing beneath the only such tree—the "upside down" tree famous in other parts of Africa but rare here—on the coastal border of Gabon's first national park, called Loango. The hundred-foot-tall tree was most likely planted by a slave merchant two hundred to three hundred years ago when this coast was amok with traders. During the past forty years, the economy of this sparsely populated country—just one million people—has been predominately oil and timber. Ecotourism is just starting to make inroads as a potential new economy. It was jump-started just a year and a half before, when this beach and the dense forest that stretches inland for dozens of miles were protected—along with twelve other national parks, a total of 11 percent of Gabon—thanks to one monumental presidential signature. We'd been on the ocean for just a couple days; the previous two weeks in early February had been spent paddling across inland lakes and up a long river, and then pulling the kayaks on wheels on an overgrown jungle trail to the ocean. Our goal was a one-hundred-twenty mile circumnavigation of Loango, the country's jewel of a national park.

In August 2002—thanks to long and impressive efforts by a variety of international environmental groups and prompted by a series of beautiful photographs and video of his country's little-seen interior—President Omar Bongo had proclaimed thirteen national parks in the country he'd presided over for thirty-six years. There had been none before. Today the thirteen parks are scattered across the country, forever out of the hands of always-eager oil and logging companies looking for new lands to exploit. Bongo's decision was perhaps the biggest conservation sign-over in history, and Fay had been a big part of the push.

"It's an unprecedented move," says Fay about the president's declaration. "You have to go back to guys like Teddy Roosevelt and his creation of 230 million acres of national forest in the U.S., which was similarly radical and the result very positive. It is not an easy country to start up eco-tourism, but Loango happens to be an extremely beautiful place. Great climate, few bugs, hippos and elephants on the beach. What we're trying to do now is show the government in a very clear and real way how you can mix the public sector with the private to create a sustainable management structure for all the national parks. We've still got lots of things to do—more beach cleanup, trawler control. But while there are still obstacles, I don't focus on the frustrations."

Since Fay had already walked across the country, we decided to see some of it from the seat of a kayak. We were five. Since 1999 I've organized sea kayak expeditions around the world, for both adventure and to learn about the lives of people who live on or near the sea, and the environments of the oceans. Photographer Pete McBride has joined me on several of those adventures. California-born Fay has lived and worked in Africa for twenty-five years; the great thing about our foray is that he'll be going places, seeing things he's never seen before. We are joined by two young Gabonese men, Sophiano Etouck, thirty, and Aime Jessy, twenty-two, who are in training to become eco-guides at the brand new park.

As we ready the kayaks at Loango's first and only lodge—Iguela, an amazingly sophisticated African safari camp, built on the lagoon seven kilometers from the sea, in full operation for less than six months but already booming—Fay is full of questions. For me: "How familiar are you with tsetse flies?" For Sophiano and Aime: "Are you sure you guys can swim?"

We push off under sultry, gray skies (no big surprise since two out of three days in Gabon are gray), and no sight of those four-meter-long crocodiles that have discouraged us from taking much-needed and desired swims in the lagoon. We will cut across the 120-square-mile N'goya lagoon before heading twenty-two miles up the N'Gove River. It is the rainy season, and the dense black and red mangrove forests that line the shores are flooded by high water. It is wild country. The Congo basin rainforest is the second largest rainforest expanse in the world; 77 percent of Gabon is covered by dense, hilly forest. The country offers a rare interface between terrestrial and marine wilderness, wild ocean, lagoons, and river mouths. There are fifty thousand to sixty thousand elephants in Gabon, many the coastal species, thus smaller, making it easier for them to crash through the thick foliage. The forests are also filled with bush pigs and lowland gorillas, sitatungas and buffalo. Along its 885 kilometers of ocean coast are an abundance of Atlantic sea turtles, dolphins, whales, and fish. Birds are in every tree, from kingfishers and turacos to twenty-six types of bee-eaters and gray parrots (the national symbol, white and gray with a red tail). This first day we cross the wide lagoon, mostly hugging the forested shoreline. A mist rises above the tall Okume trees, branches laden with squawking monkeys.

Roughly four hundred people live around the lagoon, mostly fisherman, and at day's end we pull into the camp of the local chief, who invites us to stay the night and offers us pine nuts, pineapple, and breadfruit. We trade him a newly sharpened machete for a dull, broken model. He is the chief of approximately a thousand people and his region is rich with oil. He guesses that over the years, oil companies have taken $25 billion from the area. The locals' take? Zero. Bone thin at seventy-eight, wearing only a pair of cutoff khakis, he is accepting of that status quo, rather than angered. To the chief, the national parks are a good thing, largely because they will employ many of his neighbors.

Before sunset he proudly takes us to visit a valuable icon kept in a kind of shrine, a three-sided shack partially covered by a rusting corrugated metal roof. On a rotting wooden table under the protection lies a piece of iron found in the stomach of a dead elephant more than one hundred years before. He tells us that the piece of metal grows every year, especially when a woman in the community is pregnant.

"The interesting thing," whispers Fay, out of earshot of the chief, "is that they have never doubted that it is true. It is just fact." Our upriver paddle begins the next afternoon, at the swollen mouth of the N'gove. We'll be paddling against strong currents and curves for twenty-two miles . . . , which makes me, wonder, Whose idea was this anyway?

Paddling into a light wind and rain, we stick to the shores, hugging the blooming papyrus and palms. The flooded forests on either side are haunting—dark, wet, and humid, filled with leeches and shoe-sucking mud. A meter of river water rises up the thick trunks of tall trees. During the dry season the thick papyrus—a favored elephant snack—runs right down to the river, turning the shores into "a kind of Serengeti," heavy with hungry elephants, Fay says. Late in the afternoon it's as if the animals woke up. An elephant swims across the river thirty yards ahead of us; a river tarpon rises midstream; buffalo paralleling the river crash through the muck, followed by a beautifully white-striped sitatunga. McBride and Fay paddle into the flooded forest and a manatee jumps between them. At sunset, a flock of egrets rises from an acacia, hippos and male gorillas bark. "I've never seen a manatee like that," says Fay, truly impressed. "And I've never seen a river tarpon during this season. We thought they were only up here during the dry season."

The river braids as we climb, forcing us to choose one channel over another several times. We mostly make the right choices. One very important observation we are each making is that as dusk closes in, it is clear there is very little terra firma nearby. We'll have to stop and sleep somewhere, but solid ground may still be many hours upriver. Around 5 p.m., with just an hour of light left and big rainstorms threatening, it is clear that we are not going to find land anytime soon. Fay and I confer mid-river.

"The only thing to do is paddle into the flooded forest, tie up to some trees, put our tents on top of the boats, and voilà!" I suggest. Without debate the decision is made—to sleep in our kayaks—because, well, because there's no option.

We paddle into the dark forest, bumping into hanging vines and branches, looking for a small tuft of muck we can pull the bows of the kayaks onto, maybe something sturdy enough for us to stand on, set up a stove and start cooking dinner before what will assuredly be heavy rains arrive.

Suitable muck is found at the base of a giant okume, and we pull the bows of three boats up into the mud and empty them of dry bags, portage carts, paddles, Pelican cases, tying everything to nearby trees, just in case the river should rise with the coming rains. Our tents set up atop the kayaks should be sufficient to keep us dry; Etouck and Jessy are in a bit of a fix, since they opted to bring just one tent to share. Which means they'll spend this night uncomfortably squeezed into a single kayak. We light the stoves just as it begins to rain heavily. Mike has found a huge branch to sit on, and a tiny, folding umbrella; I hunker down on the nose of my kayak snug under a rain jacket hood; Pete is still trying to drain his boat of river water; Etouck and Jessy have set their kayaks up side by side in the middle of the flooded forest. The rain makes quick work of our fire, so dinner is scratched and we crawl into our tent/boats. It is only 7 p.m. And then it begins to rain for real, the dark, fairy-tale-like forest lit up by lightning and long peels of rolling thunder, making for a long night filled with worries of rising waters and falling trees. . . . Despite all that, I sleep like a baby. We start the next morning early, just after 5 a.m., hoping to spy the same abundance of wildlife we'd caught at day's end. Which paid off. Paddling in the dark, following an unknown braid of the oxtail of the northern river, we sat beneath a tree mid-river filled with two hundred white egrets, playing an hour-long game of flying out and returning, a beautiful sight as the big flock of birds comes and goes against the just-sunlit sky.

From the tree to the head of the twelve-mile trail where we'll pull the kayaks over is less than an hour's paddle. It is an old "colonial" trail, built by early explorers as a link between inland lagoons. Its condition is unknown—it's possible we'll find it impassable, a mud fest, or blocked by numerous, elephant-downed trees, meaning we may have to return the way we came.

Kayaks and gear gingerly rigged atop portage carts and pulled by harness like a dogsled, we run across, within the first hundred feet, sizable gorilla scat, three-foot-wide elephant footprints in the mud and seven-inch, red-and-black African worms curled in the middle of the trail. If we thought it was hot on the river, now we're under a jungle canopy, pulling 150- to 200-pound loads over a very, very rough trail. Nearing heat stroke, we suck down water from dromedary bags. Our biggest concern is the big, bulbous tires on the portage carts. If they start to fail—go flat—we're going to be in big trouble.

Carrying machetes to hack at tree limbs and branches covering the path, we cross beautiful, clear streams and old overgrown bridges made from downed logs. Stopping is risky, thanks to long lines of red ants, the kind that take a piece of flesh when they bite.

By five o'clock, even Fay —whom one men's magazine recently included on a list of the world's "25 Toughest Men"—is too tired to move. "I could just fall down right here, " he admits, in the middle of the trail. Though we are now only sixty miles from his base, he also admits—happily—that we are once again in a place he's never been before.

Best sign of the day? We can hear the ocean, six miles away as the crow flies, through the jungle.

The next morning is spent repairing tires. All ten of them, thanks to run-ins with long macaranga and fagara spikes. Melting rubber over our cook stoves and applying it to holes identified by immersing the tires in a nearby stream proves ineffectual. For the next two days we'll be pulling the boats on nearly flat tires. "It's like the parking brake is on," says McBride as we set off. When we finally drag the boats into the village at Souanga, nearly three days after leaving the river, the patron of the seven-person community and his wife greet us open-jawed, yammering in Gabonese. I ask Fay to translate.

"They just kept saying 'Holy shit!' over and over."

From Souanga to the ocean takes half a day, across another lagoon (N'dogo), up another river (the Echire), then over a final lagoon, which turns out to be home to a pair of very big hippos. They're known to be very territorial, and one of the big guys surfaces just fifty feet from me, blowing a spray of pink mist into the sunlit morning, glaring menacingly, behaving like a very pissed-off monk. McBride later said he never knew I had such a "high gear" as I paddled away from the hippo, which I was convinced was giving chase.

The afternoon was spent luxuriating on the sands of the Atlantic, relishing the ocean breeze and testing ourselves in the kayaks against the sizable ocean surf. If we couldn't comfortably get off the beach and through the six-foot waves—and then back in—we had some reconsidering to do. The biggest kick of the day was watching some of the locals we met on the beach try the kayaks and get pummeled as they paddled out and back in.

The only disappointment was that twenty-two-year-old Jessy was incapable of breaking out through the surf. From the beach I couldn't tell if it was an issue of not being physically strong enough to power the boat through the series of waves, or if he was just intimidated. Either way, after more than ten tries without success, the decision was made that he would have to stay behind. Self-sufficiency on the ocean is a requisite; it is definitely not a place for baby-sitting. He'll paddle to Sette Cama, where his family lives, then fly back to camp out of nearby Gamba. It will be a race to see which of us gets back to the lodge first. Sitting on a fallen log, our backs to the big beachside baobab, we are paying attention to cooking dinner when a young male elephant wanders out of the forest behind us. Dark-skinned, his ivory tusks yellowed, he sniffs through the grass twenty feet from where we sit. We are upwind, so that he doesn't catch our scent, intent on his search for a baobab fruit he is convinced is somewhere nearby.

"Holy shit," says Fay, an unpurposeful imitation of the villager's reaction to our arrival the other day. For twenty minutes the elephant moves around the mix of grass and sand before shuffling back into the forest. We are camped on the most beautiful of sand beaches at Petit Loango, with signs of animals everywhere. A perfect point-break rolls in front of us and hippos lounge in the lagoon two hundred yards down-beach. We can easily make out the flares of oil rigs thirty-five miles offshore. A pair of trawlers pass by, just two kilometers offshore, obviously breaking the five kilometer law. With the oil industry in Gabon fading, overfishing has become a new concern.

As the night sky darkens we share only-in-Africa tales. Etouck is from one of the first villages where Ebola wreaked havoc; of his eleven siblings, the disease, one sister dying in his arms, killed eight. And it was just a few miles from here where a year-and-a-half earlier Fay had confronted a charging elephant and been gored several times, surviving only by hanging onto its razor-sharp tusks as it slammed him repeatedly into the sand. But the biggest news in Gabon these days is still the new parks. Thirteen of them are now on the maps, their borders permanently inked. There is no guarantee that they will survive the next generations of leaders in Gabon, but for the moment things look good. But environmentalists working in the country—the World Wildlife Fund, Conservation International, Wildlife Conservation Society, and more—are not resting on their laurels.

"You know what job I'd do for free, in a heartbeat?" Fay asks out loud.

"I'd run a speedboat up and down the coast of West Africa, armed with a bazooka, and take out illegal trawlers. Like those guys out there, fishing inside the limits, and in tandem, which is also illegal. Blam, blam, blam! The word would get out pretty quickly and those suckers would disappear fast, I promise. That's the kind of thing I wish we could do, right away."

Nearing Pointe Sainte Catherine and the mouth of the Iguela lagoon that will lead us back to the lodge after two weeks of non-stop paddling and pulling, on yet another hundred-degree-plus afternoon, we drag the boats over a low sand dune to the twelve-mile-long Louri Lagoon, paralleling the ocean. Paddling it will give us another perspective on the big animals we've been seeing every day along the beach.

And we are not disappointed. Filling dromedaries with tannic brownish water direct from the lagoon and munching on lunch of cashews, jerky, sardines, and Clif Bars, we are off, floating quietly down the lagoon. It's so shallow we must occasionally get out of the boats and pull them over the sandy bottom.

"Let's try and stick together," says Fay, "because we'll probably run into big buffaloes taking baths." Sure enough, around the first bend we run smack into an old mom-and-pop buffalo couple lying in the river, cooling off, attended by a pair of attentive secretary birds picking bugs from their fur. We watch for twenty minutes, just a few feet away, until they stand up and gambol down and across the river.

An hour later we are again bunched up when Fay signals toward the right bank—a big male elephant is pushing its way through the undergrowth toward the river. We hurry our paddling; the light is fading and we are a bit too far away in the dusk light to see him perfectly. Or more appropriately, them, since it turns out to be a whole family.

Two babies and two more adults follow the big male and they walk in a line across the river directly in front of us. Adult, baby, adult, baby, adult, the big ones laying their trunks on the tails of the babies to guide them. We watch under diminishing light, the fact that we've been in the kayaks for more than eleven hours this day now a minor complaint.

We end the day just a little more than a mile from the outlet back to the ocean; sometime the next day we'll be back to the lodge, where our greatest desire will be met by several tall glasses of cold, clear water.

The outlet that takes us back out to the ocean is fast flowing, like a Class III river rapid, blue and translucent, offering a fast ride between flat plains of sand. Here we finally meet the ocean conditions I'd anticipated all along—big, rolling seas, marked by twelve- and fifteen-foot rogue waves, requiring full attention. We are two miles off the beach and a flip out here would end in a long swim back to shore.

After a couple hours of easy paddling, just as we are setting up to hit the beach one last time, Fay spies a trawler working just offshore on the other side of the mouth leading back to Iguela. With an eye on the trawler, we ride the surf, landing gently on the beach. Tying straps to the fronts of the kayaks, we pull them through the shallow waters toward the pass, marked by standing waves and strong current, too strong for us to paddle through. Pulling the boats along the edge of the pass, through the fast-moving muddy brown river, we watch thick blocks of sand cascade into the water as we walk gingerly along its edge.

Fay is ahead of me and focused only on the trawler on the other side of the pass. Before I can catch up, he's off, paddling directly across the fast-moving currents rather than hugging the shoreline of the fast-moving river, as we'd planned. At risk of getting sucked out to sea, he paddles hard to gain the far side where, armed with satellite phone and video camera, he's off on foot, to document the trawler fishing illegally and put in a call to someone in the government in the capital city of Libreville to file a report. I watch his instinctual reaction to environmental abuse, and the only thing I can say to McBride is, He's not packing a bazooka in that kayak . . . is he??

Soon after our kayak exploration, Fay mounted his Mega-Flyover project which took him by air 70,000 miles over the entire continent. In 2008-2009 he walked the length of California's redwood forest to draw attention to its present and future.

TAKE THIS PARK
AND SHOVE IT

Doug Tompkins

The New York Times Magazine, 1995

It is an April day—early autumn in southern Chile—one day after Doug Tompkins's fifty-third birthday. He'd spent it quietly at his thousand-acre ranch with friends and employees, only to return to his "town" home in Puerto Montt to disheartening news. A story in the daily *El Mercurio* reported that conservative politicians in Valparaiso had denounced him on the floor of the legislature. As a result, his morning had been spent on the phone with his lawyer in Santiago hurriedly planning a week of meetings with ministers and politicians and an end-of-the-week press conference.

Between phone calls he pads around the house on Buin Street in a buttoned Scandinavian sweater, khakis, and lambswool slippers. Dark eyes sunk in his graying head, he moves his small, athletic body in a hurried shuffle. The house is pure Tompkins-esque, light and airy, well-crafted of blond woods and white paints, a museum of aesthetic perfection (a furniture maker is among his full-time employees). A twelve-foot-tall, Giacometti-like wood sculpture rises in the atrium around which the house is built. Irving Penn and Avedon and elegant color photos of big trees hang on the walls with black and white photographs. Small photographs of his mentors—Ghandi, the Dali Lama, and the father of deep ecology, Arne Naess—grace the first-floor offices. Out back are a Japanese garden and a greenhouse. Tompkins carefully designed every renovation detail of the hundred-year-old house. At Esprit de Corp, the international fashion company he started with his wife, Susie, he was officially president and CEO, but preferred the title "image director."

What has so aroused, and aggravated, a handful of Chilean legislators, most of them conservative to right-wingers, is that quietly over the past five years the multimillionaire (his now ex-wife bought him out of Esprit in 1990 for $125 million) eco-philanthropist has become the largest private landowner in Chile. Spending $12 million, he has acquired a block of 670,000 acres of pristine forest, mountains, and rivers that literally cuts the nation in two, stretching from the Argentine border to the Pacific Ocean. His intention is to turn the land into a national park—the largest private national park in the world—and one day hand it over to Chile's national park system. Until recently he had proceeded quietly (some in the government suggest secretively), purchasing parcels big and small without asking for help from or giving the government much information about what he was doing, or why. His secretiveness, or arrogance, as one legislative critic explains it, has now come back to haunt him, as the legislature launches an investigation into exactly what he's up to. "It was never a secret," he argues. "We just wanted to have all the land locked up before we went public with our plans for the park."

Big wall maps indicate the pieces of land he has acquired to date; a few he is still negotiating for and a couple tracts he'll never get. One calculation suggests Tompkins already owns 78 percent of the remaining native forest in Chile. His park—which he's dubbed Pumalin—will include the country's largest remaining alerce forests, some as old as four thousand years, as well as great bowers of coidue, tepa-manio, toneu, tepual, nirra, and lenge. Purchase of the land is almost complete: 670,000 of the 700,000-acre goal. (He had initially hoped to amass 1.25 million acres, but his foundation board, which controls the purse strings, thought 700,000 was plenty.)

Tompkins first visited Chile when he was seventeen. Since then he'd co-founded one of the world's biggest fashion retailers, made many millions of dollars, and subsequently decided to step out of the corporate world. He saw Chile as a perfect escape from the consumer culture he'd participated in but had grown to despise. It was also a place he could put into practice his take on deep ecology, the environmental philosophy that holds, among other tenants, that the life of a tree is as valuable as that of a man. In the early nineties he sold his San Francisco Victorian, put his vast monies into foundations in the U.S. and Chile, and moved to northern Patagonia. But once an entrepreneur, always an entrepreneur—soon he was buying up all the native forest around, intent on keeping it out of the hands of developers. A self-made man and born risk taker, he did not think it necessary to include the locals in his plan. Instead, he did what he had always done before when facing a new challenge, whether it was kayaking a whitewater river or building a Fortune 500 company. He simply plunged ahead. In retrospect, his independent ways may have cost him his vision. Case in point: a deal for one last strategic piece, thirty thousand acres owned by Catholic University, has recently been hung up thanks to the political denunciations. By accusing Tompkins and his San Francisco–based Deep Ecology Foundation of promoting population control (e.g., abortion), his foes have persuaded a handful of bishops to speak out against the project (one going as far as to call him an "anti-Christian pagan"). Conservative legislators have urged the university, which gets part of its funding from the government, not to sell to Tompkins.

To allay his critics, he has tried to emphasize that his goal is "ecology, nada mas." But his otherwise free-to-be lifestyle has been derailed by a coalition of politicians, businessmen, and military men in southern Chile who don't like that he's taken all that prime native forest out of play. In a country hell-bent on development, where trees are being felled by the thousands every day and turned into wood chips to be shipped to Japan to be made into cardboard boxes, preservation is not a word on the lips of too many Chileans.

Tompkins is a character. Gruff and simultaneously endearing, former employees love to hate him and vice versa. No one who knows Tompkins is surprised he is in the middle of a growing controversy. Tenacious and obsessive, passionate and compulsive, even caustic are words most often used to describe the entrepreneur-cum-ecologist. No one suggests he is ever subtle. "I want to raise the consciousness of the world," he recently told a Chilean newsmagazine. At the height of Esprit's success he confessed to another interviewer that he was obsessed with two things: "moving in places where the ordinary human doesn't go" and achieving "world-class status."

In Chile his critics see him as an interloper, a threat to development and national security. It has been suggested by some legislators that the land he's already purchased be expropriated. While he insists he's "doing a good deed," a growing number of powerful Chileans think he is making them look bad. Imagine if a Japanese megamillionaire bought one-third of Montana, and then informed the local populace he was doing them a favor. Even if true, it's a hard truth to swallow.

"The country is divided into two and the guilty party is a North American who doesn't even live in this country," warned the conservative weekly *Qué Pasa*. "His objective is, to say the least, dark, covering a vast territory from mountains to sea." Fueling the fire, one right-wing legislator suggests Tompkins "has imposed the law of his money to win the battle." The Superintendent of Region Ten, of which Tompkins owns one-fifth, keeps a thick file on the American atop his desk. The Army keeps one, too: since his land shares a seventy-mile border with Argentina, it sees him as a potential threat to Chile's national security.

A variety of rumors about Tompkins's motivations don't make his task easier. "They're trying to demonize me and the project," he complains. The most popular is that he's securing lands for a "second Israel," though he's not Jewish. He's been accused of being a money launderer, a front for a powerful transnational logging company and a variety of New Age spiritual groups. It has been reported that he intends to replace all the cows in the region with buffaloes, and that he is preparing a place to store nuclear waste. "They just don't get it," sighs Tompkins, letting slip his frustration at having to waste his time on "all this bureaucratic b.s." "Even though preserving natural places may seem ludicrous to most Chileans, I still believe it is the right thing to do," he insists.

Perhaps what bothers him most is the evidence that the powers that be in Chile simply are not interested in preserving the country's native forests. The best example of its pro-development stance is that another American operation, a lumber company called Trillium, out of Bellingham, Washington, has bought nearly as much land as Tompkins has, 625,000 acres on Tierra del Fuego, without its motive being questioned. "I don't see Trillium's CEO, David Syres, facing the 'Spanish inquisition' like I am," says Tompkins, "which seems odd to me. They want to cut down all the trees on their land. I want to preserve mine forever. And I'm the one threatened with being run out of the country."

Despite his sincere desire to simply save a big bunch of trees, rivers, lakes, and mountains, Tompkins doesn't always help his own cause; he can come off caustic, condescending. Even some of his friends are concerned that he should make more of an effort to get along, to befriend some of the small group of rich and powerful elite that runs Chile. But that is not Tompkins's style. "Some people here in Chile think he is kind of naive, with all his ranting about how 'the system doesn't work,' etc.," says a Santiago friend. "Here, we know the system doesn't work, that it's ultimately corrupt. That's a given. But talking about it all the time—like you just figured it out—makes him seem kind of . . . silly."

What he is attempting in Chile is novel. No one has ever tried to assemble a private park this big. In a country only recently emerged from beneath a military dictatorship and now geared to rampant development, here's a guy with preservationist instincts going against the grain, trying to do what he sees as the right thing. "Initially I don't think Doug knew exactly what he was doing down here, he just had a big idea," says Jib Ellison, a friend and onetime employee. "He sees this as a grand experiment, a forerunner of how environments can be protected by changing the rules, changing the approach, changing the mindsets of people."

Chile's view of environmental do-gooders is skewed by the country's incredible, post-Pinochet rush to development. Boasting the best economy in South America, its politics stable, Chile is slated to become the next signatory to NAFTA. New president Eduardo Frei, the second elected since Pinochet stepped aside in 1989, has traveled nonstop around the world since elected, returning home just long enough to report how many millions of investment dollars have been promised by foreign nations. Few in his government appear to be stepping back and looking at what this boom means for the future of the country's natural resources—air, water, forests, fisheries—which though vast are increasingly pressured. Frei has gone so far as to say that no environmental cause will stand in the way of development. "He's an engineer, a numbers guy," says Daniel Gonzalez, president of Tompkins's Chilean foundation buying the land, "certainly not an environmentalist."

"Look, every big project is criticized. That is part of the process," Tompkins admits. "That is why we must be as transparent as possible. Naturally this makes our work harder, because we need to answer to all these rumors. But every day people stop me on the street and thank me. Last week a taxi driver in Santiago recognized me from television and told me it was important to take care of what we have." While Tompkins has people who go into the bush and negotiate with farmers and fishermen, he often goes himself, by horseback or boat; he says he is willing to spend a total of $20 million to see the park become a reality.

Not everyone in the government is a critic. Ricardo Lagos, regarded as the most likely next president of Chile, has announced he agrees "100 percent" with Tompkins's goals. Veteran legislator Guido Girardi, president of the House committee on the environment, is one legislator on Tompkins's side. "At enormous economic risk Douglas is doing something the government should be doing—preserving native forests."

"Douglas' biggest problem is that he has become part of a soap opera, fed by envy, one of our great national pastimes," sighs Adriana Hoffman, a Chilean biologist and Tompkins's ally.

Tompkins's preference is for the outdoors and the company of a handful of climbing and kayaking buddies (his first business was The North Face Company, which he started in his twenties). Since his teens he has made first ascents and descents of dozens of mountains and rivers, from the Sierras to Antarctica. He first fell in love with Chile as a seventeen-year-old ski bum trying to make the U.S. ski team—he now owns his own rivers and fjords, mountains, even volcanoes, and spends most of his days piloting one of his small planes or boats between a rustic ranch at Renihue and Puerto Montt. At Renihue there is no telephone or fax; communication is by radio only. Energy comes from an eight-kilowatt electrical plant, the kitchen is wood-fired, the gardens organic. On the property is a one-room schoolhouse he had built for the children of employees and neighbors.

Since abandoning the fashion/business world he has devoted himself to ecological philanthropy. His Deep Ecology Foundation funds projects in fifty countries. He hopes his example in Chile—a private person spending personal wealth to preserve nature where governments cannot or will not—might set an example for others. Obsessed with the ecological future of the planet, he attacks this new mission with the same relentlessness he once put into making neon-colored T-shirts an international rage.

The product of Mayflower-related stock, Tompkins grew up in Greenwich Village and Millbrook, New York; his father owned a Manhattan antiques store. Kicked out of Pomfret School in Connecticut, he never went to college, moving to California instead to climb and ski. He met

Susie Russell in 1963. He was topping trees for a living near Lake Tahoe and she was working as a keno runner in Reno; he was hitchhiking, she picked him up; they were both twenty. Married, they moved to San Francisco where he borrowed five thousand dollars to start North Face, selling it a few years later for fifty thousand.

Esprit started out literally on Susie's kitchen table in 1968; by 1986 its worldwide sales had topped $1 billion. With Susie's designs and Doug's marketing savvy, Esprit was the fastest-growing fashion and lifestyle company in the world, preceding later successes of the Gap and The Limited.

Known as Little Utopia and Camp Esprit, the San Francisco-based company was the leader in neo-hippie perks, offering employees free language, aerobics, and kayaking lessons. They paid half for cultural events and sent employees rafting in the foothills of the Himalayas. The company credo was "No detail is small." (Others were "Life is entertainment, survival is a game" and "Thou shalt not knock off.") Happy employees made for fat profits: Along the way the boss acquired million-dollar collections of quilts and art, including paintings by Bacon, Picasso, Balthus, Botero, and Hopper. As the company grew Tompkins perfected what was dubbed MBA—Management by Being Absent, going off for months on climbing and kayaking adventures.

Ultimately he lost his passion for fashion, ironically about the same time the company took its first loss. He and Susie weren't getting along, and as they quarreled profits plummeted. In 1990, after several years of wrangling, she and three partners bought him out; the deal gave him $125 million, 25 percent of Esprit International and plenty of free time to devote to his new passion. Afterward Susie still opened Esprit meetings by urging: "Everybody take a minute and think about Doug, because we wouldn't be here without him." But when I call to ask if she's surprised by her former husband's recent predicament, she does not return the call.

On a late-April night in Santiago Tompkins is preaching to the converted, fifty people gathered at EcoCentro, home to an umbrella group that coordinates Chile's environmental and social groups. Though most in the audience are on his side, they too know him mostly from the headlines, and they have plenty of questions.

He responds in what the local media has dubbed his "precarious" Spanish. Dressed in black cotton turtleneck, khakis, and leather slip-ons, he takes questions for two and a half hours, gesturing with his hands when his Spanish fails. He has now done his slide show song-and-dance four times for politicos in Valparaiso, and he's fed up with the endless meetings, the bureaucracy. "I've had it up to here," he says, chopping at his neck with his hand.

He has brought his slides tonight, two carousels. The first is made up of dramatic photographs of ugly clear-cuts in North America, from Tennessee, Idaho, Oregon, North Carolina, British Columbia, and Saskatchewan. The second carousel starts out with recent pictures of logging in Chile— lots of roads cut through pristine forests, aerials of stripped hills, vast piles of wood chips. These are followed by elegant photographs taken in and around Pumalin. Tall mountains, snow-covered peaks, deep, forested ravines, tall Auracarias (the Chilean redwoods), blue lakes and fjords, all untouched. It is a powerful display, dripping with exactly the kind of imagery Tompkins knows is his best weapon.

After his talk, in a moonlit courtyard, he elaborates on how he sees his place. "Obviously the whole country can't be preserved, but this is a very special part. It is no good for agriculture or cattle. Sure, you could cut the forests and sell the trees, but once cut the land would be good for nothing. It is one of the last virgin reservoirs of the world, and I intend to see it preserved."

It has been eight years since he decided to leave business and devote himself to ecology. One concern of critics and loyalists alike is that the current hassles will turn Tompkins off, and he'll walk away. After all, he fled the fashion business when it got "boring." Is it fair to wonder if he might similarly tire of the endless Chilean bureaucracy and walk away from Pumalin? He insists no. "It's funny, because I thought they would be glad to have me here," he says. "But to many Chileans I guess what I'm trying to do must seem incomprehensible. Ultimately it doesn't matter what they think. I'm not going anywhere. This park will take the rest of my life."

That sentiment may not last. In late July the government of Chile announced it would purchase the thirty thousand acres from Catholic University that Tompkins had been negotiating for more than two years. He'd been willing to pay $2 million. Now, out of the blue, the Minister of the Interior announced the government would buy the land and get into the ecotourism/park business itself. Is it just coincidence that the piece sits smack in the middle of Tompkin's proposed park, dividing his acquisitions neatly into two pieces?

The day the government made the official announcement he called me from Santiago, excited, angry. He'd written a letter to the press and the government (in longhand, his preferred manner of communication) declaring if the government was going to interfere with his grand plan, he was no longer interested in making a park. He would continue to seek sanctuary status for his land, but would keep his 670,000 acres private, off-limits to the public.

"They (the government) jumped right in there to muck everything up. These far-right guys somehow talked the president into taking the decision to buy this piece of land. The reason they put forward—national security— is entirely stupid. We went to the Minister of Defense, and he admitted we presented no security problem.

"It is ridiculous. We've been transparent; we've been straightforward, yet all sorts of politicians have been hammering us. I've been called all sorts of names; all sorts of weird rumors have been intentionally circulated to demonize the project and me. We're sick of it. Forget the park. We'll keep the land as private property. We're trying to do a good deed for the country; we don't need this kind of aggravation. It's one thing to get hammered by some right-wing nuts, some fringe people, but when the government, right up to the president, says it's going to jump in, that's too much.

Officially, the government says it will make a park out of the land. If that's the case, contends Daniel Gonzalez, trying to put an optimistic spin on the news, "they've saved us $2 million." But Tompkins doesn't believe they'll ever follow through. "They don't necessarily want to develop this piece of land or turn it into a park. All they want to do is break the initiative. They want to sour the atmosphere for other kinds of investment like this, on principle. Preservation is a bad word to them. This is not personal, it is ideological." Velario Belasco, sub-secretary of the Ministry of the Interior, says Tompkins is off-base in his accusation that the purchase was done to spite him.

WILDEBEEST IN A RAINSTORM

Despite his heated rant, Tompkins is not exactly giving up on the park. He will spend the next days and weeks on the telephone with local journalists, meeting anyone in government he can, arguing that the government has no good reason to spend taxpayer dollars on something he was prepared to buy—and then give back to the people of Chile. But for now he's not feeling very optimistic. "People tell us that once the president makes a decision, he'll never back off. But we're holding the line. We're going to do whatever we can to make it hurt a little bit, without getting myself killed." I encourage him to watch the gas tanks of his Cessna. "You're not the first person to tell me that," he chuckles, nervously.

Three years later it is late afternoon on a spring day in the south of Chile, and I've just pulled off a bumpy dirt road into what will soon be the shiny, proud entryway to the country's newest park. Officially known as Parque Pumalin, it is roughly 670,000 acres of steep hills, snowcapped mountain peaks, deep fjords, and acre upon acre of tall primary forest. Its boundaries run from just outside of Puerto Montt south to Chaiten, and from the Argentine border to the Pacific Ocean, an almost neat rectangle literally splitting Chile into two parts. That such a pristine piece of wild land has been put into the hands of the people of Chile rather than cut, mined, and overfished by developers and the local population is a rarity in any country in this day and age. That Tompkins, an outsider, orchestrated the now-$16 million effort is little more than a miracle.

This day in late November 1997, the entrance looks more construction zone than park entrance. Forty men, locals from Futaleufu, Chaiten, and Castro on the nearby island of Chiloe, hustle to finish a half-dozen building projects at once, with a firm deadline. In less than a month the first daily ferry of the summer season arrives from the north. Tompkins wants the initial, most public impression of his new park's infrastructure to be a good one. Already they've finished a beautiful hanging bridge over the Rio Gonzalo, several camping spots, baños, trails and a refugio where locals can stay on their way to and from farming and fishing camps. There is a rush to finish the seven small cabins, a handful of other refugios, camping spots, and pair of nearby hiking trails.

But the beauty of this place is not in its manmade edifices. Standing alone in the midst of these northern Patagonian forests, looking out over a wild Pacific Ocean, surrounded by ancient forests crisscrossed by translucent blue rivers and studded with snowcapped volcanic peaks, it reminds me of a kind of emerald Yellowstone, minus the hordes.

I have been to this tiny cove many times over the years. While there has been much progress in the shaping of Parque Pumalin (named for the pumas that once prowled these hills), it has been a long time getting to this juncture. In a country hell-bent on development, the notion of preservation is not always at the top of politicians', or businessmen's, lists. The fact that Tompkins's purchases—orchestrated by negotiating one parcel at a time, from tens to thousands of acres at a pop—nearly cuts the country into two threatened many in Chile, especially considering their centuries-old concerns about land grabs made from next-door neighbor Argentina.

Tompkins and the government reached a final agreement a year ago on how the future of the park should be handled. The agreement dictates that Tompkins turn ownership of the parkland over to a Chilean foundation, which in turn will be directed by a board made up of Chileans, and Tompkins. Today he says he's looking only forward. "Our project ran into problems because it favors conservation and care for the environment, and confronts that runaway pro-development juggernaut. Any project similar to ours would have faced similar opposition, whether in Africa or Australia," he said just after the deal was signed.

"I'd say we have another eight years of serious work ahead," he says, adding that he intends to raise another $20 million to provide operating funds for the park for years to come. "The best change is that we used to spend half our time fending off attacks of all kinds—tricks, threats, and criticism. Now, we can concentrate 98 percent of our time on working on the park. That feels pretty good."

What has been ignored during all those years of political wrangling is the incredible beauty, the wilderness of the place. I spend one morning at Coleta Gonzalo slipping and sliding, huffing and puffing up a steep, not-quite-finished trail to a beautiful waterfall. Despite the thick mud, I have no complaints. All I can think of as I climb and ponder what Tompkins has done down here is, "What a perfect thing for somebody with too much money to do." A lot of other guys with a couple hundred million in the bank would focus on collecting mansions around the globe. If only others in his tax bracket would follow his example. . . . What he's created is a truly unique place in the far south for hiking, camping, kayaking, and fishing. The park also supports a couple hundred locals, making a livelihood on Tompkins-financed farms, a sound alternative to the other obvious economy, cutting down trees.

From this vantage I am seeing just a sliver of the park. Most of its land lies to the north, and is most easily accessed by water. Plans are for a dozen hiking trails covering sixty kilometers—to be built by a combination of locals and volunteers—and five visitor centers. Two more campgrounds will be built, at nearby fjords, and more small cabanas and horse-riding stables. For now, the best way to see the park is to contact the foundation's office in Puerto Montt. A handful of outfitters, including Alto Sur in Puerto Varas, are offering sea kayak tours that will lead into the heart of the park and take out at Coleta Gonzalo.

My second morning in the park, I wake up to a warm sun burning through the window of the tiny pickup truck. I crawl out, bending stiff knees and watching my breath cloud the blue sky. Roosters crow, and hammers pound under a climbing sun. I'm going to wait a little while for it to warm up before pushing my kayak into the frosty Patagonian sea.

At mid-morning, the small bay in front of Coleta Gonzalo is calm, the tide out. As I download my sea kayak, a bright, warming sun peeks over the far mountains.

Out on the water, into the cold, damp, blue sea, my first turn is left, out into the Pacific, a couple miles' paddle. I stick to the rocks, carving through the water past steep walls and the edge of the deep, deep fjord.

Initially the paddling is easy. A light breeze at my back. Across the bay I can just make out a small farm; the hills are covered with forest, the steepest topped by year-round snows. Much of the park is steep, inaccessible, and will stay that way indefinitely. From the sea I can hear wind whistling through the trees and unseen waterfalls pouring over rock ledges. Four birds, a duck, and a lone sea lion check me out. Otherwise the day paddling these deep blue seas is perfectly quiet.

Returning to shore after inspection of the interior of the fjord is a bit more difficult. The tide is coming back in, pushed by strong winds off the

Pacific. Whitecaps rise between two spits of land that guard the entrance to the fjord. Fighting small waves and stiff winds is a good workout, made easier by studying the landscape that for now is still so little known.

I pull my boat up on the ramp and lay down in the sun. The hammering has stopped. Despite the bright sun, the winds soon turn cold, and I take refuge next to the ramp, among a jumble of golden rocks that line either side. A perfect Patagonian siesta follows my first Pumalin paddle.

Parque Pumalin has been formally given to Chile; currently Tompkins has teamed with former foes, salmon fishermen, to fight the government and utilities intention to construct dams across the south of Chile and a delivery system of power lines through the park. His total land holdings are 1.8 million acres in southern Chile and Argentina, making him one of the largest private landowners in the world.

CRY WOLF

Renée Askins

Harper's, 1994

It is dawn in the lobby of the Chico Hot Springs Lodge in Montana, just north of Yellowstone National Park's northern border. The morning is cold and bright; winter's first dusting of snow came overnight. Renée Askins is settled into an overstuffed chair next to the woodstove. She's been up since before the sun, doodling in a tiny notepad, wrestling with a speech. Around her are piles of books, magazine articles, scientific reports, emptied Styrofoam cups, and photocopied poems from her Poems to Live By file ("I tend to use poetry as my handrails," she confesses).

Her blue eyes are tinted red from lack of sleep, a touch of the flu, and many long days of travel, press conferences, public hearings, and wrangling with supporters and opponents. Her long brown hair falls around her face as she writes (she has been described as looking like a western schoolmarm). Equal parts biologist, philosopher, and poet, Askins was trained in science, not speechmaking. Yet her seven-year-old Wolf Fund has been so successful that she's been forced to play a public role she never anticipated. Until her ultimate goal—the reintroduction of wolves to Yellowstone—is reached, she'll keep up the pace.

She's preparing for a pair of New York City events. The first is a Cartier-sponsored reception at which she will receive the Student Conservation Association's inaugural Conservation Award. The other is a fundraiser at which Robert Redford is hoped to "star." She's nervous; Redford doesn't often make himself available for such things. But 1994 is a big year for the Wolf Fund, and she needs money. She is uncertain this morning exactly what kind of appeal will get a roomful of hardened, big-city givers to unleash their checkbooks for wolves.

Over breakfast she describes the past years of struggle. As she tells me her story—passionately, intensely—the cornerstone of the speech she's so worried about produces itself.

"The rightness of this project is irrefutable. Wolves belong in Yellowstone.

You cannot argue that. It is the world's oldest national park, and it has every plant and animal species that existed when Europeans hit the shores—except wolves. Yellowstone is the largest temperate ecosystem in the world, a World Biosphere Reserve. Its management techniques inform and guide parks throughout the world. It should be a model."

Her argument takes flight, though no one is countering it. "Don't you think there is a certain arrogance and patronizing attitude to the conservation organizations that can ask Nepal to preserve its snow leopards or Mexico its jaguars or India its tigers, when we ourselves are not willing to preserve our preeminent predator, a vital part of the ecosystem in our first and foremost national park?"

She pauses to ponder what she's just said. "People sometimes characterize this as a crusade; I don't think it is at all. This is not my story. I am its voice; I am the storyteller. This is the story of wolves in Yellowstone. To me that story is so right and so important."

In recent years wolves have invaded the popular psyche. We've danced with them, run with them, and bought posters, picture books, and note cards graced by them. The Nature Company, for example, is selling out of everything from elegant coffee table books and calendars to wolf wind chimes and napkin rings. Just behind dolphins, wolves have become our most favored animal friend.

This despite the fact that wolves remain one of our most misunderstood animals, deeply embedded—both in mythology and in the twilight of our consciousness—somewhere between wildness and civilization. Writers as divergent as Aesop, Jack London, and Clarissa Pinkola Estés have explored the mystifying relationship between man and wolf over the centuries. Long thought of as companions to the devil, wolves have been linked in folklore with witches and portrayed in fairy tales as beasts, ogres, and evil incarnate (see "Little Red Riding Hood," "The Three Little Pigs," and all those werewolf stories).

For all the negative imagery, good wolves emerge, too. One myth holds that pricking oneself with a wolf's sharpened breastbone can stave off death; Native Americans believe that wolves' howls are the cries of lost spirits trying to return to earth; and in the story of Romulus and Remus, wolves are characterized as nurturing. In reality few species have the social sophistication that wolves have. They function in families in which all members contribute. Children are inexplicably drawn to wolves, despite the scary fairy tales. Although there hasn't been a wolf living in Yellowstone since the 1920s, in recent park-sponsored art contests in schools across the country, wolves figured prominently in students' drawings ands sculptures. It's not surprising that people are confused; even some park rangers will tell you there are wolves in the park. Not true.

Between 1600 and 1950 we killed every wolf in the West and most in the East. Financed by federal monies, the slaughter of wolves routinely brought sizable bounties. Some have called this the last tragic act in winning the West, following the decimation of the Native Americans and the buffalo. Barry Lopez, in his haunting *Of Wolves and Men*, tells of the extermination, which took place "with almost pathological determination." Wolves were lassoed and torn apart; their jaws were wired shut and they were left to starve; they were doused with gasoline and set afire. We didn't just eradicate them; we declared war. Even today, people in snowmobiles or airplanes pull up alongside wolves and blow them apart for sport. (And, to the dismay of environmentalists, a controversial "wolf control" program in Alaska is now allowing hunters near urban areas to trap and shoot wolves.)

In 1973 the Endangered Species Act required that the U.S. government take steps to bring back the wolf. Reintroduction should have happened automatically, but mighty opposition from livestock ranchers, big mining interests, and western politicians turned it into a twenty-year brawl. The fight came to a head last year. Scores of public hearings were held across the country, and though the majority of attendees favored reintroduction, the arguments against it were many. Ranchers fear that wolves will kill livestock; hunters worry that wolves will deplete large game herds; timber, oil, and gas companies fear that the presence of another endangered species may limit their access to public lands. The Wolf Fund and its supporters argue back, contending that wolves kill less than one quarter of one percent of livestock available to them in Minnesota and Canada; that Yellowstone's ungulate herds have increased by up to 80 percent in the past two decades and need natural culling; and that development would not be hindered by wolves, who are extremely adaptable and would choose to live outside the presence of man. (Some wolves do live in the U.S.—an estimated 1,750 in northern Minnesota, thirty in Michigan, sixty apiece in Wisconsin and Montana, and six thousand in Alaska. More than fifty-five thousand live in the unpopulated wilds of Canada.)

Today, after two decades of debate, the U.S. Fish and Wildlife Service has said that a wolf reintroduction in Yellowstone could begin by October of this year. One plan is to bring breeding pairs down from Alberta, Canada, with the eventual goal of 100 to 150 wolves living in the park's ecosystem. The $350,000 annual cost would be borne by the federal government. As early as next month the final paperwork will be put on the desk of Interior Secretary Bruce Babbitt. He has the last word and is on record favoring reintroduction. "I think in large ecosystems there's room for predator reintroduction, as long as we have a thoughtful way of controlling the effects off the public lands and outside the ecosystem areas," he said, days after taking the job. "We ought to be able to work it out."

If the reintroduction is successful, it will be due largely to Renée Askins and the Wolf Fund. Writing in the group's inaugural newsletter, she spelled out the case she's repeated many times since. "Reintroducing wolves to Yellowstone is an act of making room, of giving up the notion of 'bigger, better, and more,' to hold onto 'complete, balanced, and whole.' It is an act of giving back, a realigning, a recognition that we make ecological and ethical mistakes and learn from them, and what we learn can inform our actions. Thus, reintroducing wolves to Yellowstone is a symbolic act just as extermination of wolves from the West was a symbolic act."

Naturalist Alston Chase—author of *Playing God in Yellowstone*—is strident on the subject, insisting that we have a "moral obligation" to reintroduce wolves. Askins is more direct: "It is simply the right thing to do."

"Can't we have one place in America that is *wild*?" she wonders, claiming that Yellowstone without wolves is "like a watch without a mainspring."

Proponents of reintroduction are invariably proponents of the thirty-five-year-old Askins. The Wolf Fund's board of directors boasts the cream of the country's best-known environmentalists, outdoorsmen, moguls, and celebrities—George Schaller, Peter Mathiessen, Ted Turner, Yvon Chouinard, Robert Redford, and Harrison Ford.

Schaller, the world's most prominent field biologist, insists that Askins's approach "is conservation at its most basic and its best." Mathiessen, who taught Askins writing at Yale, calls her "vivid and engaging, unusually charming." Writer and naturalist Terry Tempest Williams says, "If the recovery of the wolf to Yellowstone is at the heart of saving our nation's most beloved national park, then Renée Askins is the heartbeat."

Simultaneously, she has collected a parcel of enemies. Late-night calls to her Jackson, Wyoming, office are often hateful, lewd, and violent. (She plays me a tape of one in which the caller threatens "to kill all wolves, sell their hides, and shoot the bitches that run the nonprofit group.") Public opposition is equally damning. Troy Mader, head of an anti-wolf organization called the Abundant Wildlife Society of North America, says, "Renée talks about restoring wildness. Malaria and typhoid are wild, too, but she's not talking about bringing them back." Dave Flitner, president of the Wyoming Farm Bureau, compares reintroduction to "inviting in the AIDS virus." Another opponent distributes bumper stickers declaring WOLVES ARE THE SADDAM HUSSEIN OF NATURE.

On a serene, late-fall day, lenticular clouds hover over the Tetons. Five months of below-freezing cold are just around the corner, and Tom Rush, folksinger and Askins's boyfriend for the past four years, stacks firewood outside their log cabin. Their house boasts a breathtaking view of the Tetons; through a spotting scope in the living room, elk, bison, and coyotes can be seen sunbathing on the sagebrush hills.

Inside, Askins is considering the possibility that her work may be nearly over. The Wolf Fund has a sunset clause: when wolves are reintroduced, its doors shut. She says that when the first wolves are released from their pens, she'll be happy to "just pitch a tent in the park and watch." She has studied Zen Buddhism for years and easily defines her life as Pre-Wolf, Wolf, and Post-Wolf. Comfortable at New York's Harvard Club (Tom graduated in 1963), she has also "known poor"—in the mid-1980s she shared a tepee with her dog, subsisting on packages of ramen noodles.

Askins grew up in the forests outside Boyne City, Michigan, and attended Kalamazoo College, where she wrote a paper for a theology course on the role of the wolf in religion and its historical associations with the devil. During her junior year, while participating in a wolf study, a forty-eight-hour-old pup named Natasha was put in Askins's hands, and the nineteen-year-old woman became its mother for three months, feeding it, cleaning it, sleeping with it tucked in her armpit. After Askins graduated, John Weaver, an endangered-species biologist whom she had met on the study, offered her a job in Jackson Hole, Wyoming, as a field technician. Since then her life has been nearly consumed with wolves.

In 1985 she was awarded a grant to bring a traveling exhibit to Yellowstone called *Wolves and Humans: Competition, Coexistence, and Conflict.* The popularity of the exhibit convinced her that the public would like to see wolves brought back to the park. Later that year, before heading to Yale to get her master's in wildlife ecology, Askins held the first Wolf Fund fundraiser. She envisioned "a single group devoted to a single project . . . a conservation SWAT team, very focused, very bright, light on its feet, and adaptable to a highly dynamic political scene."

The group's single focus, as well as its efforts to reach out to minorities, children, and women, sets it apart from the big conservation groups. Its founder sees the Wolf Fund serving as a kind of "herding dog," encouraging the larger conservation groups to focus part of their attention, talents, and money on her issues. Attractive, smart, and candid, she has a tendency to disarm her critics; that is one of her goals. She doesn't believe that conservationists need to be or should be confrontational, but that they must be educational. She is also unlike some of the more extreme environmentalists in that she truly understands the plight of the small rancher who is scared of wolves. The rancher's fear is that his herd of seven or eight cattle could be decimated by a couple of wolves that cross out of parkland and take his animals. Askins's mission has been to explain both sides, to try to reach conciliation. "What emerges is a genuine fear and anguish over losing their livelihoods. I live in the West. These people are my neighbors and my friends. I understand what they're going through. So our efforts have been to create a solution that protects wolves as well as people. That's why we haven't been branded as fanatical."

One cold day we go for a walk in Yellowstone, through sage-covered hills and rhyolite rock, through wolf country—Hellroaring Creek, Amethyst Mountain, the Mirror Plateau. Stopping, Askins lays back her head and howls. Coyotes answer from all directions. "I feel very hopeful, like we've crossed a threshold, that the process is under way," she says.

Still, she is upset that some of her supporters are already uncorking the champagne, celebrating a victory that is not yet certain. She's already fielded calls from movie producers and TV crews who want to be there when the gates are opened, the first wolves released. "My message to them is, 'Come now. These are the critical days,'" she says, for a myriad of things could happen to delay reintroduction, from political strong-arming to expensive legal appeals. "There is no question in my mind that there will be extremely powerful constituents who will still try to stop or sabotage the reintroduction."

People's characters are formed largely by the place they live and work, and Yellowstone has had a profound effect on Askins, both on a subliminal and a more physical level. "I feel very deeply that you must take a stand somewhere, " she says. "In some ways what I've done is a very modest stand, but it's one that is very important to this place, which is so much a part of me. And as for the species, the more intimate I have become with these animals, the more painful the compromise of dealing with their captivity. From this experience, ironically because it's a bittersweet one, comes the force of my commitment to fight for them in the wild."

Looking out over the sun-dappled hills, she peers into the near distance, straining for signs of wildlife. "We exterminated the wolf to take control. I think people are beginning to see we've taken too much control."

In 1995, 14 Canadian wolves were successfully reintroduced in Yellowstone. Renee Askins currently lives in California with her daughter, husband Tom Rush and a menagerie of animals, though no wolves.

GREAT EXPECTATIONS
Robert F. Kennedy Jr.

Men's Journal, 1995

It's an August afternoon and Bobby Kennedy and a pair of Canadian Indians are salmon fishing off Vancouver Island's Clayquot Sound. The charter is owned by one of the Tla-o-qui-ahts, whose people have been trolling these Pacific waters for hundreds of years. We're a mile off the coast and rolling waves rock the forty-foot boat. All around us bob similar craft, hopefully having better luck.

Tall, athletic and forty, Bobby sets a big pole off the back of the boat then retires to the captain's chair. He wears Nikes, a baggy swim suit covered with dollar signs, a polo shirt featuring a couple of sizable holes, a sweatshirt tied around his waist, and a Tofino Air ball cap turned backwards on his head. His gray-blue eyes are a perfect match to the summer sky.

Conversation ranges wide while we wait for a fish. Much of the talk revolves around why Bobby is here—to help the Indians strategize in their fight with the British Columbian government over logging of what they see as their land. Excited by the battle, Bobby leans forward in his chair and calls the government "criminals" for allowing the legal clear-cutting. "They should be locked up," he says. With the sun at its peak, he reminisces about the first time he visited this part of North America, when he was twelve, on a ten-day pack trip with his father and Supreme Court Justice William O. Douglas. As we reel in empty lines, he is asked by the Canadians about his siblings and he runs down the list of ten brothers and sisters. When he gets to brother David, he stares at the horizon. "He's dead, you know."

Jumping back and forth between the bridge and the deck, reeling in the heavily weighted line, sinking it back into the deep, his mood is happy, relaxed. But when conversation lags, he adapts the distant, lonely stare that indicates a lot is going on inside that he chooses not to, or cannot, articulate. I've seen this look before. His gaze masks wariness, a solitariness that comes with being born into America's most famous and perhaps most tragic family. The look reminds his Uncle Ted of RFK, a look the senator can only describe as "sad."

Bobby no longer lives up to the stereotypical "bad Kennedy" image, though for many years he epitomized the privileged, reckless, arrogant, beyond-the-law youth many often associated with his clan. With those wild days behind, replaced by a life of good works and commitment, he is on a path that allows him to try and live up to the rather large footprints left by his father. A devoted outdoorsman, he is also a daily church-goer; onshore this night he will attend a local AA meeting. His day will end near midnight with a tall glass of milk.

As we approach the dock of the small village of Tofino, Bobby offers a rare bit of public introspection. "I wish some days never had an end," he says, "because sometimes I feel like if I don't get things done today, there may be no tomorrow.

Being a Kennedy—especially a "real" Kennedy, versus growing up a Smith or a Shriver or a Lawford—means every day is a roller coaster. You grow up in a world where your name evokes royalty and is simultaneously the butt of tasteless jokes. Some days you're on top of the world, others you're racing downhill fast, nearly out of control. To be Robert F. Kennedy Jr.—heir to one of the most idolized names in American political history—has meant the roller coaster has soared higher and plunged lower than the others of his generation, twenty-nine cousins in all, taking him literally from the White House to a halfway house. But Bobby doesn't complain. "I don't look at being a Kennedy as a punishment," he says, early on a Tofino morning after a brisk swim in the ocean. "I look at it as a privilege."

Long regarded within his own family as the one with the bearing, smarts, and charisma to carry on the family's political heritage, it was expected that if any of his generation were to be president of the United States, it would be him. Such an expectation would be a heavy burden for anyone to bear—even a Kennedy—and over the years it has exacted a heavy price on the environmental lawyer, who has yet to run for political office.

Like many of his family, he has devoted himself to a public life and has essentially five jobs: he administers the Pace University Environmental Law Clinic, is a senior staff attorney with the Natural Resources Defense Council (NRDC), is the chief prosecutor for the Hudson Riverkeeper, gives twenty-five weekend-long lectures a year on college campuses (his primary money-maker), and, last but not least, he's a Kennedy, nearly a full-time job of its own. Internationally he has developed a reputation for joining indigenous groups in fighting environmental battles. In his own backyard, New York State, he has become a zealous advocate for protecting the Hudson River and upstate reservoirs that provide New York City's drinking water.

Handsome, politically savvy if not yet electorally tested, and whip-smart, he is driven by an inherited competitiveness that makes everything from diving for lobsters to building a campfire to telling a ghost story into a contest. One day on Clayquot we play touch football in the sand. With his team down by several touchdowns, it is time to go and he pulls a classic play from the book written by his father's generation. "Next touchdown wins," he crows, confident since his team is on the verge of scoring.

Those who knew his father say his namesake has a charisma to match the old man. He charms men and women, old and young, Americans and foreigners alike with a flash of his blue eyes and a hint of that patented Kennedy speech. In recent years he has become a model citizen and family spokesperson. (When a New York newspaper reported that Bobby and Jackie O. had an affair, it was Bobby Jr. who defiantly denied it; same when a biography excoriating his mother was published last year.) He seems to know everyone, from movie stars, pro athletes, and journalists to politicians and sons and daughters of foreign leaders. (When President Clinton visited FDR's Hudson River home at Hyde Park soon after he was elected, he was accompanied by just two men: one of Roosevelt's grandsons and RFK Jr.)

A skilled hardball politician, he uses his smarts and his good name to get what he wants. Like his father, he can be both ruthless and shy, driven, obsessive, and possessing of a good-sized ego. He likes seeing his name in print and never forgets a slight. Like many famous people, he can be occasionally insecure. He loves the outdoors and adventure—has jumped out of planes, speed-skied at more than seventy miles per hour and learned to kayak on some of the world's toughest whitewater—and keeps hawks and falcons on his eleven-acre estate north of New York City. Perhaps the most stinging criticism foes use against him in various environmental battles is that he's a "celebrity," i.e., a lightweight. Others who have worked with and against him cite "overzealousness" as both strength and a flaw. He's been called a carpetbagger, even in his own state. "It's one thing to be an advocate, which Bobby Kennedy is," says a former administrator of New York's Department of Environmental Protection. "It's another to be a *self-righteous* advocate, which he can be, too." Current DEP chief Marilyn Gelver says, "Intellectually, I think his arguments are often good and provocative. However, as a practical matter, he is not a consensus builder."

In the past six years I've traveled with Bobby to the sites of various environmental fights up and down the Western Hemisphere and have been witness to the burden, curse, and incredible reach of the Kennedy name. In a tiny shack off the Bió-Bió River in southern Chile, an old woman softly explained to him in Spanish why she didn't want to see the river dammed. On a wall of her modest home were two framed photos, one of Jesus Christ, the other of JFK. A few days later, getting off a bus to stretch our legs, we step into a bar for a soda; the mayor recognizes the young Kennedy and rushes home to get his camera and his wife. At a press conference in Santiago, the first question asked of Bobby (and brothers Michael and Max) is if they are afraid of being assassinated. (The answer is no.) In northern Quebec, officials of Hydro-Quebec, the powerful power company that hoped to build a hydroelectric plant that he opposed, sent a corporate jet to give Bobby—and fifteen friends—a ride back to Montreal. When he can, he surrounds himself with a fraternity of football-toting pals; at charity events in New York City adoring women have gone as far as to throw panties in his direction. His home in upstate New York is often shared with a recovering alcoholic or drug addict whom he has taken in until they get their feet on the ground.

His has hardly been a charmed life. His father's assassination sent him into a fifteen-year spiral that ended with a highly publicized drug bust when he was twenty-nine. For many years, through his teens and twenties, he believed the hype that surrounded him, listened to those who whispered, "You are like Jack, you could be president." Such confidences filled him with an invincibility that was nearly his demise. After he was arrested in the early 1980s, he laid low, wrestling with his demons, deciding his future, and laying a foundation for a career. In the last half-dozen years he's reemerged as a remade man, devoutly Christian, markedly driven. Today he travels afar to meet with opponents and colleagues, makes speeches reminiscent of his father, lends his name to fundraisers . . . assumes the mantle. Sober for more than a decade, with a new wife and a new baby, he seems to have arrived at a peacefulness not often associated with a family forever intertwined with such historical buzzwords as Chappaquiddick, Marilyn, and Palm Beach.

Yet for all the apparent calm, when you're around Bobby, there is an energy, an aura that implies a passion for being tested, that smolders inside. Comparisons between him and his father are inevitable. When his father was Bobby Jr.'s age, he'd already helped elect a president, run the Justice Department, and been elected to the U.S. Senate. Today, the-son-with-the-most-promise realizes that elected politics may well be impractical for him. Yet the question is on the mind if not the lips of everyone he meets: When are you going to run, Bobby, when?

In a small Cessna we fly over the sandy beaches, tall forests, and indiscriminate clear-cuts that dot Clayquot Sound. Seated next to John Adams, executive director of the NRDC and one of his mentors, Bobby looks out at a hill barren of standing trees and twin streams clogged by felled cedars. "That is the ugliest clear-cut I've ever seen," says Bobby. He's in a feisty mood, having just gotten off the phone with a radio host in Vancouver who accused him of being a "Yankee imperialist."

"He really thrashed me," he admits, "but I guess that's his job. The 'Kennedy stuff' wasn't so bad." Crossing borders to help indigenous people fight environmental battles has become one of Bobby's fortes. That's why he's in British Columbia. The Assembly of First Nations Indians invited him and the NRDC to come talk initially in the summer of 1993. The Indians liked what the American environmentalists had helped accomplish in northern Quebec, halting the building of a massive hydroelectric dam off James Bay that would have flooded thousands of acres of Cree land. After two days and eighteen hours of closed-door meetings, Bobby and the chiefs emerged with a battle plan, demanding—for the first time—that these Indians be consulted by the government about the future of "their" lands. Francis Frank, chief of the Tla-o-qui-ahts, assured me soon after, "It was Bobby's record, not his name, that attracted us to him." On that trip, accompanied by his eight-year-old son and namesake, Bobby was feted in a fashion growing up a Kennedy prepares you for. He was carried ashore in a dugout canoe for an outpouring of ceremonial gift giving by Indian leaders. As he received robes, paintings, masks, bracelets, and honorific gifts of cash, he was told that one gift "gives you the right to speak to the world on behalf of the Clayquot people."

"It's hard to quantify the importance of the NRDC and Bobby," Cliff Atleo, chief of the Ahousaht tribe, said. "We would have gotten where we are without them . . . but it might have taken two hundred more years." In a short thank you, Bobby insisted his biggest goal here and elsewhere is one adapted from his father: looking out for people left out of the process.

Clayquot (pronounced *kla-kwot*) Sound is 650,000 acres of ancient coastal rainforest, islands, and magnificent sandy beaches. It is the largest intact temperate rainforest remaining in North America. The government of British Columbia sold rights to log the island, and on April 12, 1993, Prime Minister of British Columbia Michael Harcourt announced that his government would preserve only 33 percent of the Clayquot forest. Much of the preserved areas were bog, marginal forest, and alpine rock—areas already under protected status. Slated for logging were giant Sitka spruce, western hemlock, and western red cedar hundreds of feet tall and hundreds of years old. With an eight-foot-round log worth fifteen thousand to twenty thousand dollars, the government had decided the trees were worth more cut down than standing. Another big reason for the decision: the British Columbian government has invested $50 million of taxpayer money in MacMillan Bloedel, the multinational timber industry giant that holds most of the tree farm licenses to log Clayquot.

Since Bobby's first visit, both sides have traded accusations as he's helped elevate the fight to an international audience. "MacMillan Bloedel has no interest in this land except to cut the lumber and run," says Bobby, "but if the Indians lose their resources, they're through." Gerry Stoney, president of the regional logging union, answered in a statement: "His support . . . is the ultimate in American-style bully tactics." Dennis Fitzgerald, environmental communications manager for MacMillan

Bloedel, cites Bobby's ability to attract a media crowd as a sly way of diminishing his effect. "The NRDC gets attention because they've got Bobby Kennedy Jr.. If it wasn't for him, I'm not sure they would get heard. He is a celebrity and thus gets media."

Bobby relishes such attacks. It means he's getting to them. "I had a strong idea about what the First Nations strategy should be from the start," he explains after our sky-view of the island. We are sitting on the deck of the Tofino Lodge, looking out at the Pacific, one of the most pristine views in the western world. "But at that point they were very tentative. Why? Because, first of all, they are just nice people and they didn't want to be unneighborly, even though it was their land. Indians sometimes don't distinguish between white people who want their land for park reasons and white people who want their land for lumber. In the view of a lot of the tribe, we were just all white people who wanted their land. Ultimately they trusted us because we were a group fighting not just for fishes and trees, but for the idea of autonomy, of self-determination."

His interest in indigenous people is inherited. As a U.S. Senator, his father became involved in affairs of New York State Indians and formed an Indian Education Subcommittee. He visited a Blackfoot reservation at Fort Hall, Idaho, where he discovered shocking rates of teenage alcoholism, delinquency, and suicide. Touring the reservation and seeing the hovels and old railroad boxcars where Indian families lived, he called it a "crime" that the "First Americans" should live in such conditions. "I wish I'd been born an Indian," he once confided to Senate colleague Fred Harris, whose wife LaDonna was a Comanche.

"When we were young, most of my brothers and sisters had Indian names by the time they were teenagers," says Bobby. "Everywhere my father went, he would take some of us with him and he would always ask if there was an Indian reservation nearby and we would go and meet people."

Despite a variety of successes in the U.S. and Quebec, he's also been involved in battles that did not end in victory for his side. In Chile, trying to stop the building of dams on the Bió-Bió, he and the NRDC ran into powerful political and economic machinery that steamrolled into concrete the first of what is expected to be five dams. Their experience trying to help native groups in Ecuador was a disaster. In 1991 environmentalists in the U.S. and around the world took offense at Bobby and the NRDC apparently mediating a deal between Conoco and Ecuadorian Indians for oil rights. An e-mail accusing Bobby of siding with the enemy was circulated internationally; a *New Yorker* story followed, in which he and colleague Jacob Scherr were branded "environmental imperialists." "They came to Ecuador for five days and then went home and sat down with an oil company and decided they knew what was best for us," complained one Ecuadorian environmentalist. "What on earth gave them that right?"

The issue was complex and his defense is too, but he'll repeat it in length for anyone who asks. He and the NRDC saw Conoco as the least of all evils and agreed to help negotiate a deal between the oil company and the Indians which could have brought many millions of dollars to the local populace. The trouble was defining which Indians to negotiate with. "Naïve" is the word the *New Yorker* used to describe Bobby's approach. He is still irked by the nastiness of the personal attacks. "It was the first time I saw that environmentalists could be bad," he says.

Liz Barratt-Brown is the other NRDC attorney working on the Clayquot issue. She recognizes the value Bobby brings to such fights, if sometimes shrinking from her occasional role as his scheduler and babysitter. ("I didn't go to law school for this," she half-jokes one day on Clayquot as she pulls him into a car, late for an interview.) What difference would it make if a smart, experienced senior attorney named Robert Francis represented the NRDC in B.C.?

"I think what surprises people is when Bobby shows up and people see he really is a compassionate guy, he really does care, and he's not just 'a Kennedy,' using these issues for political gain," says Barratt-Brown. "What we bring into this partnership is the ability to put pressure on the Harcourt government from outside. This is really Bobby's specialty— bringing about environmental change through political pressure and law-suits and prosecution.

"It is obviously what has made the Canadians fear his involvement in these issues," she continues. He also, unfortunately, gives them something to focus their attack on. They say, 'What right does a wealthy Kennedy have to come up here, kayak for a few days, and tell us what to do?'"

Over the years Bobby has learned to deflect the "just a Kennedy" criticisms, particularly if they suggest he's using Indian issues to promote himself or his own interests. He sees his involvement in these issues as continuing his father's legacy, an obligation he felt obliged to, as he says, "pick up."

"My father truly believed in democracy. That the democratic system was the only way that we were going to solve problems, because it was the only system capable of harnessing the energies of all different kinds of people. That we were really a collection of different people and that we were supposed to be an example to other nations of what people could do when they work together. That we would never live up to our own destiny if we ignored the fundamental injustice upon which this nation was founded, which was the mistreatment of the people who were here before anybody else.

"He felt we had to go back and make amends to the Indians, whatever the cost. To make sure people got their land back, or whatever proper amends was. That was totally fundamental to his worldview that this country just wouldn't work unless we went back and settled up with the people who were here first. That's the area of the work I enjoy most, in part because it is something passed down from him."

RFK loved the wilds and was an environmentalist before the first environmental laws were written. He took his family to the most beautiful natural places on earth—a pack trip to the Olympic Peninsula, whitewater rafting on the big western rivers, mountain climbing, skiing. His son remembers those times as the best days of his life and is grateful to have the memories.

"I felt a great depth of loss after he died," Bobby says now. "I cried a lot at that time, but afterward I knew that so many people shared it; one thing that made it easier was that I never felt alone with that loss. To this day, I've seen pictures of my father in the homes of rural whites in Appalachia, on Indian reservations throughout the West, and in black people's homes in Harlem.

"It's not difficult for me to talk about my memories with him. For me it was an amazing time. It was extraordinary—he took us with him every-where. . . . I made a wonderful trip with him to the iron-curtain countries, to Poland, to Czechoslovakia, and on campaigns in this country. The crowds were vast. You don't see anything like it in politics today. The streets were just jammed with people. He would stand us on the roof of a car or on the back of a train and talk to them. People would be screaming,

'Bobby!' 'Bobby!' 'Bobby!' I remember people wailing at him, even the nuns. They loved him and they'd tear at his clothes and fight just to touch him. Afterwards he'd come home bruised and his hands would be swollen from people just squeezing him and not wanting to let go. "

The son almost didn't live long enough to pick up the reins of his father's patrimony. In many ways Bobby's life began anew on June 6, 1968. He was fourteen when his father was killed. He'd gone to bed the night before after hearing the news that his father had won the California primary. He got up early to read the details in the *Washington Post*. The paper carried much different news and he fed the paper, slowly, page by page, into the fire at the family home at Hickory Hill.

"I was at boarding school at the time and the priest came in and woke me up around 6 a.m. and told me that Daddy had been shot and there was a car waiting outside for me. They took me home, and we flew out to L.A. with some of my brothers and sisters on Hubert Humphrey's plane. David and some of the other children were already out there because they had been campaigning with him. We went into the hospital and we sat with my father; my mother was there, and I held his hand that time for the last time. His head was bandaged, there was a respirator, and he had black eyes. The whole floor of the hospital was cordoned off. There were U.S. Marshals there . . . security . . . ten of us kids. We were put in one of the wardrooms of the hospital, and we all slept there together. And Joe and my mother stayed with my father, and at dawn Joe came in and told us that he was gone, and we all cried.

"I wasn't angry so much as I felt a terrible loss. But I also felt that I shared it with everybody. When we got to Washington we drove him up to Arlington Cemetery to bury him next to Jack. When we drove past the mall, it was the time of the Poor People's campaign. Hundreds of poor men were camped in shacks and tents on the mall. Ralph Abernathy was there with all of them, and they all came and took off their hats, quietly, and held them over their chests as we passed by.

"I went back to the house, and there was a reception after the funeral. I escaped from the crowd and went up to my father's office. He had a bed in there for when he would stay up late working. I just lay down on that bed and there were pictures of my Uncle Jack and my Aunt Kick and my Uncle Joe and my father when he was young, and they were all dead. I looked at those, and I just wept.

"After about an hour, Dave Hackett, who had been my father's best friend, came in. Dave was a lot like my father: He was short, he was tough, and he was a brilliant athlete and painfully shy—all qualities he shared with my father. He was quiet, and he sat in that room, and he never said anything for about an hour. And I just lay there on the bed on my stomach, crying quietly, and then he said, 'He was the best man I ever knew.' "

Being a family of enduring pragmatists, soon after his father was buried both adults and his peers began to talk about Bobby as the heir apparent, the young Kennedy best qualified to pick up the sword and run, run, run. Many told him he could be president, and—for a while—he believed them.

These are the words used to describe him as a young man: agile, tall and nimble, smart, witty, flamboyant, wiry, enigmatic, a loner by choice, leader of his generation, winner of all competitions. Lem Billings, best friend of JFK and later a buddy of RFK, became a father figure, proclaiming young Bobby "like Jack." Even Bobby Sr. contributed to the mythologizing; having once said his namesake was "just like the president." Cousin Chris Lawford put it most succinctly: "Bobby was our last illusion."

But at the moment he was a fourteen-year-old kid who felt both adrift and invincible. The combination led to more than a decade of wild acting-out. At fifteen he'd been expelled from prep school, gone to Africa on safari, and sold a story to *Life* based on his experience. At sixteen he spent days in the woods with his red-tailed hawk, at night he led a group of cousins in terrorizing Hyannis. That same year he was arrested (along with cousin Bobby Shriver) for pot possession. His mother punished her son, but that hardly diminished his feelings of invincibility. Instead, he ran. To Los Angeles, where he hopped trains, slept with tramps and vagrants. "I had no contact with home," he told family biographers, "except that every couple weeks I'd call Lem. I was riding with bums. It was good: I could be one of them and not be a Kennedy."

At Harvard he became a cult figure, attracting male friends, women, sycophants, and the allegiance of a contingency of the cousins. In his twenties he organized daring, dangerous raft trips accompanied by a legion of loyal brothers, cousins, and friends. After graduating from Harvard and law school at the University of Virginia, the wild life picked up.

In their biography of the clan, *The Kennedys: An American Drama*, Peter Collier and David Horowitz saw Bobby as a tragedy waiting to happen. "He refused to stop and look how drugs and different-women-every-night and high-life were affecting his life. Stuck in a heroic persona of his own creation—always having to outdo himself, having to go one step further than everyone else to validate his status as the Kennedy who would someday 'make it.' Unlike his brother Joe he was unwilling and unable to regard politics as a patient process of small steps. Under Lem's guidance he had in effect been an unannounced candidate for the presidency since he was 16, an ambition he held to even as his lifestyle was becoming increasingly wild and unrestrained."

The "illusion" lasted until he was nearly thirty years old, when in September 1983 he was busted for heroin possession after a stewardess on a Republic Airlines flight bound for South Dakota found him in the toilet "white as a sheet, cold as an ice cube, large beads of sweat pouring off him . . . eyes wide open and fully dilated."

The pilot radioed ahead to Rapid City to request that a paramedic and ambulance be on hand to meet the flight. When the plane landed, Bobby was helped down the steps but declined medical assistance. At first he identified himself as "Bobby Francis." Local police, however, suspected a drug overdose and obtained a search warrant to look through his bags. They found slightly less than one gram of heroin. Four days later he was arrested for possession of heroin, a felony carrying a maximum penalty of two years in jail and a two-thousand-dollar fine. It appeared that bad luck had caught up with the third generation.

After the fall, Lem Billings would say about his protégé, "I was right that Bobby is like Jack. What I didn't see was how much the world has changed. Jack was lucky; he didn't have a lot of Kennedys getting there before him. Everywhere a boy like Bobby looks, there are footprints, all of them deeper than his own."

RFK was once asked whether, given its apparent propensity for tragedy, the family shouldn't step out of the limelight. He responded, "Good luck is something you make and bad luck is something you endure."

I wonder what he would have said to his son, as he grew up--was it just bad luck, something to be endured? Would he have stopped his son, warned him, saved him from himself? We'll never know. What we do know is that this life-endangering crisis triggered a period of introspection for young Bobby much like the one experienced by his father after JFK was killed.

After his arrest Bobby was admitted to Fair Oaks Hospital in Summit, New Jersey; he completed a five-month treatment program in February 1984, a month after his thirtieth birthday, pleaded guilty, and was sentenced to two years' probation and eight hundred hours of community service. A call from a friend of the family went to NRDC chief John Adams, whose first job out of law school had been in the Kennedy Justice Department. Bobby had always been interested in the outdoors and grew up with a menagerie of lizards, snakes, raccoons, rats, and birds. He got his first homing pigeon when he was seven, his first hawk when he was twelve. He had hoped to be a veterinarian. His passion was so evident his father commissioned naturalists from the Bronx Zoo to make him a walk-in terrarium for his thirteenth birthday. He had expressed interest in environmental work and it was hoped Adams could provide some direction.

Adams offered to try. "At first, I think everybody at NRDC said to themselves, 'We can afford this, this is a good thing to do.' Not necessarily for the benefit of the NRDC, but because they—his father and his uncle— had died and here was a young man on the verge of not making it."

Bobby doesn't talk much about those years, especially around journalists. All he'll say for the record is, "I was rethinking my life around 1984 and just decided to go back and do the thing I always wanted to do." Though he's been sober for more than ten years, regularly attends AA meetings, and goes to church almost every day, he doesn't talk specifics about his recovery. Today he is heavily involved in helping other recovering addicts. In March the New York City Samaritan Foundation honored him at a dinner for his work with their residential substance program.

With an introduction from John Adams, he went to work with the Hudson River Foundation, which was building a research station in Garrison, New York. John Cronin, founder of the first-of-its-kind Hudson Riverkeeper project, was its initial tenant. Cronin was in the process of suing Exxon, and Bobby went to work for him as an investigator.

"Newburgh, across the river, was an environmental mess, known as Dodge City on the Hudson," says Bobby. "We decided to target one creek as an example. Working on weekends, I walked seven miles up this creek, from its mouth at the Hudson to the dam, and found twenty-four polluters along the way. Everybody from Mobil Oil to dye houses, mom-and-pop automobile yards to sewage-treatment plants, a tire-changing operation dumping tires into the creek.

"By then I'd gotten my license to practice law and I put together case files on each of the twenty-four. By the end of the summer of 1984, we sued all of them. Those were my first cases." He went to work fulltime for the Hudson River Foundation; his sole clients are the Hudson River Fishermen's Association (later changed to Riverkeeper). He went back to law school at night, at Pace University in White Plains, to get his master's in environmental law. He was the program's first graduate and now administers its unique environmental legislation clinic, the base from which he and his students sue polluters up and down the Hudson River. He regards his continuing work helping to protect the Hudson and the watershed that feeds it as his biggest success.

"He learned to be a lawyer, learned to be an activist, an advocate, and an environmentalist," says John Adams. "He has definitely earned his place."

By 1989 his role at the NRDC had expanded to an international level. "By then I'd developed an expertise locally, had developed some credentials. I knew I couldn't go down to Ecuador or Chile and tell people they couldn't pollute their environment without them saying to me, with a lot of justification, 'You're an American, how can you talk to us? You've destroyed your rivers and your streams and your wilderness areas.'

"But we had developed a model for ecosystem protection on the Hudson. Today it is probably one of the richest water bodies on earth, the only major river system in the entire North Atlantic that still has strong spawning stocks of its entire historical species of fish. A big reason is that people along its banks have taken responsibility, have made war on pollution. That model gave me the credentials to cross borders."

John Adams sees Bobby's carving out a niche as an environmentalist as a way of both distinguishing himself from and continuing his father's legacy.

"His father stood for something very important to a lot of people: justice. The undercounted, the underprivileged, poor people, blacks, Indians. He spoke to these people and Bobby sees this as his legacy," says Adams. "He wants to carry that message forward and he does it very effectively. He believes in these people, experiences them, and is moved by them. He is very religious and thus very philosophical about their needs, their goals. The truth is, Bobby Kennedy is more of a philosopher than anything else. "He doesn't use these people, doesn't use any of us. He's not angling, he's not promoting himself for political life. There's no other Bobby out there. You will look a long time searching for one. He is just deeply involved in his life."

The first time I asked Bobby about his plans for running for office, we were fishing on a small pond off Chile's wild Bió-Bió. Until then we'd been having a nice, early-morning conversation, about birds, whitewater, trout. When I changed the subject, he grew silent, stared into the distance, answered in short sentences, tried to change the subject. I've asked the question again since, always with the same response. I'm never sure if he doesn't *like* to talk about it or doesn't *want* to talk about it. Everyone asks, and my guess is he's probably tired of it. This is what he said the first time I asked: "I love what I do. You've seen me out here. I have a lot of fun. I just take one day at a time. I've had opportunities to take appointed jobs or run for a variety of offices, but I've had to keep asking myself, 'Would that really be better than what I'm doing?'" (The Clinton administration offered him a job as an EPA regional director; he's considered several congressional seats, going back to the early 1980s.) On another day, years later, he spoke more specifically about the drawbacks of political office. "The downside is that you spread yourself thin," says Bobby. "By having to speak out on all issues you dilute your effectiveness on the issues you really know what you're talking about. I might know everything there is to know about New York City's water supply, but not be able to talk about the long-term effects of food stamps or health care. I honestly try to run my life one day at a time. At this point, I know I'm not supposed to be running for anything today." (Not coincidentally, before his run at the presidency, some around RFK felt "he was being pushed forward by a momentum outside him, carrying on less because he really wanted to than because people told him he had to."

Peter Kaplan is a New York magazine editor, Bobby's roommate at Harvard, and still a confidant. While he is convinced his friend could raise the necessary monies and stand up to any campaign rigors, he confesses he doesn't know if Bobby truly wants to run. "It confuses him, too," says Kaplan. "I think he would like to know if elected politics is his future. But he honestly doesn't know. His indecision is not a ruse."

I get the distinct feeling political office does not hold a power over him. That he doesn't really want to run. Doesn't want, or need, to be tested. Doesn't want to have to relive or defend the past. As a nation we've gotten pretty comfortable electing people to office that admit to having smoked pot; heroin is another beast. Yet "running" is what others expect of him, so he continues to dance with the prospect. This isn't to suggest he couldn't get up for the challenge. His closest friends hope (for selfish reasons?) that he'll pick one of the races offered him. And why not? He loves the give and take of hand-to-hand politics. He likes to help. He likes to lead. He's competitive. He has an ego. He likes public respect. He loves making a speech. He thinks he has something to give. He's a Kennedy. There are pragmatic reasons for *not* running, too. Including competition within his own family. Where JFK only had to compete with brother Joe, among this new generation there are potential contenders up and down the family tree. Bobby would hesitate to join a Congress where he would now be the third cousin—brother Joe is in his fourth term in the seat once held by JFK; Ted's son Patrick was just elected to his first, from Rhode Island. In New York he could face competition for a U.S. Senate seat from either JFK Jr. or brother-in-law Andy Cuomo, both formidable names themselves.

Bobby no longer wears the false vest of invincibility. He knows better now, has learned that despite being a Kennedy he's human. His motivations have become less selfish, more pure, his priorities reordered. It may be for the best if he is never elected to political office. His strengths may be best used outside the system, an advocate with a powerful voice and incredible access. He may be too introspective, too narrow-focused to make a good politician. His willingness to look inside separates him from the pack of politicians, environmentalists, and Kennedys. "For now my own family is my number one obligation," he says, referring both to his nuclear and extended clans. "Any decision I have to make, I have to make by first considering my obligations to them."

On a rainy day last November, one day after what would have been his father's seventieth birthday and the day before the thirty-first anniversary of his uncle's assassination, we talked in his office at Pace. On the walls hang paintings of wildlife and landscapes. The only hint of family is a plaque hung on the doorframe, given to his father when he was senator. It pictures him standing near the Hudson River. Snapshots of Bobby Jr. with a cross-section of famous friends are consigned to his assistant's office: Jesse Jackson, Jack Nicholson, Whoopi Goldberg, Bill Clinton, Jerry Garcia, Bonnie Raitt, Ray Charles. A "Sludge Happens" bumper sticker is affixed to a file cabinet and a "Cuomo '94" hat sits on the floor.

It's been a big week. The Quebec government put the final stake through the heart of the James Bay hydro project, announcing it would never be built. In B.C., none other than Prime Minister Michael Harcourt has proclaimed Bobby persona non grata. In New York City he is locked in a vociferous debate with some of his colleagues at the NRDC over how to handle the city's new take on potentially limiting the watershed that provides it with water. Bobby argues they shouldn't give an inch; other attorneys are pushing to negotiate. Inside his small, crowded office the phone rings every other minute.

We talk about the role of environmentalism and its advocates. His response is quick and unique. "We're not in this to preserve nature for nature's sake. We're not preserving those great forests in the Pacific Northwest for the sake of a spotted owl. We're preserving those great forests because we believe they have more value to humanity standing than they would if they were cut down. We're not preserving the Hudson River for the sake of the striped bass, we're preserving it because we believe that the river is more valuable as an economic resource, as a cultural and spiritual resource, the way it enriches us, the way it enriches humanity, if it is pure and pristine and healthy than if it's polluted and there are no fisheries.

"We can't really call the shots, we can't make the decisions, and we can't even speak for nature. This planet was given to us by God and it's arrogant for us to destroy it because we're going to lose our ability to sense the divine, to understand who we are and what we're doing here and our own potential as human beings."

He is on the edge of his chair now, twisting a bottle cap in his hands. Gone is the distracted look you get when you ask if he still wants to be president. "If you look at the great religions throughout history, there's a connection to nature in all of them. In the Koran all of the great prophets come out of the desert and all of them are shepherds. In the Old Testament there are numerous references, consider the Garden of Eden and Noah's Ark. In the New Testament, Christ is born in a manger surrounded by animals. He finds his divinity for the first time while he's in the desert, communing with nature for forty days. Virtually all his parables are taken from nature: I am the vine, you are the branches; the mustard seed; the little swallow scattering the seeds on the fallow ground; the fig tree; lilies of the field.

"That's not an accident. He did that because that's how he stayed in touch with the people. They would confer the truth of his wisdom by looking around themselves and verifying it in the things they saw every day and knew he was speaking the truth.

"Our values don't come to us from nature. Nature is not God and you make a mistake by confusing the two. God is God, but nature is one of the ways that He communicates with us and tells us what right from wrong is."

He stretches long legs and looks out the window at the gray suburban skies. After JFK's death, out of his anguish, RFK was said to have taken on an evangelical bearing. Now his son, having endured, having survived, sounds a lot like his father.

"We don't get our values from nature, but nature confirms our values," he says. "If we lose touch with the seasons and the tides, those things that unite us with the generations that went before, we lose part of who we are. We lose the ability to confirm the truth of God's wisdom. And we lose some of our humanity, too. At that point, we become capable of anything. I do not want to see the world come to that."

A few years ago we were in a small town in Chile and Bobby gave a warm, emotional after-dinner speech in honor of the outfitter who had brought together politicians and environmentalists to see this endangered river. He extolled him as an example of the kind of hero his father thought was the best kind: the understated, unselfish kind, motivated simply by doing right for others.

I wonder if the father would see his son as a hero.

"I don't know," Bobby says, looking out the big window, taking on that faraway gaze. "I'm not sure what he would say or what kind of conversation we would have. Of course it's a conversation I would love to have. But I think he might say something he often told us as kids: 'To whom much is given, much is expected.'"

Robert F. Kennedy Jr. is senior attorney for the NRDC, chief prosecuting attorney for the Hudson Riverkeeper, and president of the Waterkeeper Alliance, which boasts 160 organizations around the globe. He is also a clinical professor and supervising attorney at Pace University Law's Environmental Litigation Clinic and co-host of Ring of Fire *on Air America Radio.*

RUMORMONGERING AMONG THE INSECTHEADS

Wangari Maathai

Nationalgeographic.com, 2004

The first thing Wangari Maathai did when she regained consciousness was call a press conference. When she came out of her club-enforced daze, she was in a Nairobi hospital (March 1991), having been badly beaten by Kenyan police during a demonstration the day before. It was a Saturday and I was one of a dozen friends and journalists who showed up to hear her side of the conflict.

The police had already been to the papers, claimed the outspoken environmentalist-cum-political activist had "incited" them. Upon hearing her clubber's account, Maathai couldn't help but smile over its ridiculousness. She looked a mess—one eye blackened, her forehead labeled with a knot the size of a Spalding. The thrashing administered her fifty-one-year-old legs made it hard for her to walk to the bathroom, where she vomited blood. The morning's paper carried other stories of a kind found only in Kenya: a pair of Maathai's friends had been jailed for "rumor-mongering," and local bus operators had decreed that anyone heard talking politics on their public carriers would be handed over to police.

The day before had begun typically for Africa's best-known environmentalist. Maathai had joined a long-planned protest by mothers of political prisoners, calling for the release of their sons. The outspoken Maathai felt a responsibility to the jailed men, who had been locked up for the crime of speaking out for democracy in a country run by autocratic thugs.

Merely showing up at the rally made her a target for authorities . . . once again. This was not the first time the founder of Kenya's fifteen-year-old Green Belt Movement had been hospitalized thanks to government goons. In the past few years, as her worldwide notoriety has grown, as she's traveled abroad to accept award after award for environmental and political heroism, she has come home to be harassed, arrested, beaten, and threatened with rape. Her Nairobi office was first ransacked, then "confiscated" by the government. On that day she'd come back from lunch to find security forces from the president's office throwing her papers and books out a second-story window onto a crowded downtown street.

Her activist roots were mild in First World terms. The first Kenyan woman to earn a PhD (in anatomy) and the first to become a professor at the University of Nairobi, Dr. Maathai took on a formidable challenge in 1977: to hold back Kenya's advancing desert. Rampant tree cutting and unchecked population growth had stripped much of the country's land, playing a hand in generating both hunger and poverty. Her response, dubbed the Green Belt Movement, was a national tree-planting program run by women. "Because women here are responsible for their children," she explained at the time, "they cannot sit back, waste time, and see them starve."

With Green Belt's support, women across Kenya established nurseries within their villages and then persuaded farmers to accept and raise tree seedlings. Green Belt paid the women two cents for each native plant they grew; exotic species were worth one-fifth as much. Farmers received the plants for free. In a decade she had recruited more than fifty thousand women, who had spurred the plantings of 10 million trees. While the seedlings took root, Maathai traveled the country speaking out for women's, and human, rights. She has been rewarded for her efforts with a bevy of awards and acclaim from around the world for environmentalism and political activism. None of her activities were looked upon favorably by Kenyan President Daniel arap Moi. Her gravest sin—either her biggest mistake or success, dependent on whose side you take—came three years ago when she very publicly scuttled Moi's plan to build a sixty-story office in Uhuru Park, adjoining downtown Nairobi. The building was to be flanked by a large statue of the seventeen-year president. Both were to be paid for by foreign aid monies. By personal plea and public rally, Maathai persuaded donors that the project was environmentally, aesthetically, and fiscally unsound, and Moi's dream was defeated.

While that victory may have earned her popularity among the workers who used the park, it assured her the eternal enmity of the ruling party, in particular Moi and the government-owned newspaper and television stations that were to have gotten luxurious new offices in the building. The day after the project was officially announced dead, headlines in the *Daily Nation* accused Maathai of "having insects in her head." A year later, when she won the prestigious Goldman Environmental Prize, CNN International broadcast a story about the six winners from around the globe. Government-employed censors edited out the three-minute segment on Maathai when the piece was aired in Kenya. She is rumored to be on Moi's short-listing for either extradition, or . . . an "accident" (not out of the question from a government whose finance minister once threw a political opponent out of a helicopter).

Yesterday's beating was part of a constant campaign of harassment against Maathai. Soon after his office building was KO'd, Moi ruled that foreign assistance to women's development projects must be channeled through the state women's organization, effectively cutting off outside aid to the Green Belt Movement. She is currently awaiting trial on charges of incitement and "rumor-mongering." Yet she continues to be publicly critical of the police state that her homeland has become.

After reading the front page of the newspaper, sitting up in her hospital bed, Maathai looks up at the crowd gathered in her hospital room. "They don't understand, do they? I'm not being critical of the government, I'm just talking the truth. Perhaps President Moi believes I should protect the image of our government, just because it is our government. But I know that I am talking about a government that does not like to be criticized. That is why I have been in trouble."

Despite her bruises, she comes off more steadfast than scared. "I know I am in danger and I know that the government has tried to push me aside. At the moment, because of the political turmoil in my country, one cannot rule out the possibility of the worst, so I do feel that I need to take care of myself. I need to stay away from 'dangerous ground.' But that doesn't mean that I will back down. I will not just 'go away,' which is what they would like. Because this is where I am needed most. My message has not shifted, if anything it has become less subtle."

Wangari Maathai was the first African woman to win the Nobel Peace Prize, in 2004.

IS CAROL BROWNER IN
OVER HER HEAD?

Carol Browner

Audubon, 1993

Framed photographs of her favorite Florida landscapes—elegant renderings of Everglades National Park and Big Cypress National Preserve—sit stacked on the floor of Carol Browner's office. The bookshelves are empty; her desk ("where I never sit") is piled with papers, *National Geographic* videos, and plastic toys (property of five-year-old son Zach). The coffee table is laden with half-filled water bottles, paper coffee cups marred by lipstick, and a half-eaten bowl of grapes. "Fresh fruit is the only advantage of having our offices above a Safeway," she jokes. The Environmental Protection Agency's Washington, D.C., headquarters leave much to be desired. Crowded, crumbling, and in a rough part of town, the office is far, far from Washington's corridors of power.

Just back from a quick trip to the White House, where she announced a novel energy-saving program created by a young EPA employee, Browner sheds her jacket and launches into a story about her recent three-day weekend in Montana with her husband and son, her first break in more than a year.

It has been quite a year. In August 1992, Florida governor Lawton Chiles asked her to do double duty, helping to coordinate the state's response to Hurricane Andrew while continuing to run its Department of Environmental Regulation. On the heels of that, she was tapped to assist in the transition of a former Senate employer, Al Gore. And then came the unexpected interview for the EPA administrator's job, the offer, the confirmation hearings, and the move to Washington. In Montana she'd spent several hours just watching hawks soar. "One problem with these office jobs is that I rarely get to see the places I help save," she says.

Her new assignment—as the eighth director of the U.S. Environmental Protection Agency—is destined to provide her with *real* complaints.

Charged with overseeing 17,738 employees and a $6.9 billion budget, she inherits an agency that operates on the fringes of power in D.C.. Despite the presence of the environmentally correct vice president and his push to make environmental concerns part of every agency's agenda, the truth is the EPA is still a bit player in the new administration.

Browner knows this well. She spent eight years working in Washington, first as an environmental lawyer, then as a Capitol Hill staffer, for Senators Chiles and Gore. From her new seat she has called this period in the twenty-three-year-old agency's history "pivotal." She understands that it's an uphill battle. One environmental-group leader summed up her challenges this way: number one, all the easy things have been done; number two, she has no money.

Browner's EPA is squaring off on a myriad of sizable legislative environmental battles. Three laws that help form the foundation of U.S. environmental policy are up for renewal in the next two years: the Clean Water Act, the Superfund law, and the Resource Conservation and Recovery Act. The new administration would like to see the EPA elevated to cabinet status, which will require Browner to navigate past congressional skeptics uncertain that more bureaucracy equals a cleaner environment. She was named to the post just six days before her thirty-seventh birthday, and her friends and critics alike wonder if she has the experience and political savvy to wrangle these laws into shape for the next century.

For the record, representatives of environmental groups speak mostly in niceties and platitudes about the new administrator. ("First-rate," says Jay Hair of the National Wildlife Federation.) But off the record there is a common concern: "*She's in over her head.*"

These worries were exacerbated during her first weeks in office, in February, when Browner jumped into one of the most controversial issues facing the agency, the debate over the amount of pesticides that should be allowed in processed food. When she indicated that she might ask Congress to relax a law that prohibits food from containing trace amounts of chemicals that cause cancer in animals, a complex issue that congressional Democrats have labored over for years, it sent environmentalists into a tizzy.

Still, the insiders in the environmental community are behind her, at least for now. "It's like a breath of fresh air after twelve years of choking smog," Sierra Club chairman Michael McCloskey said after Browner's appointment.

"She's off to a solid start," says Peter A. A. Berle, president of the National Audubon Society. "I think she has broken out of the mold of her predecessors. She wants to make the EPA an integral part of government, not an adjunct." For example, Berle noted, Browner is working with the Defense Department to make sure environmental cleanup is a standard part of the process for closing military bases.

"My experience with her is that she is quite thoughtful and willing to learn," says Natural Resources Defense Council executive director John Adams. "When she first came in she seemed very tight, but I think she's loosened up a lot. It's easy to say, 'Well, she doesn't have enough experience' or 'She's not good enough.' She's a smart lady. She'll figure it out."

Despite such enthusiasms, several environmental leaders contend that there are some things Browner simply doesn't know, because she just hasn't been around the capital long enough. Many of these environmentalists are as much a part of the Washington establishment as the politicians they deal with, and they have been involved in these issues since the EPA was formed and the nation's first environmental legislation drafted. It is a close-knit community wary of newcomers. While hopeful about Browner, some question whether she is tough enough to get rhetoric turned into law.

Seated on a couch in her penthouse office, the sun glaring off the Potomac in the near distance, the first impression Browner imparts is equal parts self-confidence and awe (as if to say, "Can you believe I have this job?"). Despite several warnings from her peers that she could be blunt, I found her warm and anxious to talk. Tall and rail-thin, one moment she is inquiring about the status of the NBA playoffs and the next joking about the other lofty new Clinton appointee from Miami, Attorney General Janet Reno—who so far has gotten considerably better press.

The first question I ask—"How did you get this job?"—raises her hackles. "I've worked in this area for almost ten years; I got the job because of my record," she says and then runs down her impressive resume: secretary of Florida's Department of Environmental Regulation (DER) for two years (1,370 employees, a $700 million budget), top U.S. Senate aide, legal counsel to the Florida legislature, associate director of Citizen Action, a Washington-based advocacy group.

"Believe me, I was as surprised by the job offer as anyone," she admits. "I went for one of 'those' interviews, you know, like right out of *Doonesbury*. I got the call and then had an hour-and-a-half interview with the president, whom I'd met just briefly before.

"This isn't one of those things you plan for. I was very happy in my job in Florida. In fact, it was very hard to leave that job, because after two years I was going to start seeing some return on a lot of things I'd worked on. "Once confirmed, she moved back to the house in Takoma Park, Maryland, where she, husband Michael Podhorzer—who works for Citizen Action—and son Zach had lived before she took the Florida post.

"I could not imagine myself ready for this job without those two years in Florida," she says. "The interesting thing about me is I am the only person to serve in this job with both the policy, i.e., the Hill, experience and the hands-on regulatory experience."

Back to the point—how did she get the job? Common wisdom holds that the answer is very simple: "She's a friend of Al's." It is hardly coincidence that the two highest-level purely environmental positions in government both went to Gore people. (Katie McGinty, the thirty-year-old director of the new White House Office on Environmental Policy, became Gore's top environmental aide shortly before Browner left his staff in 1991.)

Despite her two years in Florida, around town Browner is remembered belittlingly as "a staffer": the perception among some in Washington is that she is "Gore's girl." But after I hear a variety of takes on the "in over her head" theme, it is hard not to wonder how much Browner's gender figures into such concerns. Washington can be a sexist place, no matter how enlightened the administration. If a thirty-seven-year-old man— a lawyer whom everyone agreed was smart as a whip, who'd successfully run one of the largest state environmental agencies in the country—had gotten the EPA post, would he be regarded as a wunderkind rather than a risk?

In Florida, Browner was best known for finding trade-offs—letting all sides win something in the battle between industry and environment— and was praised for her political skills in working to settle a federal lawsuit over pollution in the Everglades and passing a gasoline-tax increase to pay for environmental cleanups. She also got credit for rejuvenating a demoralized staff, decreasing regulatory burdens, and increasing community involvement.

"A new breed of ecologist," the *New York Times* declared after she was nominated, noting that she is as concerned with protecting jobs as with protecting spotted owls. Clearly, Browner is no extremist; her reputation has been built on compromise and pragmatism. As secretary of Florida's DER, she won changes in regulations to shrink the amount of time it took to review permits for developing wetlands or expanding manufacturing plants. Business groups had long sought such changes, but some environmentalists were angry. "The whole concept of it is to make it quicker, easier, and cheaper for developers to get approvals," says Linda Young, publisher of the *Pro Earth Times,* a Florida environmental newspaper.

Perhaps the most prominent deal Browner struck was a compromise agreement under which the Walt Disney World Company agreed to spend $40 million to buy and restore an 8,500-acre ranch near Orlando in return for state and federal permits to fill in four hundred acres of wetlands for Disney development projects. Under the agreement, Disney will be allowed to build new theme parks, roads, mass-transit systems, and an entire town over the next twenty years. In return, Disney will buy the ranch and donate it to the Nature Conservancy, which will preserve it as a wildlife refuge. "This approach is so much more rational," says Browner. "Disney is happy. The environmental community is happy. We did this because we all came to the table in a non-adversarial manner."

What does she make of this "new breed of ecologist" brand? She dodges, saying she doesn't understand it. "I absolutely believe it is important to protect our health and our children's health, and to protect resources, and that hard decisions need to be made. But we must be mindful of the consequences of environmental protection. We need to use economic incentives to encourage businesses to make the right decisions. We need to look at the true cost of the actions that we take—not just what it costs today, but what it is going to cost over, let's say, the next ten, twenty, forty years and beyond."

As for the high expectations accompanying her appointment, she readily admits that no one can really manage 17,738 employees: "The best you can do is manage twenty people. The question is, Can you instill in people a vision and provide the leadership to achieve that vision? That's what these jobs are about—giving people something to think about and work towards." Perhaps the most severe criticism of her early tenure was that appointments of several key assistant administrators dragged on for months, rendering the agency vastly inefficient. When we spoke in June, seven of the ten top assistant secretaries at the EPA had not yet been named—although at least four of those appointments were being held up by the White House.

As for her key goals, she lists pollution prevention; protecting ecosystems; building partnerships with state and local governments, nonprofit organizations, and the business community; and addressing the issue of environmental racism. She seems realistic about the challenges ahead. "In the past twenty-three years the pendulum has swung back and forth a few times, but essentially we have tended to focus our energies on end-of-the-pipeline regulatory schemes. We've had some successes—our water bodies are cleaner, for example. But if we are going to do what we need to do in the next twenty years it won't be through end-of-the-pipe. A vast majority of the gains to be gotten through that kind of regulation have been gotten. Now we need to focus our energies upstream to prevent the stuff from occurring in the first place."

For environmentalists, all this sounds good. And the new administration has taken some steps to live up to its "green" promise. Perhaps most prominently, President Clinton has reversed Bush-administration policies by announcing that the United States will follow a specific timetable to reduce the threat of global warming and will sign an international treaty protecting rare and endangered species.

But there have been missteps. For example, during the campaign Gore promised to investigate why one of the country's largest toxic-waste incinerators, in East Liverpool, Ohio, was built in a densely populated community. The month after the election, Vice-President-elect Gore vowed to block the incinerator. But in March it was announced that the administration would not oppose plans to begin operating the plant. "We have not found a [legal] basis for revoking or modifying the permit," said Michael Vandenbergh, special assistant to Browner. (Browner withdrew from involvement because her husband's employer, Citizen Action, was associated with the case.)

One of the most significant actions yet taken by Browner's EPA was the imposition of an eighteen-month moratorium on the building of new hazardous-waste incinerators. ("There are a hundred and seventy-one industrial furnaces burning hazardous waste with temporary permits, yet by act of law they are allowed to operate," said Browner. "For us at the federal level to continue to allow new facilities to be built while those hundred and seventy-one have never gotten final permits is ludicrous.") She also threatened to cut off federal highway funds to California and other states that were considering defying the Clean Air Act.

Her first major national publicity since taking office came with the June announcement that the EPA, along with the Food and Drug Administration and the Department of Agriculture, would push to reduce the use of agricultural pesticides, a move aimed at protecting the health of children. When asked about her future priorities, she cites the addition of 170 more chemicals to the Toxics Release Inventory, reauthorization of the Clean Water Act, and extensive administrative changes in the Superfund program.

Browner has hardly shirked from criticizing the agency as she found it. "I'm appalled by what I've learned about the EPA's total lack of management, accountability, and discipline," she told a House subcommittee in March. "I have reviewed audit reports and received briefings from staff that clearly describe poor management practices, serious violations of rules, and intolerable waste of taxpayers' money."

Harsh words. Some, including her immediate predecessor, William K. Reilly, think her evaluation has gone overboard. "You have to make sure that before you criticize the agency, you understand and respect what it does," says Reilly, now ensconced as a lecturer at Stanford University.

Browner backpedals a bit as she explains her analysis: "Don't get me wrong. The agency is filled with wonderful, committed people. And the administrators that served during the last twelve years were also very committed. But those twelve years were very difficult. You had a White House that didn't see the environment as important, that didn't think protecting resources for future generations was something they needed to spend a lot of time or money on. That has been a very tough experience for this agency. We are trying to move beyond that, to respect the quality of work done here and to move forward."

Criticism of the EPA is hardly news. Everybody from the General Accounting Office to the EPA's in-house inspector general agrees it is a mess. Critics have pointed to major problems such as contract abuse, inefficient procurement practices, and poor management of the Superfund program, which both industry and environmentalists agree is failing to clean up the worst hazardous-waste sites. As the nonprofit Center for Resource Economics put it in a review of the agency: "The EPA is besieged by mismanagement."

Browner concurs. "The EPA too frequently does not bring an issue to a close," she says. "That contributes to the lack of credibility with the public, with business, and with others. I've found business leaders don't oppose strong environmental programs; what drives them crazy is a lack of certainty. We can change that."

Money, or the lack of it, is Browner's biggest headache. Despite the new administration's pledge to make the environment a priority, the agency's budget has been cut 8 percent from the last Bush budget. Given fiscal constraints, many feel that it's going to be difficult if not impossible for the Clinton administration to keep its environmental promises. "More money would make things easier," admits Browner, "but that's not going to happen. It is a common phenomenon faced by people in our generation who will assume responsibilities, and it's one I accept."

The legislative change Browner is now paying most attention to is the potential elevation of her agency to cabinet status. On May 4 the Senate approved, 79 to 15, a bill that would give the EPA cabinet status and a new name: the Department of Environmental Protection. The Clinton administration is firmly behind the elevation (as was George Bush), and Browner is already treated as a cabinet member, attending all meetings.

The logic behind the move is simple to Browner. "You cannot continue to marginalize environmental issues," she says. "They have got to be part and parcel of the decision-making process of all debates. The environment is a very important part of the overall quality of life in this country, and it deserves to be there with Education, Labor, Justice, and Commerce. We cannot continue to have a process at this senior level of government where a decision is made and afterwards someone says, 'Oh yeah, what's the environmental consequence?' Having that equal seat at the table is important, regardless of who is in the White House."

The House Energy and Commerce Committee are now considering the bill. Its chairman, John Dingell (D-MI), a longtime EPA antagonist and a strong supporter of auto-industry interests, opposes the legislation on the grounds that the agency currently is too badly managed to accept any more responsibility.

Browner's handling of the cabinet legislation in its early stages irritated even some of her most loyal supporters. When the Senate argued the bill, Browner was at a United Nations meeting in Switzerland. Environmentalists wished she'd been around to help them lobby for changes in the bill. As for Dingell, he is a powerful opponent who could kill the legislation. At a May hearing, with Browner in attendance, he referred to the EPA as a "cesspool"; the new administrator listened and did little to defend her agency, much to the chagrin of some EPA employees.

Since taking office Browner has attempted to appease the Michigan congressman. As a candidate, Clinton called for raising auto fuel-efficiency standards to forty miles per gallon by 2000. Browner's first outreach to industry was a trip to Detroit—at Dingell's request—to have dinner with top executives of the Big Three automakers, a meeting at which she promised to consider alternatives to such standards. In fact, Clinton has backed away from his tough campaign stance, and it is likely he will instead seek a voluntary agreement with automakers.

Browner says that the meeting was "very important to begin a dialogue. The real purpose of the meeting was to see if we had any common ground. We won't always agree, but at least now, when we have to make tough decisions, we'll have a framework in which to make them.

"I plan on doing the same with other industries. Face it, they don't even know who Carol Browner is."

It is the end of another pell-mell day, yet even as the sun sets over the Potomac, Browner and her staff must soon hustle to another meeting. When she realizes our time is about over, she gets suddenly reflective, personal. "This job is something I feel very strongly about," she offers. "Some of us are given an opportunity, for a period of time in our lives, to perhaps make a difference. I've been given that opportunity, and I take that really seriously. It's exciting. It's a tremendous responsibility. If I don't make a difference, I will have failed."

Browner's childhood home sat on the edge of a big city; today the south Miami neighborhood, from which she could as a young girl bicycle into the Everglades, sits amid urban sprawl. "That has made me realize we are at serious risk in this country of not being able to give our children the same quality of life that we had," she says.

"But I'm optimistic. I have a five-year-old, and when I went to his kindergarten class to tell them about my job—I told them, 'I save things'— I was amazed that each of them knew about recycling, and most could name an endangered species. It means that all our efforts are working, that there is hope, that our job is worth doing."

Carol Browner was chosen to be energy czar in Barack Obama's adminstration.

HEAVEN CAN WAIT

Brady Watson

Nature Conservancy, 1995

The Land Cruiser rocks along the mud-river path toward San José Bocay, headed toward the end of the road, the edge of Nicaragua's northernmost jungle. Brady Watson—forester, anthropologist, and good-humor man —is singing Sandanista theme songs intermingled with Willie Nelson covers while expertly dodging chickens, pigs, dogs, brahma bulls, and six-foot-long snakes that wander across the trail.

We plunge up and down, from highland to riverside, through dense woods, across swollen rivers, slipping and sliding in the axle-deep mud. This is a man who clearly loves his work. It's a good thing, because the challenges he faces—trying to protect and preserve land in a country largely devastated by a ten-year civil war—are big. We are on our way to a reserve called Bosawas, the biggest primary tropical forest still standing in Central America, covering 5,400 square miles, or 2.5 million acres. Bosawas is an acronym, drawn from the rivers and mountains that are its borders: Bocay-Saslaya-Waspuk. Its preservation was initially suggested in the 1970s by the JFK-originated Alliance for Peace. But Bosawas wasn't officially designated a sacred place until November 1991. Made up primarily of mountainous upland rainforest, the parkland ranges from 650 to 2,400 feet in elevation and is the native home to Sumo and Miskito Indians. That it is extremely difficult to reach helped save the area from the ravages of war. That it was also headquarters to the rebel Contras helped protect it, too.

Today, though the war is over, Nicaragua sags under the weight of an enormous rebuilding effort; it is the poorest country in Latin America. Bosawas—as well as Nicaragua's seventy other protected areas—faces a variety of threats, including several hundred thousand refugees returning from Honduras and Costa Rica hoping to homestead, i.e., cut down some trees, have a little farm, and raise a few cattle. The region is also ripe for logging, gold and copper mining, commercial cattle ranchers, and hunters.

It is also still rife with land mines laid during the war and not yet discovered.

As we jar along the road, Brady is thinking out loud, suggesting ways government money could be earmarked for conservation. Like a nation-wide property tax, just $5 per hectare, to be set aside for preservation. Or some kind of productivity/market tax that could raise $10 million a year to be administered by MARENA, Nicaragua's EPA. While Brady talks and sings and smokes, I listen and gaze at the roadside attractions. The primary lesson you take away from spending so many hours driving these muddy roads (it takes two days to get from Managua to the end of the road) is that WOOD IS THEIR LIFE. All these people—Sumo, Miskitos, Mestizos—are, it would appear, born with machetes in their hands. Stacked all along the roadside are piles of wood for cooking and heating. Big trees, cedars and walnuts and rosewoods, are felled right in front yards, their branches hacked off as needed, for kindling. Everything these people possess, except the clothes on their back, is culled from the forests that surround them: Houses, the furniture inside, the saddles on their bur-ros, even the crosses hung over each door.

There is an innocent yet mistrustful look in the eyes of these people, a result of the war that ended in 1990. In many respects the war destroyed this place, killing more than 25,000, displacing another 700,000 and cost-ing the government nearly $2 billion. Ironically, while Nicaragua's people were suffering, the environment was getting some relief from a long history of assault and exploitation: For a decade, trade in gold, mahogany, cedar, animal skins, sea turtles, shrimp, and lobster nearly ceased. Forests and grasses grew over many of the plantations, state farms, and ranches that had produced bananas, coffee, cotton, and cattle.

But as the military confrontation subsided, destructive environmental and wildlife exploitation began anew. Foreign boats have overfished the waters and reefs; contracts were cut with Sweden and Costa Rica for the export of large quantities of logs and lumber, and large-scale cattle-ranching schemes were planned. And though some indicators suggest Nicaragua's economy is slowly improving, it and the current political stability remain fragile.

"It's a good thing I'm an optimist," says Brady with a sad smile as we watch a pair of teenagers whack at the last small tree standing in an other-wise cleared plot.

Bosawas was loosely recognized by the Sandinistas; they understood the public relations value of saying they were for preservation. Truth was, they couldn't afford to "save" anything. To illustrate just how bad things were under their leadership, Brady cites his own salary experience: when he went to work for the forest service in 1969, he was paid three hundred dollars a month; in the 1980s, when he'd risen to its directorship, he was making thirty dollars a month. With the new government in 1990 came a recommitment to preservation. In her inaugural address, President Violeta Chamorro promised to renew efforts to "guard and protect and defend our environment." Preserving the still mostly pristine Bosawas was to be one of her government's biggest environmental challenges.

Bosawas is TNC's first investment in Nicaragua, part of its Parks in Peril program aimed at helping to protect two hundred key sites in the Western Hemisphere covering more than 100 million acres. The hope is that by strengthening the ability of local conservationists to manage their own natural areas, parks and other wild lands may be preserved.

Brady was hired by TNC and USAID to oversee their combined $2.5 million, four-year effort in Bosawas. The main job for him and his staff is to work with indigenous communities and Mestizos, as well as other conservation groups and the government, to try and maintain Bosawas's biological diversity, as well as protect it from the myriad of threats. Perhaps most importantly, the Conservancy project is trying to secure land rights for the small indigenous communities that border the reserve. Populated by Miskito and Sumu Indians, living in small communities along the rivers, they are of little threat to the reserve since they clear less than a square mile of forest for their own use. The hope is that if land rights can be secured from the government—for entire communities, rather than for individuals—they could form a kind of buffer zone around the reserve, protecting it from the advancement of big farmers and cattle ranchers. At the same time, the government and conservation groups are trying to develop economic projects on the edges of the parkland, for obvious reasons: if there is no other way for these people to make even a meager living, there's no reason for them not to continue the slash-and-burn techniques that have leveled two-thirds of Nicaragua's forests in just fifty years. I first saw the massive reserve from the sky, the best way to understand both its scope and its threats. From Managua we flew over

Lago Nicaragua—the biggest lake in Central America—then up the Rio Bocay to the Rio Coca, which parallels the Honduran border. As we fly over the jungle, a trio of brightly colored parakeets, wings of blue and orange, soar between the dew-covered canopy and us. Brady points out the window, explaining how he's most excited about getting a team of volunteers into the reserve to take inventory. Relatively little is known about the interior—what kinds of plants, how many, what kinds of animals, how many, etc. The biggest threat to Bosawas evidences itself prominently as we fly out of Sunui, a village of eighteen thousand on the reserve's southern border. In just the past fifteen years, small clear-cutting has caught on big. As a result one cleared patch abuts another and another, all the way back to Managua. That patchwork of small farms is Bosawas's future if Brady and his counterparts are not successful.

"The threat is not from the Sumos and Miskitos. They know their limits," says Brady. "It is the Mestizos, the Spanish-speaking farmers from the south, looking for new farmland, new grazing lands. Despite the natural boundaries—the rivers—the southern boundary is just imaginary, it's not defined on the ground. Part of our problem is that the Mestizos are moving in and moving the imaginary boundaries to their liking.

"The established farmers and cattle producers know exactly what they are doing, attempting to buy land from the Sumos and Miskitos. For them, the forest is an obstacle. What they need to see is grass growing.

Staring out the small plane's window, Brady pushes back in his seat. He is obviously affected by the "growth," the destruction below. "Bosawas is really our last opportunity," he says. We sit in the bar/restaurant/diskoteck (*sic*) in San José Bocay, posters of blondes in lingerie and red Ferraris covering the walls, and Brady chain-smokes Lucky Strikes. Outside the plank walls, firecrackers—essentially newspaper wrapped around gunpowder—explode every few minutes, many right at our feet. It is just three weeks before Christmas, and locals are celebrating La Purisma the Catholic holiday honoring the Virgin Mary.

Nearby sits a table full of Contras, or perhaps more appropriately, ex-Contras. In fact the first man we met when we arrived in this muddy village at the end of the road was the president of the local road-building association, a well-known Contra chief. While post-war Nicaragua has slowly become more peaceful, there remains an unsettled feeling in the countryside, especially here in San José, a major Contra headquarters during the war. Early the next morning we prepare to head downriver, to rapids just below the tiny village of Aylapa. The day begins by dragging Brady's boat—a forty-foot-long, seven-hundred-pound dugout cut from a solitary cedar, painted green with a white stripe—into the river. To get it to Rio Bocay a hundred feet away, we must winch it with the Land Cruiser and drag it across the flats.

Henry, Brady's boatman and local aide de camp, is a Miskito. Sinewy and muscled, with thick black hair and the inevitable machete, he proves a virtuoso at running the forty-foot boat through shallows and rapids. Aided by a nineteen-year-old bowman armed with a six-foot-long pole for measuring the river's depth and pushing off rocks, the pair handles the ungainly craft with an élan that would be the envy of the best white-water raft guides. It takes two hours to reach the border of the reserve and along the way we pass farm after farm that not so long ago were jungle. Some of the clear-cuts have been recently burned, others are already planted with beans, sugar, corn. Most farms run right down to river, ignoring the Nicaraguan law, which says clear-cuts can't come within two hundred feet of the riverside. The result is that the Bocay is muddy from erosion and run-off. Another irony is that clear-cutting is not illegal per se. These lands are all privately owned and legally cleared by government permit. The sad irony is that the officials back in Managua who grant the permits never venture from behind their desks to assess the result of all their "permissions."

As we near the reserve land, we begin to pass big trees (cabal, cedar, mahogany, bamboo, walnut, rosewood, rubber, chiclet, and one they call Comanegro, or "black man killer"—it is so hard to cut down it generally ends up falling on and killing one of its attackers). Birds are everywhere—herons, swallows, toucans, hawks, giant crows, parrots, parakeets, and a variety of fishers, which hover like helicopters then dive below the surface for fish. We spot a half-dozen crocodiles, and a pair of five-foot-long snakes called Santa Maria ("they bite you and twenty minutes later you die," says Brady). Out of sight in the now-dense jungle are tapirs, chameleons, boars, monkeys, deer, waterdogs, and jaguar. Since no inventory has taken the breadth of the plant life, medicinal and otherwise, it is still mostly a secret. The only people we see are in boats being poled up and down river, some of them carrying small cans of gas and chain saws. Clear-cutting continues through the buffer zone right up to the sign put up by Sumos declaring this spot the beginning of the reserve.

What Brady is trying to ensure is that this "growth" doesn't intrude upon Bosawas. But starting from scratch on such an education/environmental program here in the jungle is very difficult. Especially in a country left bereft by civil war—impoverished, corrupt, underemployed, undereducated, under-skilled. "Clear-cutting, lack of rainfall, erosion are affecting all the park's borders," he says. "The campesinos remember before the deforestation that the soil was good, but now they say to me, 'The rocks are growing.' That's how they see it, that the rocks are truly growing, rather than the truth, which is that the soil is being washed away." At fifty-three, Brady has only recently opted out of government employ. For more than twenty years, in two different stints, he worked for Nicaragua's forest service, eventually becoming its director.

He is in many ways an oddity in Nicaragua, largely due to his upbringing as the son of a Moravian minister. One of fourteen kids, he spoke English and Miskito before finally learning Spanish in fifth grade. Because of his father's work, the family moved around the Atlantic coast region every four years. Today his siblings, ages thirty to fifty-five, are scattered from Minnesota to Costa Rica. One sister is a nurse; a brother was a Contra commandante. Two are dead: a brother broke his neck in a bicycle accident; a vengeful spray of Sandanista machine gunfire killed a younger sister while she was sitting on her porch in Puerto Cabezas. A soft-spoken, smooth-skinned black man, his father's family was Jamaican, his mother's a blend of Spanish and Miskito. Under Nicaraguan racial standards, Brady is judged a black Creole, but his fluency in Miskito gives him entrée with the natives that most outsiders could never gain. His voice carries a Caribbean lilt, and when he talks, he emphasizes by snapping his fingers, or whistling through his teeth. He quotes liberally from sources ranging from Longfellow to the Bible. He is not above a little tango while waiting in a line or softly breaking out in snippets of song, from Sinatra to Willie Nelson. A self-confessed "ship-rat" (he has built two small boats), his hobby is planting indigenous and non-indigenous flowers and trees around his house. His family was very poor, and Brady had to alternate years in order to finish school—working for a year, schooling for a year, etc. As a result he didn't get out of secondary school until he was twenty-three. He'd considered a career in agriculture, but when a teacher announced two scholarships for forestry, he quickly applied, even though he had no clue what "forestry" was. When he discovered it was about growing trees, he thought it sounded okay. The scholarship took him to Texas and Canada (where he learned to fight fires). When he returned to Nicaragua, he went to work for the government, based in the forested plains of the east. In 1979, when the Sandanistas took over, he was called to Managua to help restructure the forest service. Soon after, he also took on management of an $8.5 million IDB project overseeing reforestation in the eastern region.

He left the government in 1986, as a result of being followed, bugged, interrogated, accused, and harassed, largely because he remained an honest man in a corrupt system. (That one of his brothers was a well-known Contra commandante, based in Costa Rica, didn't help—though Brady insists he remained apolitical throughout the war.) His biggest problem with the Sandinistas was they couldn't believe he wouldn't simply "turn over" the millions in aid money he oversaw, nor the trucks, jeeps, and pickups under his command. They went as far as to install a "minister" over him, to try and gain access to his largesse, but Brady resisted.

"I learned a simple lesson very early on," he says today, "that honesty is the best policy. And so I quit." A post with the United Nations Commission on Human Rights followed (accompanied by a much-needed raise, from thirty dollars a month to eight hundred), and then a stint consulting for a Swedish aid group. When the Sandinistas were voted out in 1990, an old friend who offered him a management job in Bluefields, where he'd grown up, lured him back to the government's environmental protection office, MARENA. When he quit the government for good early in 1994, it was, he says, to make room for "young blood." Today his wife of twenty-three years works as a program coordinator with the United Nations Development Programme. They live with their four children in the hills above Managua, in a compound big enough to include an extended family (sister-in-law and kids, mother-in-law) and a pair of big German Shepherds.

TNC's Kathy Moser, regional director for Central America, first met Brady in Washington in the mid-1980's, when the conservancy was seeking a director for the Nicaragua program.

"Everybody mentioned Brady," she says.

"Brady *is* this project," she says. "I can't imagine anyone else running it. And the last time I saw him, he told me that for the first time in his life, he really feels like he's doing something for the area he came from."

As we pound back upriver, jumping out every few rapids to push the big boat over the rocks, the small Mercury engine whines. Rain comes and goes, and at day's end there is blue sky to the south and heavy rain-clouds storming from the north. Over the jungle an *arc colores* rises, spreading horizon-to-horizon. Symbolic? I ask out loud. Sure, says Brady. Important? "Por qué no," he laughs.

In a twist, Brady believes Bosawas and the issue of native claims could become a major election issue in 1996. "The opposition, primarily the FSLN, the Sandinistas, are talking it up, which means the Chamorro party will probably adapt it too," says Brady. As the issue becomes more public, it buys Brady and other conservationists working on Bosawas time to iron out plans for getting the Indians proper title. (Ironically, Brady has been asked to be the first indigenous presidential candidate, one of perhaps as many as twenty parties that will vie for the office. A few days after we leave Nicaragua, he will fly to Miami to "entertain" such a candidacy, at the request of Nicaraguans living there.) For now, Brady keeps his optimism about Bosawas's future. He insists things are improving in his native land and is comfortable too with his own contribution.

"In my years I've seen a lot of bad times and some good. In the past year I've consulted books and religious teachers, trying to decipher exactly why I was put on earth. I think it was to help save things. Not souls, that was for my father. But living things . . . people, forests, rivers, animals. So far, I guess I've done what I could."

Brady Watson died of cancer in Nicaragua three years after we traveled with him. He considered but never ran for the presidency.

AFTER THE FALL

Claudio Cristino

National Geographic Adventure, 2007

I f Easter Island is the eeriest and most extraordinary speck of land on the face of the planet—and a very good argument could be made that it is—then the dormant volcanic crater at Rano Raraku is the heart of its sublime spookiness.

It's just after sunrise, and I've climbed the outer slope with my companion, Claudio Cristino, a veteran Easter Island archaeologist. As we look down toward the South Pacific, shining blue in the morning light, one of the world's most compelling sights spreads out on the hillside below, the maternity ward for more than 95 percent of Easter Island's grand moai. These are the gigantic stone figures that famously dot this remote island like chess pieces. The grassy slope is littered with unfinished statues of all sizes, as well as the empty niches from which hundreds of others were carved out. From this vantage point it is impossible not to ponder all the usual questions Easter Island provokes: How did the islanders carve these massive figures? Why did they make them? And what caused a civilization advanced enough to create such idols and transport them miles across uneven terrain simply to vanish?

Sprawled out before us, half-buried, is a seventy-foot-long statue weighing close to three hundred tons. It lies on its back, never finished. Cristino knows as much about this place as anyone alive. He has walked every meter of Easter Island and studied its relics for three decades, digging up thousands of clues about its lost society. Standing in the ocean wind before this breathtaking view, above this immense symbol of a civilization's mysterious rise and precipitous fall, I sense that Cristino is going to offer some profound insight into what it all means.

He points to the monster and smiles. "I think they may have gone a little bit over their limit with that one," Cristino says, and walks off down the hill.

On Easter Island, I'm learning, you're left with more questions than answers.

Across the vast swath of ocean and atolls that loosely defines Polynesia, there is no more improbable place for humans to have settled than Easter Island. At only fourteen miles across, it is an impossibly small target for even the most proficient navigators and is one of the more isolated habitable spots in the world. The nearest neighbors are on Pitcairn Island, 1,290 miles away. The mainland of Chile, which owns and governs what it calls Isla de Pascua, is more than 2,200 miles away—farther than Montreal is from Vancouver.

And while simple geography kept the clans of Rapa Nui, as the island is known in the local Polynesian language, insulated from the outside world for centuries, that has changed dramatically in recent years. Thanks to near-daily flights from Santiago and Tahiti, the virtually inaccessible isle is now within reach of anyone willing to endure a five-hour plane trip. Over 45,000 travelers visited last year, up from 6,000 in 1990. In response, hotels, restaurants, and guide services have sprung up by the handful, and tourism, an almost laughable concept just twenty years ago, has become the primary industry.

Much of the recent interest is the result of geographer and writer Jared Diamond's 2005 best seller, *Collapse*. Diamond, who won the Pulitzer Prize for his 1997 book, *Guns, Germs, and Steel* (and who is a National Geographic explorer-in-residence), posits in *Collapse* that societies that develop in fragile environments are likely to be the agents of their own destruction due to the mismanagement of natural resources. In Diamond's suspenseful telling, Easter Islanders' unregulated exploitation of animals and plants—in particular, trees used as material for boats, as fuel for fire, and as sleds to move moai—led to the extinction of essential species. Lack of resources created tensions between the clans, and wars broke out. Ultimately, the population plummeted. To Diamond, the disappearance of Easter Island's once thriving society around four hundred years ago could foreshadow an unpleasant future for all of planet Earth.

I visited Easter Island twice last year, arriving both by ship and by plane, to spend time with some of the island's top archaeologists. The Diamond Theory was hard to avoid. Half the tourists in restaurants and on trails seemed to be carrying well-thumbed copies of *Collapse* and quoted liberally and loudly from the book, citing the author by name as if he were a friend. (I hadn't seen this phenomenon since Alex Garland's novel *The Beach* stoked the slackpacker invasion of Thailand a decade ago.) Diamond's kindly face—he looks more like an Amish elder than an anthropological bomb thrower—doesn't yet appear on T-shirts in the shops of the main town like Darwin's does in the Galápagos, but that day may not be far off.

Some longtime island residents, including Cristino, take issue with Diamond's thesis, which has been knocked around in various forms for the past hundred years. They don't disagree outright; rather they suggest that the demise of those early Easter Island peoples was more complicated than simple death by deforestation. Locals complain about what they call the "cowboy archaeologists" who've been landing in their backyards since before Thor Heyerdahl popularized the island a half century ago. With perhaps a touch of professional jealousy, they also grumble that Diamond's weeklong visit in 2002 seemed a bit short for him to make such definitive pronouncements.

If tourism is the number one industry here, then the minting of experts must be a close second. The rapid, unexplained decline of the island's sophisticated civilization has proven irresistible to the writers of thousands of speculative dissertations, studies, and popular books. After decades of debate, scientists generally agree on a few basic historical facts. The first peoples arrived between 800 and 1,200 years ago from the Polynesian islands of the Pitcairn, Marquesas, and Gambier groups. When they beached their ocean canoes, they found a near-perfect isosceles triangle of rock, a moonscape formed by the lava pouring from craters at each corner, which later softened into hills; the highest, Terevaka, rises to 1,669 feet. Instead of the spare, rolling grasslands that greet travelers today, the first visitors found a veritable Garden of Eden. Lush forest covered the island, thriving in its temperate South Seas climate. Rich volcanic soils could be easily worked to grow taro and other staples. Abundant fisheries provided more than enough food. Palms towered more than eighty feet tall and grew six feet in diameter, yielding sap for sugar, syrup, and wine and supporting a variety of fauna. Other trees were perfect for moving giant statues and carving seagoing canoes.

In such a welcoming environment, free from invaders, the population boomed. Clans grew and spread around the island. This battered chunk of lava rock nurtured a society that created sophisticated woodworking, tattoos, rock art, the semblance of a written language—and the most spectacular frenzy of religious building known anywhere in Polynesia. The fruits of this compulsion were the giant statues and platforms that have become icons around the world.

Between 1200 and the late 1600s, Easter Islanders carved some nine hundred giant stone-faced figures. Roughly four hundred of them were placed on a hundred or so colossal stone platforms ringing the coast in an almost unbroken chain. The tallest was thirty-three feet and weighed more than eighty-two tons. Referred to as "public works" rather than "monuments" by archaeologists, no two are exactly alike. All of them have nicknames like "Twisted Neck," "Tattooed One," and even "Stinker."

The moai have baffled outsiders since the Dutch first arrived on Easter Island in 1722. Apparently all the carving, transport, and erecting had been done without wheels or animals, using only the muscle power of hundreds of men and thousands of felled trees. To this day no one knows for certain the purpose of the moai—the most common hypothesis is the expression of a near-obsessive ancestry cult—yet their artistry seems to have been competitive, with clans living in different parts of the island trying to outdo one another. The wealthier the clan (the better fishermen with the biggest boats), the grander the statues.

Then something went horribly wrong. Eighteenth-century European visitors to Easter Island recorded that many moai stood intact as sentinels but that not a single palm tree or native creature larger than an insect was to be found. By 1877 the statues had all been knocked over and the population had dropped to 111, from a high of 25,000 in the 1500s. Somehow over the course of a few centuries, wars had broken out, sacred statues were toppled, and people were forced to live in caves, ultimately turning to cannibalism. Even if the islanders had wanted to leave during this collapse, they couldn't have: The absence of trees made escape by canoe impossible. In the end Easter Island's culture was strangled by the same isolation that had allowed it to flourish.

One morning Cristino and I drive to the ceremonial village of Orongo, one of the archaeological centerpieces of Easter Island. The remains of a dozen stone buildings are dug into a narrow spine of earth. On one side the vast crater lake of Rano Kau spreads out as if in a cauldron; its dark waters are nearly covered by a thick skin of totora reeds. On the other side the spine drops a thousand feet straight down to the Pacific Ocean. It is a site of such beauty, it literally draws the air from your lungs.

Orongo was the home of the Birdman cult, a relatively late development in the history of Easter Island. Though not much is known about why the cult emerged or how it exerted its influence, archaeologists have revealed one of the most grueling physical trials known in Polynesia. Every year warriors would assemble at the ceremonial village. When the signal was given, they would climb down the perilous cliffs and paddle out a mile to three small islands on handmade rafts in search of the egg of the sooty tern. The first to find an egg would be anointed the Birdman and led away to live a semimonastic life.

Today this long-gone spectacle draws thousands of tourists. Indeed, Orongo is one of the few archaeological sites that are roped off on Easter Island; the rest are nearly unmanaged. While Cristino and I look out over the ocean, vans of travelers pull up to the site. If Orongo were anything other than stunning, this would be a distraction, a nuisance even. But here atop an ancient crater rim, with the Pacific stretching to the horizon, there is a sense of spirituality unlike anyplace else I've been.

On a Saturday in October, the dusty main street of Hanga Roa is crowded with locals and tourists, the latter shuttling from storefront to storefront looking to rent cars, horses, guides. Archaeology is the primary draw for visitors, but once they reach Easter Island, they're confronted with a host of other options. Surfers have started to gather at the big breaks around the island, gunning for position on swells that have seen no obstruction since hurtling out of Antarctica. Divers come to explore underwater formations, great arches and pillars, in what many claim is the clearest water in the world; 130-foot visibility is an average day, though in the right season it can extend to an unheard-of two hundred. And because Easter Island is small, with mostly rough roads, mountain bikers have begun to patch together trips that mingle adrenaline-charged runs with seldom-visited archaeological sites.

At a café inside an artisan's market, where mini wooden moai are the top sellers, the locals drink Nescafé, slather sweet caramel onto fresh bread, and debate the pros and cons of the island's only economy. "The tourists are mostly a good thing," says Patricia Saavedra, who's lived here for forty years. "The only bad is the social stratification that has arrived too, as some people on the island have gotten very, very rich . . . and others have not."

For much of the twentieth century, Easter Island was leased to a multinational company that used it as a sheep farm; today about a third is national park, while another third is government ranchland. What is not controlled by bureaucrats on the mainland is passed down between Rapa Nuian families. Lately there has been talk that the government will give away some of its holdings in one- and two-acre parcels. The Chilean congress is considering a "special statute" that would grant Easter Island political autonomy, giving its government greater control over land use and finances. There is a fear that such a policy shift might promote more regimented development and kill off the loose island spirit that still predominates here. Horses outnumber humans and roam unhindered in groups. The entire island is essentially an archaeological site free of docents or minders. Fearing the Aspenization of Easter Island, some locals are trying to revive their cultural roots. The native Polynesian language, Rapa Nui, is now mandatory in elementary school. In the hills, local versions of Rastafarians—los Yorgos—live a hippie's life, dressed in camouflage and colorful bandannas.

Cristino and I stop for coffee along the main street. At the curb in front of us, a man tinkers under the hood of his car as two others ride by on horseback, metal horseshoes sending sparks off the brick paving stones. Cristino wears his work uniform of khaki pants and shirt and wide-brimmed leather hat, jet-black hair jutting out the back. He was born in Santiago and worked as a professor at the University of Chile until he was exiled to French Polynesia during the Pinochet years.

Cristino came to Easter Island as an assistant of William Mulloy, a University of Wyoming professor and one of the very first Easterologists. Cristino and his wife, Patricia Vargas, also an archaeologist, thought they'd be here six months. They've now been on the island for more than thirty years, trying to connect the migration and population dots. Together they've identified twenty thousand different archaeological sites, directed the standing of fifteen giant moai back on their feet at Ahu Tongariki—a massive stone platform some three hundred feet long—and published a 450-page "summary" of their work. Yet they readily admit that they still haven't decoded Easter Island's secrets, and probably never will.

"People come here because they are fascinated by the big statues," says Cristino, lighting a Marlboro. "All the popular literature claims to have 'solved' the mysteries of Easter Island. To get research grants, to get book contracts, you have to say, 'I found this! I am right, they are wrong!' But they are wrong. We still know almost nothing about what happened here between 1500 and 1700.

"Patricia and I have concentrated on an island-wide archaeological survey, counting not just the moai, but trying to re-create the lives of the people," Cristino says.

"Think of it this way. If New York City was destroyed and archaeologists arrived some three thousand years later, they could easily re-create the city based just on the remnants of the churches and big monuments. But how many people lived there, how they lived, et cetera, that's another job—and that's what we have undertaken on Easter Island."

Cristino is not wild about the tourism boom, evident from the dozens of vans streaming up and down the island's one main road, ferrying visitors from site to site. "From an archaeologist's perspective, tourism is a catastrophe," he says, with mixed feelings, since four of his eight children live here and participate in the tourist business; even he occasionally works as guide. But, he says, "The island needs tourists to help make it sustainable. Nonetheless, we are at critical levels. Forty-five thousand visitors each year to Orongo, the site of the Birdman cult, is far too many. It is fragile and will be destroyed by all those footsteps. We need Galápagos-style policing to stop its destruction, but we are not very organized at that level."

We finish our coffee and drive out toward the white sands at Anakena, one of two beautiful beaches on the island. Sun dapples the soft green, treeless hills, and a spring breeze rattles dry lucerne pods. A red-tailed tropic bird soars high above as tourists arrive by the busload and wander among the statues lining the coast, encircling the island. In many respects Easter Island will never be about its current inhabitants but rather the spirits of those long-gone people—the statue-makers, their chiefs and families. Ethnographer Kathleen Routledge, who came from England in 1914 and wrote the bible of the island's early settlement, suggested that "the shadows of the departed builders still possess the land." It is the presence of this absence that continues to give Easter Island its aura of mystery.

"Everything was not as simple as Diamond and others paint it," says Cristino. We are standing at the edge of the Anakena beach, where the first settlers pulled up their double canoes. He and his teams have spent years on this beach digging through middens—the mounds of shells, bones, and other detritus left behind by ancient visitors—attempting to pinpoint when the Polynesian invaders arrived and puzzle out how they lived.

Cristino chooses his words carefully when talking about the popular deforestation theory, which discounts other possible causes of the society's devolution: Did diseases brought by Europeans accelerate population loss? Was there a drought? Could a natural disaster have devastated such a tiny, fragile ecosystem? "In my opinion, current models put too much weight on human factors," Cristino says. "It was more than just man impacting the environment. Maybe El Niño, or too much rain, or maybe lack of rain.

These theories don't give enough weight to a variety of other debilitating elements, including earthquakes, the arrival of Europeans, and warming ocean temperatures."

Cristino doesn't seem convinced that Easter Island's example is a harbinger of terrible things to come for modern-day societies. He's worked and traveled all over French Polynesia and has seen that all cultures degraded their environments to some extent, even in Hawaii and New Zealand. The deforestation and resulting depopulation on Easter Island was not that unusual, he insists. Most Polynesian islands were stripped of trees, including Mangareva and Pitcairn (both of which Diamond also cites as environmental collapses). When Captain James Cook arrived at the big island of Tahiti, his men had to travel nine miles inland to find trees.

"The idea that humans destroyed Easter Island because they were not environmentally conscious is nonsense," Cristino says.

Later that night at a downtown restaurant, we sip pisco sours. We've been joined by Cristino's longtime colleague Edmundo Edwards. One of his ten children owns the restaurant, so we are treated well as we wait for a table.

"You want answers, I've got the answers," Edwards says, laughing, when I mention Cristino's professorial reluctance to formulate a grand unified theory. Mainland-born, to one of Chile's most powerful families, Edwards has lived and worked on Easter Island since the 1960s. Together the pair is the Laurel and Hardy of the archaeology world. Where Cristino is dark and handsome, Edwards wears thick glasses and a gray goatee, resembling an Oxford professor on walkabout. The tattoos on his chest, arms, and legs offer a counterpoint, testifying to his having, in Cristino's words, "gone native."

Cristino and Edwards basically agree on what happened to the Easter Islanders but occasionally reach conclusions via slightly different paths. Edwards is more insistent that the current popular theories are flat-out wrong.

"Easter Island has become a 'showcase of failure,' but the reality is very different," he says. Part of the problem, he continues, is that so many of the models are based only on histories and research written in English. He's pored over many original archaeological and anthropological studies and found evidence that points in a variety of directions. He argues that the biggest harm to Easter Island was the "fatal impact" of the Europeans' arrival, which brought with it disease, slavery (raiding parties from Peru kidnapped islanders in the 1860s), and violence.

He's not overlooking natural phenomena either. "For several years I worked with engineers studying the possibility that earthquakes knocked the statues over, which is suggested in some of the interviews done by Kathleen Routledge in 1914. When you look at the fallen statues with that in mind, it is very clear that is a possibility. Sure, some were knocked over during wars, but not all." More recently, an earthquake caused a tsunami that pushed several moai hundreds of feet inland.

Edwards is also convinced that during the 1800s the island was not completely deforested, as most contend, and that a largely peaceful population of fifteen thousand still lived on things they could grow. Though the stone-statue building was finished, they continued to create tall woven statues of reed and bark to deify their ancestors.

One major concern shared by both Cristino and Edwards is the land giveaway to registered Rapa Nuians planned by the government. Various hotel chains have noted the spike in tourism and are eyeing property. Chilean investors have even talked about building a casino. With so many questions unanswered, increased development could obscure the truth once and for all.

"This land is still covered with archaeological remains," says Cristino. "I know what's going to happen. The new landowners are going to say, 'I'll take care of these remains all right—get me a bulldozer.' They wouldn't do that with a statue, of course. But the foundation of a stone house, a cave home, these things are just as important to us."

Growing populations. Rising tensions. Environmental concerns. Is there any worry that Easter Island may be doomed to repeat its own history? As is always the case here, consensus is hard to come by.

"Easter Island is headed for another collapse if we don't learn to take better care of it," cautions Cristino, eliciting a grunt from his colleague. "I think it will survive now for a long, long time," counters Edwards. Based on what I've seen here, I'm tempted to side with Edwards. People around the world have proven extremely adaptable. I want to believe that the human experience on Easter Island has taught us something.

I suppose the only experts who know how things will end are the moai, who have seen all this before. But as usual, they're the only ones not talking.

Claudio Cristino and his wife Patricia Vargas continue their work on Easter Island, and as professors at the University of Chile in Santiago.

THE ARTISTES

"I still think Africa is a great place, affording the greatest evolutionary perspective, the last chance to have your feet on the ground where we began. I think the thing to do is just sit back and enjoy it and know that it is the greatest show on earth. It might be the last show, but it's the biggest, the most exhilarating, phantasmagoric, riveting, devastating, great."

—Peter Beard, *Wild Man in Africa*

WILD MAN IN AFRICA

Peter Beard

Condé Nast Traveler, 1993

Peter Beard has been both applauded and chastised during the forty-plus years he's lived in Kenya. But perhaps his greatest accomplishment, which no one can contest, was following the dream that took him to Africa as a teenager. While every one of us imagines setting sail, escaping to the wilds, of leading a life filled with adventure, few manage. Beard made his dreams real. As a result, he has lived a life matched only in fiction.

The product of a wealthy, patrician New York family, Beard first visited Africa in 1955 when he was seventeen. He was looking simply for adventure, desperate to immerse himself in this place so different from the streets of Manhattan and the summerhouses of Long Island. He was drawn initially, after reading Isak Dinesen's *Out of Africa*, to the life of a great white hunter. He sought out and met the last remaining characters Dinesen made famous—Bror Blixen, Philip Percival, "Cape to Cairo" Grogan, even Dinesen herself. He hunted on some of the last great safaris to leave from Nairobi's Norfolk Hotel (in the footsteps of Teddy Roosevelt). He lived for months in the bush with just a native tracker as a companion. He hunted big game, for food and pleasure and in the name of science. He followed on foot herds of beasts for days on end, camera in hand, learning about the animals, and himself. Granted unique permissions by park administrators and wardens, he roamed the savannas and forests of Kenya like few had before.

When hunting was outlawed, Beard picked up his camera and captured some of the last images of Africa as it was at the turn of the nineteenth century. A self-acknowledged remittance chum, Beard has never loved life as much as he did through the 1960s and into the early 1970s. Since 1962 he has made Hog Ranch—a forty-five-acre camp on the outskirts of Nairobi—his home. Around its campfire, in its studio, or atop one of the half-dozen tree houses scattered around the property, he has hatched his photography and acclaimed books. *The End of the Game*, its first draft written while he was still a student at Yale, stands as a classic documentation—in words and pictures—of the fast-evolving relationship between rapacious man and the diminishing wilds. *Eyelids of Morning: The Mingled Destinies of Crocodiles and Men* and *Longing for Darkness: Kamante's Tales from Out of Africa* are books only Beard could have assembled, both eclectic and prescient, part history, part scrapbook, crammed with existential anxiety and doomsday forecasts.

No matter the medium—words, pictures, or films—his take on Africa serves as an intriguing introduction for the laymen as well as a record of just how fast his adopted home has changed since he arrived. Everyone who has crossed his path has a different take on Beard. One friend says of him, "An American born into wealth and privilege, a charter member of the jet set, he could easily pass as a romantic figure right out of Solomon's mines. He has the looks, the bearing and the natural assurance and flamboyance of the Hollywoodized 'great white hunter.'" Next door neighbor and photographer/biologist Ian-Douglas Hamilton insists he's a "scavenger"; Kenyan Dr. Harvey Croze dismisses him as a lousy ecologist. *Newsweek* once dubbed him "Tarzan with a brain." Over the decades he has been diversely labeled a naturalist, fashion photographer, prophet of doom, stoic, diarist, garbage collector, felon, bum, racist, anthropologist, social chameleon, raconteur, celebrity, schizophrenic, court jester, despiser of mankind, and eighties existentialist. All and more are true.

Nothing irks Beard more than when he's dubbed "a jet-set socialite." Yet he's done little to evade the tag. Since he was old enough to drive, he has courted, been linked with, even married to some of the world's most famous models, actresses, daughters (and wives) of billionaires, *Playboy* centerfolds, and royalty. Most people recognize his name for marrying America's sweetheart Cheryl Tiegs, and many of his friends are household names. One day at his stateside house in Montauk, during the course of a couple hours, he fielded phone calls from Lee Radziwill's biographer (Jackie O's sister was a longtime sweetheart), Terry Southern (with whom he wrote a screenplay), and Lauren Hutton (one of Hog Ranch's most frequent visitors). The years of wild life have taken a physical toll. Today, at fifty-five, he bears the weathered look of an aging movie actor or beach bum. While he appears younger than his years, he's starting to wear down from years of bush life and hard living. His stomach is bad and most mornings begin with a slug of Maalox. He prefers "soft" food because his teeth are literally worn away from incessant nighttime grinding (he claims he can't afford to see a dentist). He often cups a hand behind his right ear to hear and can no longer read without glasses. An unaccountable, incurable skin disease he calls "African crud" rashes his ankles. Most photographs he takes are with a point-and-shoot automatic.

What has saved Beard from ignominy and perhaps even an early death is his passion for his adopted home. Though regarded by some as a loose cannon, he can be a forceful spokesman on the fate of Africa, the future of its people, and the end of the game. He hangs on in Africa because— like his hero Isak Dinesen before him—he regards it as the last great place from which to watch evolution. On a 1954 trip to England with his family, sixteen-year-old Beard read Karen Blixen's *Out of Africa*, which she wrote under the name Isak Dinesen. He credits this singular book with triggering his lifelong obsession with both the authoress and the place she loved. With what he describes as "an incredible amount of luck and a lot of pushiness," he would eventually meet Blixen, at her home in Denmark. To this day, he speaks of her reverentially. "*Out of Africa* was the first meaningful book I'd read and clearly the best," he once wrote. "All the dark mysteries of nature finally found a voice in one of the few outsiders who had the intelligence to go to Africa to listen rather than to tell. She was lucky, of course she made her luck, to be in one of the greatest places on earth and at possibly the greatest time."

Beard first visited Africa in 1955, accompanied by Quentin Keynes, grandson of Charles Darwin. They saw Madagascar and South Africa, the grand parks at Umfolozi and Hluhluwe, and made short forays into Tanzania and Kenya. "Everything I knew about the place came from books," he says. As a boy he had filled his rooms at home and college with antlers, horns, and the stuffed heads of various animals. "I thought of Africa as a place where there was still plenty of room, where you could actually live life rather than have your life run by a world where you wake up in the morning to a traffic jam, rush to catch a bus, struggle to get to the office . . ."

His timing was fortuitous. He arrived in Kenya when the nation was entering an era of incredible shake-up, politically and environmentally.

He was fortunate to meet and befriend the last generation of settlers before they died. He quickly assimilated himself into the group of young white Kenyans—politicians, scientists, entrepreneurs, hunters—who would emerge as the country's leaders in the years to come. When Beard first moved to Nairobi, he took a room at the New Stanley Hotel, where the action was. He would come down in the morning, get a small table at the Thorn Tree, buy the papers, and before long, several tables would be pulled together and fifteen to twenty people would be drinking coffee, eating, and sharing their most recent escapades. Some of them are still among Beard's best friends in Africa: Tony and Betty Archer; Bill Woodley and his wife, Ruth Hales; John Sutton; Glen Cottar; John Fletcher; Murray Watson; Mike Prettyjohn. From those long brunches he latched on to the best safaris of his life.

In 1961 Ruth Hales worked for the safari company Ker & Downey, which had a kiosk at the hotel. Knowing that Beard was looking for a guide to the bush, she introduced him to Douglas Tatham Collins, one of the most colorful hunters in Kenya and a former district commissioner of Somaliland. An incurable romantic and confirmed bachelor, he first helped Beard purchase a fourth-hand Land Rover and a cheap 9.3 mm gun. Pooling their resources—Beard's brought the Land Rover loaded with food, Collins's the native trappers, gun bearers, and cook—they set off for the first of many tours of the Greater Shag, Kenya's northernmost desert and bush country. In Collins' company Beard saw virtually every hectare of wild Kenya. From the open plains under Mt. Kilimanjaro to Tsavo West and then northwards, through Makindu to the desert of the Northern Frontier District (NFD). They spent months away from Nairobi. Along the way Beard sought out the last living remnants of the pioneering days. He interviewed, photographed, and learned from these men whose reputations had been secured in the writings of Blixen and others. He listened intently to their tales from the past and forecasts for the future. He had come to Kenya in many ways a blank slate and on these first journeys his mind was indelibly chalked.

Every day brought new encounters with a plethora of beasts, including black rhinos, lions, cheetahs, hippos, buffalo, and massive herds of elephants, reticulated giraffes, gazelles, dik-diks, and warthogs. He suffered through the hot desert life of the NFD, discovered the mystery of the African night and heard strange legends about snakes that could slither as fast as men and elephants with tusks so large that they had to walk backward. Along the way they hunted for sport and food. In fact, hunting was one of the primary reasons the young Beard was so excited about Kenya; he admired the lives of the great hunters and was anxious to experience something akin to what they had. He had learned to shoot as a boy in Alabama and Long Island, and was an excellent marksmen. His first kill in Africa was a hippo at Donya Sabuk. Mbuno handed him a .375 and he took careful aim using a tree as a rest. "It wasn't a hard shot, but it had to be done right, within about two inches of the ear," he recalls. "Up came the head of the cow with its distended eyes. A rifle crack ruptured the silence; a thud and a monstrous sinking. Not a bird or anything stirred. The kill had been too quick for me to know exactly how I felt; it was strangely exciting. The result was two tons of meat, which was carved up for workers on a nearby estate." Following kills were more dangerous and exhilarating. (One rainy evening he shot a leopard with a .375 broken in half and at the last minute tied together with a rope. The leopard jumped five feet in the air and then fell to the ground dead; the rifle shot knocked Beard to the ground and bloodied his eye.)

These were not big-money safaris. When they ran out of food or grew tired of trying to eat zebra (often cooked in a can of sand and gasoline when no wood existed and no thorns burned), they survived on spaghetti, passion fruit, posho, biscuits, and Fig Newtons. Hungry and in search of dinner, one Sunday Beard made a long, hasty shot at an impala, wounding it. In the hot pursuit that followed, he tripped in a warthog's hole, breaking his left ankle in two places. "The impala died nearby, and I crawled up to watch these two hungry Turkana boys pulling it apart and gobbling up the kidneys raw. They broke the bones to suck out marrow, the sound of which was beyond description." When he and Collins split up after three months, Collins continued on to Somalia. Beard headed for Laikipia, two hundred miles north of Nairobi, to learn the intricacies of "game control." He took a job on the ranch of Gilbert Colvile, who had begun with eight Boran cows in the 1940s and twenty years later had amassed a herd of ten thousand. Unfortunately cows and wildlife could not coexist in the same fields due to tick-born diseases transmitted by the non-domesticated beasts. The only alternative for farmers anxious to squeeze profit from the now fenced-in land, was to eliminate the competitive game. As well as being challenging hunting, this was to serve as a first and firsthand introduction for young Beard in the effect on wildlife when humans move in.

The work was hard, stalks long, the shooting fast and usually from quite a distance. Unlike trophy hunting, in which the target lies in a single vital area, in control work, after the first steady, calculated shot, everything is on the run. The shooters' main targets were zebras, buffalo, and cattle-killing lion, and they shot plenty of each. A day's hunting began with a painstaking, tedious stalk until a skittish herd was within range. They made certain that each gun could bring down two or three animals. Back at camp skins were pegged down for salting, and dried ones from the previous day were stacked. Dinner was around seven o'clock and sleep came soon after dark. It was arduous, dangerous, enlightening work. (Though Beard calls it "work," like virtually all his experiences in the bush, he was never paid, per his request.) He remembers one day in particular, running after buffalo full out, carrying heavy guns. "Bryan Coleman, a professional hunter carried a fourteen-pound .577, which could stop a buffalo by sheer impact. I had a slightly disintegrating Husqvarna 9.3 millimeter I had bought from an elephant-control officer in the New Stanley's Long Bar. It might seem that running through the narrow, 'wait-a-bit' thorn-pulling tunnels would be the most exhausting part of the ordeal, but it was not. There was an intense exhilaration as we plunged on faster and faster, snapping branches and pulling through vines, soaked with sweat, thinking of nothing but how that bull would look, how long the dogs could hold it at bay, how far apart the horns would be, how big and how mean it would be.

"Ahead of me Bryan fired two shots. Unbelieving, we froze and all at once a blackness burst through the branches. . . . I turned and let off two shots from the hip and then felt an explosion from behind. Another buffalo, wounded and down on its front knees, was circling with its hind legs before collapsing in a heap. Bryan lay between us a few feet away in the dirt, dazed. I hadn't seen him because he was run over by the first black, wounded form. As he rolled over, yet another buffalo appeared, a cow with her head down, and he got off a perfect heart shot as she turned."

Man versus nature. It was a theme that would become Beard's primary focus. He wrote at the time: "In the fight of men and domestic animals against nature and her complex balances there is no compromise. In areas where there is a winner, the winner is absolute. In an environment ruled by nature's balances, man cannot play around without expecting unsavory repercussions. For instance, on the Fletcher estate not far from Colvile's, a successful anti-vermin fence had so protected the reproduction of Thomson's gazelles that seven thousand of them had to be shot. And when they built up again in a year or two, someone had to buy another seven thousand rounds of ammunition."

At first Beard had hunted for pleasure, for sport. In the mid-sixties, he hooked up with several of the numerous scientific outfits studying wildlife in Africa and from them learned the work of a slaughtering hunter, shooting hundreds of crocodiles, hippos, and elephants. The purpose of such hunting was to gather enough scientific evidence, after dissection, to better understand the animals mating, reproductive, nutrition, and aging processes. Game was plentiful, and cropping made sense and was usually paid for by governments anxious to learn how to better manage the wildlife they hoped could one day pay for itself. Carrying his camera with him everywhere, he documented cullings of hippopotamus and elephant populations in Uganda, Tanzania, and the Congo, animal populations suffering from overgrazing and overcrowding. It was fascinating if occasionally dangerous work, and it introduced him to a wealth of wildlife professionals.

The Kenya national parks, organized in 1946, were run by a small, army-trained band of wildlife adventurers. Beard befriended them all— Mervyn Cowie, David Sheldrick, Peter Jenkins, Bill Woodley, Ian Parker. He purchased property from Cowie; walked every step of the Abedares with Woodley; lived for months with Sheldrick and his wife, Daphne; attended drunken bashes with Jenkins, Parker, and the others after long days and weeks in the bush. They welcomed Beard for his outsider's humor, bush sense, and photographic achievements. Bill Woodley is both Beard's mentor and best friend in Kenya; he remembers his young protégé in near-mythic terms. "Peter could run faster, walk farther, shoot straighter than anybody. If hunting had lasted, he'd have been a great hunter. But he loved the bush . . . with or without a gun."

Perhaps his most thrilling months were spent in the company of a grizzled, eccentric rhino trapper named Ken Randall, a South African whom

Beard still calls "the craziest man I ever met." Randall made a living on government contracts, catching rhinos in the hunting blocks and releasing the adults in Tsavo National Park. Beard remembers those chases—which entailed bouncing around on the running board of a Ford Bedford through the baobab and commiphora forests at forty miles an hour while attempting to lasso two-ton beasts—as "my first and best job in Kenya." The rhinos—black and five feet tall at the shoulder—were difficult to spot from the ground in the dense scrubland, which meant running into game was often sheer luck. Randall refused the assistance of airplanes, so ropers and spotters balanced precariously on the roofs of the lead truck, followed by an ambush vehicle carrying a crew of ropers, diggers, pullers, and general helpers. Day after day the crew bumped along from dawn to dusk.

When the chase commenced, the chief priority of the spotters was watching for burnt-out baobob stumps—vast black pits, sometimes twenty feet across—into which the entire catching truck could disappear. Uncaring, slightly mad, the begoggled Randall would floor it over blind gullies, termite hills, boulders, rocks, Acacia stumps, and thirty-foot trees. The windows of the truck had long ago been broken out, its cab was filled with tree branches, dirt, and leaves. Once captured, the rhinos were trucked eighty miles into Tsavo, where they were disinfected, dewormed, deticked and kept in log pens, made from great tree trunks dug deep into the ground and wired together with sturdy crossbeams. (On more than one occasion Beard paid natives to construct the pens out of his own pocket.) At first, each beast would hurl itself against his commiphora prison, shaking the pen and frightening the captors. The irony was that once released into their new home, nothing stopped the rhinos from running right back to their old stomping grounds in the hunting block. "This was conservation at its crazy best," he wrote.

In the mid-sixties, Beard and biologist Alistair Graham spent parts of several years living on the shores of Kenya's Lake Rudolf, hunting, dissecting, and documenting the lives of crocodiles. Graham had been hired by the Kenyan government to study the Nile crocodile, a previously ignored and little-probed creature. Their job was to assess the biological status of the lake's crocodile population in order to help the game department shape a policy toward an animal traditionally despised as a dangerous pest. Though contracted by the government, Graham received no money to pay for the survey, so Wildlife Services would have to finance its study out of what it could get for the skins of the five hundred crocs to be killed for investigation. Beard signed on as Graham's partner. "His devil-may-care manner was a tonic for the rest of us, though he clearly confirmed the Turkanas' suspicion that all white men were completely crazy," wrote Graham at the time.

The pair of white men and a half dozen Turkana helpers set up camps on either side of the lake, at Ferguson's Gulf, Moite, and Alia Bay. At the time the region was menaced by shifta—roving outlaws hostile to Kenya and sympathetic to the neighboring Somali Republic. Because of the risk of banditry, the scientific team kept as mobile as possible while on the east side, storing gear when not in use on the west side, at Kalokol. This meant crossing the lake every month, for skins had to be turned into cash regularly in order to keep the study going. Continuity was essential, so for a solid twelve months in 1965–66, Beard and Graham rarely left the lake. Beard's main assignment, other than photographing carcasses, was hunting, day and night. His limitless energy and enthusiasm were indispensable catalysts to a sometimes-flagging project; often he managed to turn mishaps into laughter.

Throughout their year together Beard constantly amazed Graham. "When Peter sees a dangerous situation, he has to get involved. What he likes most about Africa is to do your own thing there, a way of life you create with no plan. To Peter, something is creative only if it happens by surprise. He can't—won't—accept the normal responsibilities of society."

Horrendous conditions nearly made the crocodile study impossible. Lake Rudolf—once part of the Nile—is deceptively treacherous; winds average twenty to thirty miles per hour across it and whip up on a whim to fifty or sixty. "It's just like an ocean," says Beard. "We often saw crocs being tossed about in ten-foot waves." On the first day of what was to be more than a year on the lake, their boat sank. During the course of their study, its replacement, Graham's nineteen-foot converted lifeboat known as *The Curse*, was swamped four times and eventually sank.

For shelter they designed blow-through canvas sheeting rigged on steel frames; tents would have been too heavy, too wind-resistant, and unbearably hot inside. These open shelters offered the only shade, and so served as dissection room/bedroom/storeroom. Sand was in everything and flies were a major annoyance. By day the black volcanic shore was furnace hot, interrupted randomly by violent whirlwinds, which tore through the camp like miniature tornadoes, scattering anything not weighted down with stones.

Their diet was mostly catfish and tilapia, supplemented by Ritz crackers, Hellmann's mayonnaise, bread-and-butter pickles, condensed milk, and a few treasured tins of grapefruit. Soup was concocted from grand-sounding packets like Egg-drop, Mushroom, and Chicken Noodle, but the vile alkaline water polluted everything. Black volcanic sand was in every mouthful of catfish, perch, turtle, zebra. "The cook's forte consisted of dropping slabs of catfish, some fat, and plenty of sand into a pan and heating it for an indeterminate period," remembers Beard. "The result was then dumped, wordlessly, before us. There was, to be sure, nothing to say." The natives existed primarily on crocodile meat. (Beard: "I have eaten nearly every kind of wild animal meat and found all of it good with the single exception of croc. It has an oily, pungent flavor however cooked, cut up, or disguised.") Occasionally they were treated to Nile turtle or croc eggs. Their teeth turned brown from drinking the alkaline lake water, which Beard claimed tasted "like melted jellyfish." Hyenas and lions stole and ate several fresh croc carcasses even though they'd been anchored well offshore. Scorpions crawled into sandals, damp-skinned toads were found in every jar and metal box, poisonous night-traveling carpet vipers hung from tent frames. They could not have picked a more difficult and dangerous location for a scientific survey.

Alia Bay was where Beard and Graham engaged in some of their best crocodile hunting. Using .270 silver-tipped bullets, they learned much about crocodiles simply by pursuing them. Their goal was to shoot a minimum biometric sample of five hundred during their stay, or forty to fifty crocodiles each month. (At the time it was estimated there were thirty thousand crocs in the lake, plenty to cull from.)

It proved an arduous task. They needed a random sampling of ages and therefore shot any adult available. The bigger, older, and smarter, the better, but "monster pebble worms"—as Beard and Graham referred to those over thirteen feet long—were rare. Most ranged from six to ten feet.

Hunting day and night was a necessity. "We had hoped to hunt from a boat, but the wind ruled that out," wrote Graham. "Then we found that because the lake was shallow a long way out, most of the crocs were out of range of a hunter walking along the water's edge. So we had to go in after them. Our technique was for one of us to walk in front with a torch, followed closely by a rifleman. Behind him came one of the men to tow our kills along. This was necessary because if we left them on shore the lions or hyenas that followed us when we were hunting at night quickly stole them. "The torch bearer would cast around for crocs, whose eyes shone red in torchlight. Finding a suitable one, we would try to approach without alarming the wary animal, which more often than not would silently submerge and disappear. Once down (underwater), a croc can last up to an hour without breathing. Although the light dazzled the crocs, many things worked against us to warn them of danger. It was essential to keep downwind, for their sense of smell is extremely good. Their hearing is keen, too, and this was our greatest problem, for the ground underfoot was seldom easy to traverse soundlessly. Mostly it was vile ooze studded with sharp chunks of lava and rocks. Every now and then someone would plunge into a soft patch, for it was a constant struggle to keep upright. Many were the crocs lost at the last moment as somebody subsided noisily into the lake. Scattered about were hippo footprints, deep holes in which the lava chunks clutched at you like gin traps. A shoe torn off deep beneath the mud was almost impossible to retrieve without alarming a croc floating a few feet away."

Close calls were almost a daily occurrence. Graham shot one big croc, walked up to it, and was surprised when it began thrashing about, snapping its jaws viciously. Stumbling, he felt it whip around and its jaws close on his leg. He let out a muffled howl and managed to wrench his leg clear with no damage but deep gashes. On another night Graham was bitten by a spitting cobra. Luckily it was only a scratch; he jumped aside at the last second and the fangs only grazed him. Two teeth marks about a centimeter apart were the only evidence of the strike; from each tiny wound trickled small tracks of blood. Beard remembers the twenty-minute journey back to camp as chilly and uncertain. "We all expected him to keel over, dead," he says.

On yet another night a twelve-footer came like a torpedo from more than thirty yards off shore straight at the flashlight, which Beard was holding. Graham was so surprised that his two or three shots failed, then the gun jammed. "Scared stiff, I held the flashlight out to the side and ran around in tight circles," says Beard, "waiting for a finishing shot. Alistair hurled his rifle to the ground, took out his trusty Colt .45, and, at point-blank range, fired again and again. The scaly leviathan was on auto-pilot and it took several loads to weigh it down with lead." Another night one of their native hunters was grabbed from behind by a ten-foot croc on Central Island. He managed to get away after a grizzly tug of war that sent him to the hospital in Nairobi with massive injuries. Animals weren't the only beasts they had to watch out for. Merille, Rendile, and Boran bandits passed by their campsites many nights, looked them over, and kept walking. They were lucky. In Loiyangalani, near the southern tip of the lake, Somali bandits with automatic weapons raided the only fishing lodge on the lake. A Catholic priest was killed, the lodge's manager shot in the back of the head, and an Italian driver speared and skinned.

The crocodile survey ended in typically Beardian fashion, with the sinking of *The Curse* on September 17, 1966.

Three crocs short of five hundred, Graham dropped Beard and a knock-kneed skinner nicknamed the Wildman on Shingle Island. They were to spend one last cold, windblown night hidden in trenches scooped out of the sand, waiting to shoot anything that came ashore early the next morning.

When Graham returned in *The Curse* the next morning to pick up the hunters and the last crocs, the wind was blowing twenty to twenty-five miles an hour, covering the lake with whitecaps. Celebrating the conclusion of a year's hunt, they decided to make one last trip rather than two and loaded the boat with all three crocs, gear, and men. Two miles from the mainland the winds worsened and green waves began pouring over the narrow stern of the wooden boat. They quickly jettisoned the crocs, but it was already too late. In seconds the boat filled with water, and sank. The trio found themselves adrift in rough seas. Worse yet, the Wildman, who could speak neither English nor Swahili, could not swim a stroke. "His eyes were wide and rolled back, searching Heavenward," remembers Beard.

Graham quickly disconnected the gas tank and emptied it of fuel so that it would float. Pushing it toward Wildman, they spent the next frantic minutes trying to teach him to swim, by madly kicking his feet while clutching the tank. The wind was now blowing about thirty miles an hour, and the air a foot above the choppy sea was full of spray. Swimming in what they hoped was the right direction, the Wildman and Graham, who was desperately trying to hang onto his glasses, headed back for Shingle Island. Beard stayed behind. His diary was in the sunken boat and it contained the only records of the yearlong crocodile hunt. He found it after four dives into the metal cockpit of the boat, which lay twenty feet under. "For the first time one of my diaries contained something irreplaceable: all of Alistair's croc data, markings, measurements and tail-scale sequences for age-criteria studies. This made it vital to save," remembers Beard.

His swim to Shingle Island was a blur. Clutching his diary he swam against the current and waves. The island, a sand bank the length of a football field lying very low in the storm, was barely visible above the chop. He tried not to think about the thirty thousand crocodiles that hungered in the lake. Eventually on shore ahead of him he spotted his two friends, apparently hugging, slapping, rubbing, and shaking each other. When he stepped ashore, he understood their frantic behavior. The high-octane aviation fuel dumped into the sea had badly burned their skin; the wind onshore immediately brought the resulting pain to their attention. Assessing their options—stuck on the island with no one within a hundred miles to miss or rescue them—Beard decided he could make the two-mile swim to the mainland. With the red fuel tank as his float, he set off at 2 p.m. and he paddled and kicked for hours to reach shore. The next day, his skin sore and scabbing from gas burns, he rigged a larger float. He tied the fuel tank and an empty jerry can together, then flattened another jerry can to serve as a sail. After affixing emergency rations of Skippy peanut butter and honey, he set off for Shingle Island. If he misjudged the position of the tiny island, he risked being blown past it into forty miles of open lake. After another several-hour long swim, he found the island. He and Graham then kicked the makeshift craft back to the mainland. The next day Graham would retrieve his plane, borrow a boat from Ferguson's Gulf, and go after the Wildman. The survey was indisputably over. By taking just one chance too many, they had brought it to an abrupt halt three crocs short of their goal of five hundred. To top it off, they had lost their boat, engine, guns, and all other equipment.

Today Kenya's fast-swelling population is touching Beard in a personal way. As the country nears implosion, Hog Ranch is threatened by the imploding Nairobi populace. Together with neighbors Beard has paid for a ten-foot-tall chain-link fence to wrap a communal 150 acres, in an effort to protect what is left of the Mbgathi Forest from fast-encroaching development. But that is merely a Band-Aid. Roads are being surveyed and wells tested all around Hog Ranch. It is a matter of time before the expanding metropolis devours his once-private domain. "If things get really bad, we're on to the Congo, the Riviera of Africa," he says only half in jest. One evening, sitting on the porch of Hog Ranch's kitchen, I ask Beard if he ever thinks about leaving Kenya and not returning. Thoreau, after all, left Walden after just two years and never went back. Karen Blixen was in Kenya for seventeen years, then retreated when the going became too difficult. Beard has been here for more than thirty years. I wonder out loud if perhaps he has stayed in his paradise too long. Around every corner he has found the end of something and it has soured him. "I disagree," he says when I suggest my theory. "I still think it is a great place, affording the greatest evolutionary perspective, the last chance to have your feet on the ground where we began. I think the thing to do is just sit back and enjoy it and know that it is the greatest show on earth. It might be the last show, but it's the biggest, the most exhilarating, phantasmagoric, riveting, devastating, great.

"Mostly I feel like the wildebeest out there in a rainstorm . . . you just put your head down and wait."

Peter and Najma Beard split their time among homes in New York City, Montauk, and Paris. He rarely visits Africa. His commissioned artworks sell for hundreds of thousands of dollars.

REBUILDING PETER BEARD

Peter Beard

Men's Journal, 1997

Prone in his hospital bed, Peter Beard pulls up his kikoi to show me the results of his "tusking." A foot-long, just-stitched scar snakes along the meat of his left thigh, matched by a just-smaller wound on the backside of his leg—compliments of a three-ton elephant trying to turn him into a human shish kebab three weeks earlier. The fifty-eight-year-old wildlife photographer smiles as I run my finger along the wound. Hiking his skirt even higher, he shows off his man-inflicted scars, the incisions made by doctors at Manhattan's St. Vincent's Hospital in an attempt to repair a pelvis fractured in five places. Ten hours, four plates, and twenty-five screws later, they predicted Beard would walk again. He is more optimistic. "I don't even anticipate a limp," he laughs through a slight Demerol fog.

I spent a few hours with him two days after his surgery, entering the room with his wife, Najma, and daughter Zara, to find him flanked by a pair of young model-babes. He seemed his exuberant, ranting, charismatic self. We talked of African politics, conservation scams, shared trips into the bush, the usual Beard subject matters. On the surface it would seem the crushing had barely fazed him. But the "accident"—I guess that's the best thing to call being chased down and skewered by one pissed-off pachyderm—has definitely sobered the wild man.

It wasn't just the sutures and hardware that had added new weight. Something else had changed. An as-yet-unarticulated introspection, perhaps. "This was no laughing matter," he admitted. "I am extremely fucking lucky to be alive." On the way to the hospital in Nairobi—the trip took four hours via Land Cruiser and Cessna—he nearly bled to death and had to be pumped full of whole blood upon arrival. I ask what went through his head as the elephant was puncturing him. "It's odd. Instead of seeing my entire life flash before my eyes, I saw only the bad things. That was a total drag." His gaze turns to eight-year-old Zara, a dark, striking beauty, and he fixes her with a smile that suggests he will be forever thankful to some higher power for just being allowed to look into her eyes again.

His Greenwhich Village hospital room overlooking the Hudson River has been transformed into quintessential Beard. A red kikoi is draped over the fluorescent light, and a late-afternoon autumnal sunset washes the private room. Dangling from the pull-up bar above his bed (so he can readjust himself), are photos of Peter with Zara and a stuffed Babar. The room's bulletin board is covered with snapshots—Beard in Nairobi Hospital, a Masai medicine man working his magic in the bush, a photo of Salvador Dali at a car crash, and color photocopies of Beard as painted by Francis Bacon. Pasted over the stock hospital art is a Beard photograph of a giraffe head lying next to one of his infamous diaries. His narrow bed is piled with newspaper clippings, books, and magazines. Within arm's length are glue and scissors and his latest diary. A plethora of flower baskets line the radiator; catered dinner from Nobu, the pricey Manhattan sushi restaurant, is on its way, compliments of a friend.

Despite his doctors' attempt to keep the room quiet, a string of friends check in throughout the day. A young photographer Beard met just days before brings by color prints he'd taken during the ten-hour surgery—fingers prodding gaping holes in flesh, cold steel being inserted, Beard anesthetized. "You have made my week, friend. The whole episode wouldn't have been worth it without this photographic record!" A doctor stops by with a Ziploc bag full of metal parts installed in Nairobi and removed in Manhattan. It is on its way back to Africa. "They don't have much surplus," jokes Beard.

This is not the first time Beard has had a run-in with elephants. On many occasions during his forty years in Africa, elephants have stepped toward him, flapped their ears, bellowed, made typical demonstrations to warn him off. This time was different. Very different. Walking just behind fourth-generation white Kenyan Calvin Cottar, a thirty-five-year-old safari guide whom Beard has known literally since Cottar was in diapers, Beard approached this herd with due caution. "Just out of curiosity," says Beard, who was not even carrying a camera. "She charged the first time and it looked 'sick,' not typical," he remembers today, looking out at the sun setting over the Hudson river. "I should have recognized then that something was wrong. Then she repeated it. Right then we should have run as fast as we could."

For posterity's sake there is a partial videotape record of the accident. Partial, since the young Frenchman carrying the Hi-8 camera dropped it as he too ran from the charging cow.

This is what the video does show: On Monday, September 9, Beard, Cottar, Cottar's wife, Amanda, their two children, and Amanda's father, were in the southern part of the Masai Mara National Park, near the Tanzanian border. The area is hardly new to the Cottar family, which has organized hunting and photo safaris in this territory for eighty years. Ironically, in 1940 an angry rhino killed Cottar's great-grandfather nearby.

They were on their way to a picnic lunch on the Sand River when they spotted a herd of twenty elephants and stopped for a look. It was noon on a perfect blue-sky day. Beard tested the wind by plucking tall grass and dropping it. The elephants definitely knew man was present; on the videotape you see them look straight at Beard and Cottar as they approach from three hundred yards away. But the big animals—males, females, kids—continued to stroll casually away from the men, so passively that Beard and Cottar decided to continue their "walk up" on the herd, to get as close as they could, for observation's sake only. No one carried a gun. "We had no intention of risking our lives in that open country," recalls Cottar. "We were enjoying the experience of being with these magnificent animals. We were not getting 'bad vibes' from them."

Suddenly, and unexpectedly, one of the females turned toward the approaching men. She brayed, flapped her big ears, and then charged toward them, stopping after ten yards. Assuming she was just trying to put a scare into them, Beard and Cottar turned and began to jog away, watching intently over their shoulders. So far, it seemed typical. She then charged again, closing another twenty yards, feinted . . . and kept coming, downhill. Beard and Cottar were now running for their lives.

Beard went left; Cottar right. Beard turned the corner around a six-foot-tall anthill hoping to elude the big gal; he tripped and fell. Before he could get up, the elephant was on him, her tusk sinking through his left leg. It was the elephant's massive forehead that crushed Beard's pelvis, the weight nearly imploding his organs and lungs. "For three or four minutes it felt like a freight train was running over me," says Beard. The smart thing he did, instinctively, was sit up and grab onto the elephant's leg, which prevented him from being ground beneath its foot like a cigarette butt.

From where Cottar had fallen, he could see what was happening to his friend. He picked himself up and ran for help (i.e., the car). "I looked back and saw some of the herd had now come down to join the angry cow and were milling around Peter. I thought with that tonnage of pissed-off pachyderms, there was no way he could still be alive," says Cottar.

When the car pulled up to where the ellie had left Beard for dead, he was struggling to catch his breath. Momentarily blinded, his first words were, "I think my hip is broken . . . my left leg and hip are fucked. . . ." Helped by Cottar and the others into a sitting position, he moaned with pain, surprisingly articulate given his condition. Obviously in shock, his lips and mouth were bloodied, dirt jammed beneath his fingernails from the struggle. "She was determined, wasn't she?" he quipped. In the background, Amanda was on the radio to Nairobi, attempting to arrange an air rescue. "Don't worry about anything . . . ," moaned Beard, ". . . just drive me quietly to a hospital . . . don't get on the airways and get everybody riled. . . ."

Very Beard-like, trying to calm those around him while he's the one in dire need, he then trotted out a joke. "Curly, don't worry. I'm not going to sue," he said, addressing Cottar by a childhood nickname. The joke was a reference to the 1987 accident in which Beard and veteran guide Terry Mathews were chased down by a pissed-off rhino, resulting in a nearly fatal goring of Mathews and followed by a six-year legal battle over who would pay the hospital bills. (Funnily, when this quip was first translated to friends around the globe, it came out as, "I'm not going to screw" . . . which may yet prove true, too.)

Once Beard struggled painfully into the backseat of the Land Cruiser, they drove forty minutes over bad roads to the closest airstrip. The agonizing moaning on the videotape is almost unbearable to hear. "I'm afraid my hip is so, so crushed," wails Beard. "I wish someone would just put an end to it. . . ." Cottar on the radio with the flying doctors, describes his friend's condition: "His stomach is turned up . . . his leg and pelvis may be fractured . . . we need a stretcher . . . and lots of morphine . . ."

By 4:30—just four hours after the goring—he was on the operating table at Nairobi Hospital, literally bleeding to death. He had no pulse, no blood pressure. After pumping him full of new blood, staunching the internal bleeding, and securing his hip bones to an external scaffold by placing pins through the skin, the doctors pronounced that he would make it. Two weeks later he was flown to New York for further, extensive repair. Before parting company at the airstrip, Beard and Calvin had made a pact. They theorized that the elephant had charged because park rangers had recently been culling elephants nearby. This big female, perhaps realizing these humans were not carrying guns, decided enough was enough, that she was going to mete out a little payback. Beard and Cottar agreed not to tell anyone where the accident occurred, concerned that the elephant would be hunted down and exterminated by rangers. By keeping silent, they saved the elephant's life.

No stranger to close calls in the bush, over the years, whether photographing, hunting, or just out for a piss, Beard's had his share of run-ins with buffaloes, rhinos, elephants, crocodiles, and lions. Close calls are not unusual when you live in Africa. He has always been turned on by the contact, the risk, confident he could read (or outrun) the big animals. Some of his most memorable game photos were the result of his being willing to get closer than anybody else in their right mind might.

That's not to say he is careless in the bush—a criticism some in Kenya have made in the past, and again post-accident. "Peter's been fucking around out there long enough, teasing the big animals to get a good picture," one old friend of Beard's told me last week. "It was just his turn."

My assessment is that in the past he has been both good—and lucky. This, for example. One day in the early sixties he was working in Uganda with a pair of scientist/hunters, Ian Parker and Lionel Hartley, tracking and shooting elephants, employed by the Nuffield Unit of Tropical Ecology. Late in the afternoon, armed with rifle and camera, Beard found himself separated from the others. He could hear Parker and Hartley shooting on the far side of the hill when an angry bull came charging over the hill, directly at him. He stood his ground, for while the elephant appeared intent on skewering him, Beard curiously welcomed the experience of being charged. Meanwhile, Parker and Hartley had come to the top of the hill, but were a hundred yards away. They both knew that a shot to scare or wound the big animal would be extremely difficult, yet Hartley shot once anyway. Miraculously, he dropped the elephant and it skidded to a halt, dead, just feet from Beard. Instead of being thankful, Beard's response was irritation. He was unshaken by the charge but infuriated by the shooting. "I wasn't ready to run," Beard yelled at Hartley. "It just wasn't time yet." Dangerous-if-exhilarating, a life-enhancing near miss—a perfect recipe for fun in the bush, à la Beard. Today his two hunting friends still shake their heads in amazement over his attitude and confidence.

The Terry Mathews accident was much more traumatic. While making a television special for ABC (*Peter Beard in Africa: Last Word from Paradise*), Beard and Mathews, who'd known each other thirty years, were tracking a mother and baby pair of rhinos through Nairobi National Park. As two cameras filmed them approaching the rhinos, a vanload of boisterous tourists distracted the big beasts and the mother advanced toward the humans on the ground. Beard reversed and started running; Mathews stood his ground, desperately picking up stones off the ground and hurling them at the two-ton animal, shouting at the top of his lungs, "Bugger off! Bugger off!" As the rhino closed, Mathews turned to run but tripped and fell to the ground. When he stood, it gave the rhino a clean shot. ABC filmed—and aired—pictures of Mathews impaled like a rag doll, being tossed high in the air. Beard was the first to reach Mathews. Barely alive, he had his kidney and spleen sliced by the rhino's horn, which plunged up under his ribs and stopped a quarter of an inch from his heart. His left leg was fractured and three vertebrae broken. Doctors had to split his body open from neck to knee to repair him and he spent months in the hospital. He later sued ABC—and Beard—claiming they were responsible for his injuries. The ensuing legal fight split white Kenya, some siding with Mathews, others with Beard. (The suit was ultimately settled, in Mathews's favor.)

Beard and I have talked endlessly about the accident, and the ensuing *fitina* (gossip). It was beyond him that Mathews would try and hold anyone else responsible for what was simply an unfortunate accident. One night at Hog Ranch, Beard's pastoral home outside Nairobi, Tony Archer, an old friend of both men, cracked, "The smartest thing you did that day, Peter, was wear better running shoes."

Ironically, one of many who came to visit Beard in Nairobi hospital was Terry Mathews. Beard was touched. "That proved it wasn't as personal as it seemed at the time. It was about getting his legal bills paid."

While there is an inherent level of machismo at play anytime a pip-squeak human attempts to get close to big animals in their own habitat, in Beard's defense elephants are known to charge hunters and photographers all the time. "If you're working out in the bush, being intimidated like we were by an elephant is hardly unusual," says Beard. "What is unusual is that she kept coming."

As he shows me the tusk wound, he details what it felt like to be on the sharp end of the ivory.

"I went down behind this giant anthill, fell down actually, and there she was, on top of me. To keep from being completely crushed, I tried and was successful at grabbing her leg as she gored me. Funny, I couldn't feel her tusk going right through my leg.

"Then I just lay still, for maybe three, five, or ten minutes. Playing dead, hoping she'd go away. Instead, a whole bunch of her friends joined around, for a look I guess.

Today, he thinks the crushing was a good thing, not surprising considering his "any experience is a good experience" philosophy toward life. The love and concern that emanated from friends around the world post-accident reminded him just how many good friends he has. Still, during my first visit he makes several references to life "starting over again" and about how very, very lucky he is to be alive. "You know what today is?" he teases his daughter. "It is the first day of the rest of your life." At the moment he's vowing to change his own life—new playgrounds, new playmates, even no more cursing (the last at the behest of Zara). We'll see.

The next few months are big ones for Beard. The biggest show of his career, a retrospective at Paris's Centre National de la Photographie, opened the first week of November. On the art market his work, particularly his one-of-a-kind collages, are selling for ever-higher prices. In New York and Paris he can't stay out of the gossip pages. An admitted master at "flogging his own crap," Beard—and his handlers—are savvy enough to realize there is publicity value in "almost" being killed, especially by an agitated elephant in the African bush rather than by an angry bouncer outside a Manhattan nightclub. (The latter run-in left him with a broken arm just last winter. . . .)

I am a friend of Beard's and a fan of his work. I think he, and it, are daring, one-of-a-kind. But I have always found his life in Africa far more interesting than his stateside existence. When he's in Africa he seems more comfortable, more content, which makes the rumor that, coincidental to his accident, he is selling his forty-five-acre Hog Ranch foreboding. For many years, Beard has been afraid that the Kenyan government could seize Hog Ranch. He's recently been negotiating with a neighbor to buy the property, granting him some kind of life-tenancy deal.

I get him on the phone a week after he's been let out of the hospital. He's just come back from his daily physical therapy session ("lots of stretching and heavy, heavy massage," he says), and admits to being in a lot of pain. "I'm not doing very well today, because I'm trying to get off some of the painkillers . . . a very bad cracked rib scene going . . . I can't breathe . . . it's really a drag." He's expecting to endure rigorous therapy for at least four months; for now he's getting around only in a wheelchair. I ask if all this pain and hassle might put distance between him and Africa.

"NOOO FUCKING WAY," is the slurred-if-emphatic response. "Not at all. I want to go back as soon as January, do a safari that starts where the elephant situation occurred. . . . Then I want to go up on top of the hills and see the laibon, the Masai medicine man. No, this won't stop me. . . . I'm going back as soon as I'm able." Good, I tell him. Because Beard out of Africa would definitely signal the end of the game.

BAD BLOOD

George Butler

Premiere, 1989

Aslab of Brie in one hand, a glass of fresh New Hampshire cider in the other, George Butler paces the floor of his apartment on New York's Upper East Side as the fading light of a late-afternoon sun pours across his path. It is autumn 1988, and Butler is not happy. "I just don't know what Teddy wants," he snaps. "He wants me to change the name of the film? Fine, I'll do it, I'll come up with a better one. He wants me to take a scene of him and his son out? Done. Same with the one involving the shooting of the lion. And he still wants to add a rejoinder at the end of the film, saying he did not approve of the crocodile hunt. I'll tell you, I'm about up to here with the guy." Red in the face from his tirade, he kicks a pointy cowboy boot into the thick Oriental rug and drops into a rocker.

Of course, it isn't just any Teddy who's vexing Butler. It is Theodore Roosevelt IV, the great-grandson of the former president, whose African safari in 1909 was the inspiration for Butler's movie. Right now, both Butler and Roosevelt wish they'd never gone to Africa to retrace the great hunter-conservationist's steps, at least not in the same Land Rover. Since the pair first ventured to Tanzania in the summer of 1986—joined by an odd mix of blue bloods, gun collectors, professional hunters, children, Masai tribesmen, and filmmakers—many of the elements of Butler's movie, which he expects to get into theaters later this year, have changed.

The name of the movie was to have been *African Game Trails*, after Teddy Roosevelt's 1910 book recounting his eleven-month safari. Now it is called *In the Blood*. The stars of the film were to have been Roosevelt and his ten-year-old son, "Bear," Teddy Roosevelt V. Now the stars are a Great White Hunter named Robin Hurt and Butler's thirteen-year-old son, Tyssen. Originally, the film's executive producers were a couple of avid gun collectors with no filmmaking experience. Now one of the men who bear that title is a former secretary of the treasury. Before filming began,

Butler was set to collaborate on a companion book with Bartle Bull, a former publisher of the *Village Voice*. Now that book has been published, without Butler's contributions or consent. And when Butler and TR IV first arrived in Tanzania, a professional hunter named Bilu Deen was alive. Now he's dead.

The making of this quasi-documentary has been one fiasco after another. Yet Butler still thinks *In the Blood* will be a success. "There are 40 million hunters in this country, and I think they'll want to see this film," he says hopefully. In truth, though, Butler is stalking bigger game: he wants *In the Blood* to do for hunting what his best-known film, *Pumping Iron*, did for the sport of bodybuilding—namely, bring it into the cultural mainstream. But in *Pumping Iron*, Butler had the services of a cooperative, charismatic star: Arnold Schwarzenegger. For his safari movie, Butler had a considerably more recalcitrant Teddy Roosevelt IV.

Why did TR IV agree to be in the film only to back out soon after? Well, he's not talking. (Roosevelt declined to be interviewed, saying in a letter that he preferred the movie to speak for itself.) Friends say he initially hoped his involvement as an investor and "star" would help promote conservation and big-game hunting in East Africa—and that his role in the film might secure his own place in a famous family. But instead of reveling in his film debut, TR IV has spent much of the past two years attempting to have his image removed from the movie.

What began as an effort to make a $2 million film documenting one hunt in Africa—an adventure that cast and crew alike took to calling *Wasps on Safari*—now bears a striking resemblance to a bitter Park Avenue divorce. Yet Butler, even as he paces his living room cussing that famous name, remains cautiously optimistic. He smiles, a handsome, mannered grin. "I still think the movie will be better than the story of its making," he says. "Maybe."

Rather than seek a third term as president in 1908, Theodore Roosevelt went hunting. With the support of the Smithsonian Institution (and a fifty-thousand-dollar advance from *Scribner's Magazine*, for whom he would write about his adventure), TR and his son Kermit spent eleven months slaughtering their way across Africa. Bringing with them a "pigskin library" of Dickens and Browning—and enough firepower to take on a battalion— father and son shot and killed more than five hundred wild beasts:

elephants, lions, leopards, cheetahs, rhinoceroses, hippopotamuses, buffalo, and more.

Roosevelt was an early convert to the power of the moving image. On his travels, he brought along a Smithsonian cameraman, who documented the hunt in black-and-white stills and moving pictures. There's Teddy, foot resting atop a downed Cape buffalo. Here's young Kermit, seated in front of their Stars-and-Stripes-bedecked camp. And there's Teddy again, gently lifting a flower to his nose as he admires a double-barreled rifle. After his return, Roosevelt wrote his articles for *Scribner's*, which helped make his book, *African Game Trails*, a best seller. Film clips of the hunt toured the country accompanied by a lecture to be delivered by the local theater manager.

The inspiration for the late-1980s version of *African Game Trails* came from a couple of non-filmmakers looking for a free safari. A Connecticut gun collector named Larry Wilson was having dinner with one of his friends, former Columbia Records vice president Arma Andon, in the late spring of 1985. Andon wanted to go on an African safari and asked Wilson to investigate the costs. When they discovered just how expensive a two-week adventure was, the pair hit on a plan they hoped would get them a free trip: they would make a documentary of the hunt and sell the television rights to HBO, PBS, or another cable outfit. They contacted two filmmakers for help: Ken Walz, a veteran music-video director who had also worked for *The American Sportsman*, and George Butler. Wilson and Andon made their pitch at the Stanhope Hotel in May. Walz begged off, saying he was too busy. By the end of the evening, Butler had more or less turned them down, too. "They wanted to do essentially a vanity film about a safari," remembers Butler, "and I was leery about making any film about hunting." But Wilson lobbied Butler hard. "We really wanted George's help," Wilson recalls, "because we knew he was a specialist at taking unfamiliar and unpopular or misunderstood subjects and making them into films."

Wilson flew Butler to San Francisco to meet another gun collector, Greg Martin, who showed him one of Teddy Roosevelt's African guns: a Holland & Holland double-barreled .500/.450 nitro express. It is believed by some to be the most valuable gun in the world: Martin had recently been offered $375,000 for it.

Butler's interest was piqued—and by the end of August, he began to envision a potential film, though one that was very different from Wilson and Andon's project. Butler was himself a hunter, and he'd long been curious about hunting's role in late-twentieth-century life. He was also intrigued by the relationship between fathers and sons who hunted together, such as Teddy and Kermit Roosevelt.

"The first thing my father did was teach me how to hunt," says Butler, who spent his boyhood years in the African outback, the son of a Bostonian blue blood and a British army officer. "My brother and I would hunt all day. What we shot was for the table—mostly birds, because there were no beasts in the country. Even my mother became a hunter. In fact, one of my most vivid mental images of her as a young woman is heading out the back door with a shotgun."

Early that fall, Butler met with one of Africa's best-known professional hunters, Robin Hurt. Hurt told Butler that in his view, licensing hunters and stringently enforcing hunting regulations diminished poaching—indeed, that hunting was the only thing that could save the wild animals in Africa. Butler found himself agreeing with Hurt. For Butler, the project offered the chance to do another of his nonfiction films about a subject that was dear to his heart. "What has always fascinated me about hunting is what you can learn by observing nature and animals. I've always wanted to take my sons to Africa, teach them to hunt like my dad did with me. So when this project evolved, I promised Tyssen I'd take him along." But he felt that the project needed one more element: "I was convinced that we needed a Roosevelt." As it happened, he had a Roosevelt in mind.

George Butler had known TR IV since they were thirteen. The pair had roomed next door to each other at Groton and for the past three decades had traveled in overlapping New York social circles. According to Butler, TR IV's career path had been solidly laid: Harvard, Vietnam, the Navy's diplomatic service in Western Africa, Harvard Business School, and Wall Street. He was a very private man, but like his great-grandfather he'd been an ardent hunter and conservationist all his life.

To Butler, TR IV may have represented just the Schwarzenegger-like character he needed for his film: a sympathetic figure to serve as the movie's guide to the changes in attitudes about hunting. Butler invited TR IV and his wife, Connie, to dinner in September 1985 to explain his ideas for an updated *African Game Trails*. "By the end of dinner," Butler recalls, "things were beginning to click all over the place." Butler introduced Roosevelt to Larry Wilson, who along with Greg Martin agreed to finance part of the film. Over the next few months, a limited partnership was drawn up, with Butler, Martin, and Wilson as the general partners, and an outline of the film was written and approved by TR IV.

The project gathered steam as the months passed, and a safari was scheduled for late summer 1986. In October 1985, TR IV was filmed at a Christie's auction admiring collectible guns. In February 1986, he assured Butler in a letter that he was eager to take part in Butler's film, as an investor and—along with son Bear—as a participant in the safari, scheduled for East Africa in the summer of '86. In March, Butler filmed Roosevelt at the Holland & Holland factory in London.

In April, after dinner and a game of touch football at Roosevelt's home, Butler asked him again if he was committed to the film. "Do you realize that if you pull out of the film, I'm going to be in some difficulty?" is how Butler remembers their final conversation of the evening. Don't worry, he recalls Roosevelt replying, I understand how important I am to the film and would never pull out and let you down. In Butler's mind, their subsequent handshake cemented their deal.

The first whiff of trouble came on July 29, 1986—just twenty-four hours before Butler was to leave for Tanzania—when a two-page letter from TR IV was hand-delivered to Butler at his Manhattan office. In the document, TR IV asserted that the principal objective of the film was to increase the American public's awareness of the plight of East Africa and its diminishing wilderness. He also detailed several concerns he had about the movie, especially that it might not represent the original Teddy Roosevelt accurately. TR IV said firmly that he did not want the film to imply that he had come to Africa as an homage to his patriarch. He also ruled out any exploration of father-son relationships, either between TR and Kermit or himself and Bear.

Butler's heart sank as he read on. The letter stated emphatically that neither TR IV nor his son were to be used to advertise the movie or any related product and that he would have the final say over which scenes of him or his son would be included. He closed with what Butler regarded as a thinly veiled threat: if Butler breached this agreement, Roosevelt would have the right to sue to prevent the film from being released.

Efforts by Butler to meet with TR IV before Roosevelt's plane left the following night for Africa were futile, and he signed the letter, which formalized the partnership. Butler did reach Roosevelt by phone, and he attempted to soften their pact by requesting that Roosevelt put in writing any objections he had to the filming at the end of each day. Butler was eager to bend over backward to appease his old friend, in light of the constricting letter he'd signed before leaving. Unfortunately, once they were in Africa, their relationship went downhill fast.

On the second day of filming, with Butler's cameras rolling, TR IV shot and killed a lion. Perhaps the kill would have seemed more heroic if the lion hadn't been dozing. The safari's leader, Robin Hurt, had prepared a barn-door-sized blind and baited the lion for Roosevelt to shoot and Butler to film. Several members of the crew wished that somebody had at least thrown a stick at the beast to make it fair sport. But that didn't seem to bother TR IV; over lunch, he gave *People* magazine reporter James Wilde an excited interview about his first kill of the safari.

But the day after he shot the lion, Roosevelt began demanding that the footage of him shooting not be used in the film. Roosevelt was urged to take up the issue with Butler by Bartle Bull, another pal of Butler's, who had come along to write the book that would accompany the movie. Butler attempted to talk Roosevelt into confronting his own inner wrestling about the kill on camera, but TR IV would have none of it. That began three weeks of dissention-wracked filming. The battle pitted the "stars" of the film in what was essentially a class struggle—Greg Martin and Larry Wilson, the nouveau-riche gun collectors, versus Roosevelt and Bull, the old-monied traditionalists. Butler and his crew were caught in the middle.

The next day, Butler, Roosevelt, Bull, and crew went out in search of buffalo to hunt and film. Meanwhile, Greg Martin; his wife, Petra; two gun bearers; a skinner; and an Indian professional hunter named Bilu Deen went off on a picnic and hunting adventure. Deen seemed to be an emotional mess; both his wife and his girlfriend had recently left him. He tried to impress the Martins by driving forty miles an hour through herds of buffalo. Throughout the morning, Deen ordered the gun bearers to set small grass fires, an accepted practice among African hunters. (Game is drawn to new shoots of grass, and the hunters encourage growth by burning acres of plains.)

Unfortunately, Deen's timing was a bit off, and when the Land Rover got stuck on an anthill, walls of flame quickly surrounded them. Martin, who had worked as a firefighter in his college days, dug a fire line and led his wife and the skinner through the burning brush. But Deen, for some reason, ran in another direction—and the fire overtook him. Martin then led the survivors, including the two gun bearers, who had also escaped, on what would become a grueling nine-hour hike toward camp, with no water, no guide, no compass, and only a few bullets among them. As night fell, lions roared in the distance, and Petra Martin was forced to pour her own urine over her body to stave off dehydration. Finally, they were picked up—exhausted and flame-singed—and brought back to camp. The death of Bilu Deen stopped filming. Local police officials and Interpol heard rumors of foul play and interviewed the gun bearers, the Martins, and Robin Hurt. A memorial service and funeral were held. While Greg Martin was applauded for leading the others to safety, his reaction to the tragedy quickly earned him the wrath of the rest of the crew. Three of his guns, valued at $200,000, had been lost in the fire, and one of his first actions after arriving back in camp was to ask Hurt who was going to pay him for his uninsured guns. Deen was an employee of Hurt's, Martin argued, and had acted recklessly. Thus he was convinced that either Hurt or maybe the government of Tanzania, which had licensed the hunt, was liable.

The mood surrounding the film worsened from there. It was obvious to everyone that Roosevelt and Bull had developed an animosity toward Wilson and Martin. Martin had never been hunting before, and even Butler tired of his "ungentlemanly conduct" regarding guns and the safari. "If he'd pointed his gun at me one more time," says Butler about Martin, "I would have taken them all away from him." For their part, the gun collectors, both longtime admirers of President Roosevelt, were greatly disappointed in his heir. "He's a poor, wishy-washy guy," says Wilson.

"He's a very insecure individual," says Martin, "and he wears his name like the Shroud of Turin." At one point, during the filming of a contest in which each contestant used a rifle to shoot at a swinging coconut, the tension nearly broke into fisticuffs, with Bull screaming "Racist!" in Butler's face and Roosevelt threatening to punch out Hurt.

"It was quite clear that Bartle and Ted were retrenching while we were in Africa," says John Karol, a filmmaker and lawyer who acted as second cameraman. "I think they generally constructed their outlook while we were there, which became increasingly antagonistic and alien to George's. I also think Ted became very concerned about his name and his image and differences he perceived between his own background and the predispositions of both Larry and Greg. He just didn't want to be seen on the same screen with them."

Roosevelt was also taken aback by what he perceived as the "chaotic" nature of the production, says a crewmember. "There didn't seem to be a plot to the movie, which may be endemic to documentaries. We were just shooting scenes, and I'm sure it was hard for Teddy to see exactly what the movie was going to be about." Karol concurs: "You had to give [Roosevelt and Bull] some degree of understanding, because there was a lack of predefinition. But that was part of George's creative effort."

They wrapped after three weeks of filming. They'd spent $800,000 thus far, most of it Martin and Wilson's money. The seven-person crew had wrangled fifty-seven cases of equipment into the remotest corners of Africa, five hundred miles from the nearest airport or electrical socket. Even though the cameras had bounced around in the backs of Land Rovers, fallen in swamps, and been immersed in dust, the filmmakers brought back thirty-five hours of perfectly exposed film. Butler was convinced they had captured a telling story about big-game hunting in the late twentieth century. He felt they had shot the "real" Africa, not the gel-coated, Hollywoodized images of *Out of Africa*. Despite the hassles, he felt he had his film. To pacify Roosevelt, Butler reassured him that he wouldn't use the "sleeping lion" scene in the film. Cinematographer Dyanna Taylor assured Roosevelt that she had many "wonderful father/son scenes" of him and his son, Bear. "Really moving stuff," she told him. With the bitter clashes that haunted the filming now past, Butler and crew were confident. "In an on-camera interview the day before he flew home, Teddy said this was the "most extraordinary experience in his life and that he had had a wonderful time," remembers Butler. "He shot fourteen animals, got a free safari ride with his son, and even got a lion for his Brooklyn apartment. When I talked to him at the Nairobi airport, he was flying home with Bull and my son, Tyssen, and he said he was satisfied with the filming."

But by the time his plane landed at Kennedy Airport, something or somebody had changed Roosevelt's mind. Even before he left the airport, he was on the phone, starting efforts to disengage himself from the film. Ten days later he mailed another letter to Butler, in which he excoriated what he considered the boorish behavior of Martin and Wilson, claiming that they planned to use his name for profit. Harkening back to the letter he had sent before the trip, Roosevelt gave the partners notice that neither his nor his son's image could appear in the film and that any investment he had promised was canceled. Butler had lost his Schwarzenegger—and, it seemed, his film.

"By comparison, Arnold was great," Butler says. He would say, 'Okay, George, what are we going to do tomorrow? Let's stay up for another hour and figure out what we're going to film.' He'd come into the editing room and make suggestions, and he'd be right. With Ted Roosevelt, it was more like, 'George, you don't know what you're doing.'"

It is September 1988, and Butler is eating grilled swordfish at a posh new café not far from his Manhattan office. Almost two years to the day has passed since he received a letter from his old prep-school friend informing him he was out of the picture. As a result of that withdrawal, Butler went back to Africa and spent another $350,000 to replace TR IV's role in the film. Robin Hurt and Tyssen Butler, along with a dozen clips from the original 1910 Roosevelt footage and the Holland & Holland gun, will become the stars.

It would be an understatement to say that Butler is disappointed in his old friend. He spent 1987 trying to talk Roosevelt out of his complaints, replacing the investment he'd lost when Greg Martin also removed himself from the film, wrestling with Bull over control of the companion book, and scrambling to raise money to finish the project. After receiving Roosevelt's letter in 1986, Butler and other members of the crew attempted to straighten out whatever misconceptions the stockbroker had about the film. John Karol wrote Roosevelt a long letter, hoping to explain the crew's side of the shoot. "I suggested that he shouldn't panic. I thought he was probably equating the chaos of production with the final product, and anyone experienced in film knows that no matter how well planned your shoot is, there is always more chaos than you would anticipate." His letter was never answered.

After several screenings of the work in progress, Butler finally wore down some of Roosevelt's complaints, though it seemed that every time he answered one, another cropped up. Roosevelt asked that several intimate scenes between him and his son be cut. And he requested that a crocodile hunt that was also filmed be excused or that he be allowed an on-camera denouncement to be included at the end of the film.

Greg Martin convinced Robin Hurt to pay him thirty thousand dollars for "emotional damage" he and his wife suffered in the fire. He then sold the Holland & Holland rifle to former Secretary of the Treasury William E. Simon. Larry Wilson, who has bought and sold guns for Simon in the past, arranged the sale for $750,000. A crafty investor, Simon hopes the publicity given the gun in the film will drive up its value. "I'm keeping my fingers crossed," says Simon, who has seen the film and calls it "exciting."

With Simon's name attached to the project, money raising proved easier. And Butler thinks he's calmed Roosevelt enough to keep him from enjoining the film. But in Butler's eyes, it is Bartle Bull who has encouraged most of Roosevelt's protests. (Bull declined to be interviewed for this article, as did his attorney.)

"I don't know why he turned against me," says Butler, "but I have to think it's because he wanted the book for himself." The original contract—which was drawn up but never finalized—called for Bull's book to be illustrated with Butler's photographs, for Butler's name to be on the cover, and for royalties to be shared. On two occasions Bull, who heads a forty-member law firm in Manhattan, attempted to buy the book outright from Butler.

But despite arguments from Butler, his agents, and his lawyers that if Bull published the book without Butler's consent it would constitute severe copyright infringement, Viking Press distributed *Safari: A Chronicle of Adventure*, illustrated with stock photos, in November 1987 in England and the United States. Butler did not sue; he is convinced that if he had tried to stop publication of the book, Bull would have done everything he could to destroy the film.

Butler's literary agent, Peter Riva, likens the pissing match to a divorce. "It appears that at some point Bartle's idea of what the book should be diverged from George's, and he decided to take it his own way," says Riva. "It's been a long friendship, and George is extremely hurt. I'm pretty damn sure Bartle will be, too."

Butler is even more damning of his old friends. "The problem is, these are guys who have good jobs and houses in the country, belong to all the right clubs, have dinner with Mrs. Astor whenever they please, and drive Mercedes, but they've never taken the kind of risk I take. They don't understand that risk, and quite honestly I think they're a little envious of that."

It's October 1988, and Butler is locked in a Times Square editing room, wrestling with a two-hour rough cut. For all the Teddy-and-Bartle hassles, he has assembled a potential, if curious, success. Roosevelt and Bull are now bit players in the movie, as are Greg Martin and Larry Wilson. Robin Hurt emerges as the film's hero, a spokesman for the need to continue licensed hunting. It is a very pro-hunting film, laden with lush pictures of the African landscape as well as scenes of violent kills by both man and animal. The subtext of the film is the coming of age of Tyssen Butler, who, taught by Hurt and filmed by his father, chases down and kills his first buffalo. Hurt dips his hands into the animal's blood and paints the young hunter's face. One of the film's final images is of a "blooded" Tyssen staring into the camera.

After many letters and several screenings of the film, Roosevelt and Butler have reached a guarded agreement. "Essentially I outwaited him and outlasted him," says Butler, "and now there is nothing in the film he's going to object to." Butler is adamant that if he'd had all his deals in writing—releases for the film and a contract for the book with Bull—it wouldn't have made a difference. "If we had had to go to signed contracts, the trust wasn't there in the beginning to support the film," he sighs. But even his most supportive friends think Butler realizes the error of his ways even if he won't admit it.

"In a perfect world, a handshake would be all that was needed," says John Karol. "But in our world, both a contract and a handshake are necessary."

Patricia Beard, who is working on a novel based on the making of Butler's film, suggests that Butler is at fault for letting the film slip out of control. "Any director who can let things get out of hand, who goes off without signed releases—no matter what kind of friends they are—starts out on shaky ground. That he didn't stand up and hold the thing together is very indicting of him."

Butler remains chagrined but righteous. "The greatest irony of the film," he continues, staring at the small screen on the editing bench, "is that at the beginning of the shoot in '86, I had a meeting with the film crew. I told them, 'After dealing with bodybuilders for eight years, finally I'm taking some people of my own ilk out, and a handshake is the law. You don't need contracts with Ted Roosevelt.'

"The crew hoots with laughter today, remembering that speech. Because Roosevelt and Bull have behaved worse than anyone I've ever dealt with in my life, with less honor and less integrity and less honesty." Others would, of course, see things differently—but in Butler's mind it is his movie now, and when he looks at the screen, it is his son's image that stares back at him. "I did learn one lesson, though: you cannot trust your best friends in America these days. I think maybe I'll go back to bodybuilders next time."

George Butler has made several IMAX films, most recently Roving Mars. *In 2004 he collaborated with college classmate John Kerry to make the documentary* Going Upriver, *which documented the then-presidential candidate's war experience.*

BONES OF CONTENTION

Gillies Turle

Arts and Antiques, 1993

On a sunny afternoon two years ago, I drove with an acquaintance to the top of a grassy hill overlooking the Great Rift Valley, thirty miles from downtown Nairobi. The aging Datsun hesitated as it performed off-road duty for which it was not designed. We passed grazing cows and a handful of their native keepers. Midway up the hill a Masai man emerged from behind a lone tree, we slowed, and without a word he climbed into the backseat.

When we topped the rise, the car stopped, and the trio of us—collector, salesman, and observer—walked to the brink of the ridge, looking around to make sure no one was watching. The Masai, in his mid-forties, was most nervous and understandably, since everything about this meeting was illegal. He was dressed in a fashion typical of the modern-day African. A red blanket was thrown around his shoulders, his ears sagged with big loops, and he carried a spear in one hand, an umbrella in the other. On his feet were cheap sneakers and argyle socks. A Swatch watch wrapped one thin wrist. We sat on rocks and he produced his wares from beneath his cloak. They were like nothing the collector had seen in his decade of searching. Magnificent objects and pipes, actually carved from giraffe bone and rhino horn. The collector took them in his hands, rubbed and smelled them, and smiled. He spoke a few words of Swahili with the seller, then produced from his pocket a thick wad of tightly rolled shillings held by a rubber band. The price, like the clandestine meeting place and time, had been set weeks in advance. With the exchange the meeting was over; the encounter lasted fewer than five minutes. The collector and I walked back to the car; the Masai disappeared quickly and silently down the green hill.

"These are incredible," said the collector as he folded the half-dozen items into a blanket in the trunk of his car, "and incredible that so few have seen them."

WILDEBEEST IN A RAINSTORM

For most of his adult life, fifty-one-year-old Gillies Turle, the collector, lived that of a typical post-colonial Kenyan. He had come to Africa in 1965 as a military attaché for a British diplomat. When his boss was killed in a plane crash, he opted to stay on in Nairobi. He worked as a safari guide before opening an antique store in downtown Nairobi, filling his shop with European goods bought off the estates of the white colonials who began to flee East Africa once it became obvious that black rule was going to last. Married, with two kids and a house in the suburbs, Turle lived the good life. But in the early 1980s he endured a life change. He left his wife, two-story house, and polo-playing pals and moved into a tent on the outskirts of town (on land owned by American photographer/raconteur Peter Beard). By coincidence Turle says his primary occupation shifted at the same time, from collecting the remnants of white colonial society to the artifacts of black African culture, in particular rungus, pipes, and paraphernalia of the Masai wise men. Today Turle insists he has made a valuable discovery of a previously unknown African art. His book about his experience, *The Art of the Maasai*, will be published by Knopf this month (October).

The collection and book have already raised intrigue in the art world. Enid Schildkrout, director of African Studies at the American Natural History Museum in New York, has examined pieces of the collection and is anxious to acquire several for her museum. Roderick Blackburn, an associate with the Institute of African Study, the Museum of Natural History, and the National Museum of Kenya, calls Turle's collection "legitimate ethnographic artifacts of real cultural significance."

But the collection has also raised the ire of a very important Kenyan, anthropologist Richard Leakey. While the art world waits to see the collection, Leakey has hindered its unveiling by pronouncing parts of it "faked." Turle is in the middle, caught between possessing perhaps one of the greatest cultural and artistic finds in African history and simultaneously defending himself against accusations of encouraging forgeries.

The singular piece that began Turle's obsession was a rungu (club) made from rhinoceros horn. A Masai who had once sold him ivory snuffboxes brought it to him. The rungu had been shaped by sword, the rough cuts sanded down by damp leather dipped in coarse sand and polished by leather soaked in urine or by ashes in the palm of the hand. He was told it was "several generations" old and had been kept buried under wood ash to protect it from voracious white ants and rubbed in cow fat to preserve its texture, which brought out the horn's individual color. The Masai explained to Turle that this unique rungu had belonged to an elderly medicine man no longer in need of the tools of his trade.

Unfortunately for Turle, buying, even possessing, the rungu was illegal due to the 1977 ban in Kenya on buying or selling anything made from wildlife parts. Though Turle knew of the ban, he had never seen anything like this rungu and encouraged the man to bring him other artifacts of like quality. When word got out in Masai-land that this white man was willing to risk breaking the law, a dozen Masai "suppliers" began making regular appearances at the door of his shop. Turle rationalized his law breaking because he viewed the artifacts rarely before seen by white man as cultural history, not souvenir trinkets. He saw his role as preserver of culture, not profiteer.

He began to spend weekends and every off-hour deep in Masai-land, studying the culture, learning the language. Months turned into years, and he developed rare connections with the last of the traditional Masai elders. At first the artifacts he was offered were ordinary, like goat neck pendants, fly whisk handles carved out of warthog tusks, bone and ivory finger rings, leather bags, beaded skirts, wooden stools, rungus made from giraffe bone, and bells made from tortoise shells.

Once his trustworthiness had been established, the elders who either no longer had need for the antiquated tools, or their sons and grandsons who had never learned the meaning or use of the pieces, brought out elaborate pipes carved from ivory and rhinoceros horn and the leg bones or vertebrae of hippopotamus, giraffe, eland, elephant, gazelle, cattle, and calves. Turle had read about these pipes, in the writings of turn-of-the-century Masai experts. Some had nozzles with thick holes for smoking or sucking down powdered medicines, others fine holes through which the laibon (medicine man) puffed to get powders burning in the bowl. The rising smoke wafting under the patient's nose was thought to heal everything from snake bites to broken bones, as well as to fend off lion attacks on the Masai's cattle. The pipes were augmented by vertebrae bones of elephants and rhinos, their scooped tops used for holding the ceremonial powders and pestles made from stones, wood, bone, and rhino horn. Part ceremonial, part practical, part spiritual, these artifacts, Turle says, are "the last great East African art," pre-dating the abstract work of Picasso, Matisse, and Gauguin.

The collection absorbed Turle. He sold his house and his car and nearly lost his shop as every shilling he had went into buying from the Masai. His money turned several of his key Masai connections into "bush yuppies"; today his best suppliers wear suits, ties, and shoes. "To us, it may seem like they're selling out their culture, but that's not true," insists Turle, with a soft-spoken British accent. "The Masai are crazy for machine-made things: clothes, watches, plastic bowls, tin plates, barbed wire, and money. These things mean progress to them. They are selling me their artifacts so they can go out and buy a watch or a pair of good shoes, something they've got their hearts set on. Whereas our hearts are set on the beautiful things they've made with their hands . . . because we've already got the watch and good pair of shoes. It's just a balancing act, really."

Due to the gray area his burgeoning collection occupied, were they illegal trinkets or cultural discovery? He shared it with few. Those he did show had two basic questions: Why hadn't anyone seen this stuff before? And, How old were they? He insists the reason no one had seen them before was because no one had asked. "The Masai have an absolute code of revealing nothing unless you ask," says Turle. The laibons kept the items in bags hung in the dark corners of their dung-and-acacia huts, or buried under ashes. As for age, Turle claims most of the pieces he collected have been passed down from generation to generation.

The flaw in this story of discovery is Richard Leakey's insistence that some of Turle's collection is fake, that greedy Masai hungry for the cash offered by the naive antique dealer in fact manufactured some of his "artifacts." Chief of the Kenya Wildlife Service (KWS), Leakey is also the longtime chairman of the National Museums of Kenya and a powerful voice in global anthropological circles. He insists Turle's collecting has encouraged poaching, contending that when word got out among the Masai that Turle was buying things made from ivory and bone, they proceeded to kill game animals to satisfy his desires. Ironically, it was Turle himself who brought his collection to Leakey's attention. In 1988 he acquired permits for seventy pieces from the KWS Game Department. Such permits are required to possess any bone or ivory artifacts; KWS maintains a full-time inspector and office to consider such applications. Turle donated 144 pieces to the National Museum of Kenya in 1989, and the museum's deputy director of ethnography thanked him by letter and speculated that some of the artifacts "were being used for medicine and divining purposes between the 1850s and 1940s." The letter said the museum was "looking forward to displaying the artifacts in the future."

Turle then ventured to New York, where he sold his book about the art to Vicky Wilson at Knopf. Late that year, he filed another application for permits for more than one thousand pieces. A year went by without any response to that application, so he arranged a meeting with Richard Leakey to ask why.

Turle knew from the beginning that his collection occupied a legal gray area. The Masai knew, too, which is why nearly all of their transactions were done surreptitiously. Under the 1977 law, they could be jailed for selling any pieces made from bone and horn. With the passage by CITES (the Convention on International Trade in Endangered Species of Wild Fauna and Flora) in 1989 of the so-called ivory ban, the dealings became even more risky.

When Turle met with Leakey in September 1990, the KWS chief took one look at the basket laden with rhino horn and ivory rungus and pronounced them "fake." (Despite that, the deputy director of the National Museums of Kenya, a twenty-year veteran appointed by Leakey, had accepted them as real.) Three weeks later Game Department officials visited Turle at his tent and confiscated more than one hundred pieces of his collection. Turle immediately wrote the licensing officer and asked for an explanation: were they going to keep his stuff or authenticate it and return it? His answer came two weeks later, in November 1990, when the police came to his tent with a search and arrest warrant and seized more of his collection. He has not heard a word about either confiscation since.

Leakey repeated his charge of fakery in 1991 to Albany-based anthropologist Roderick Blackburn, who has studied the Masai for more than twenty years. "That stuff is an artful mix of the fake and the authentic," Leakey told Blackburn. He accused Turle of having the stuff "manufactured."

Blackburn did not agree. He has studied Turle's collection and taken pictures of the artifacts into the bush. There the Masai have recognized the pieces, told him the native words for the pipes and produced similar pipes made from ivory. During his months of visiting Masai elders in Kenya and Tanzania, Blackburn has accumulated a catalogue of 120 different kinds of objects, many similar to Turle's. Most, he says, "are at least eighty years old" and were made for and used by the laibons until about sixty to eighty years ago. They were shaped by hand from ivory and game bones by the poorer of the Masai, who did not have cattle and so had to make a living hunting wild animals and making things for trade.

"Since most of these objects are made from game bones, ivory, and horn in Kenya, they are suspect as technically illegal, even though most if not all were from animals shot when it was legal to take them, before 1977," says Blackburn. "The concern of wildlife preservation people is that these objects may become 'popular' and thus may stimulate fakes being made from bones of animals killed for that purpose. So far I have not found any direct evidence of this being done, but I would not preclude the possibility that some objects can or have been faked so well that it is not possible to tell them from the earlier ones without sophisticated technical examination." Blackburn says that preliminary tests of Turle's collection have been inconclusive.

For final evidence that his collection is valid, Turle points to similar rungus donated to the British Museum of Natural History in the 1920s. Ironically, they were collected and donated by Louis Leakey, Richard's anthropologist father.

In response to questions put forth for this report, Leakey faxed this "no comment": "I have some serious questions and reservations about the whole thing and I fear that someone, somewhere is involved in a most unfortunate game on this issue." Turle argues that Leakey's concern about poaching is valid, if wrong, since raw ivory and rhinoceros horn traded on the black market would bring ten times what he could pay for a pipe or rungu that would take months to carve and shape. The biggest stumbling block is the lack of proof of the age of the rungus and pipes. Turle has shown them to forensic experts in London and New York, but carbon dating has so far proven insufficient. Turle insists all of the artifacts are "authentic." "Some of them look newer because they are unused and have been hanging in a bag for twenty, thirty, or forty years. But there's not a single piece that is not authentic. I have two or three times come across pieces made by young hustlers and they jump out at me by a mile.

"But I love it when people say, 'If this stuff is authentic, how is it nobody's ever come up with it before?' For me, that is the excitement of all this. This is a true discovery."

For now the seized parts of Turle's collection sit in boxes at the National Museums of Kenya and in Leakey's office. In the meantime Turle has endured several years of uncertainty, unsure whether the rest of his collection will be confiscated or whether he might be arrested and charged with a crime. He still has hundreds of pieces spread among various safe spots in Kenya and Tanzania. Given the ban on trading ivory, the artifacts cannot be exhibited in Kenya, nor moved from that country. Upon the book's publication, he expects to be criticized for not being an anthropologist, and for questionable record keeping. "But if I had gone in there with a pencil behind my ear, it would not have worked," he says. His biggest concern is that given the current anti-ivory sentiment in Kenya, the part of his collection that has been seized could go up in smoke. Twice before, Leakey has made very public showings of burning poached ivory confiscated by KWS. "It is becoming very difficult to preserve cultures," says Turle. "Imagine if someone had taken what the ancient Egyptians were doing, using, and making and burned them for some naive reason. We would never know how they lived. Now they're threatening to do just that to the culture of the Masai.

"Surely laws can be devised to allow and indeed encourage the preservation of historical artifacts. Who knows what fascinating artifacts are being eaten by white ants now because their owners are in fear of the law."

Artifact rich and cash poor, Turle's hope is that his collection will be bought by a well-to-do financier, who will then donate it to the museum he dreams of building on the edge of the Great Rift Valley overlooking Masai-land. He wants to turn his efforts and the artifacts into both an accolade to the Masai culture and a tourist attraction. The spot he has picked for his museum is within eyeshot of Richard Leakey's home.

Gillies Turle lives in Kenya; he was never able to successfully validate — or sell or display — his collection.

THE SPORTSMEN

"The more you are out there adventuring, the more adventures you survive. If something does go wrong, you have developed some instinct about how to survive, how to deal with whatever comes up. It's exactly the same with business. There is a very, very thin dividing line between survival and failure in both. You've just got to fight and fight and fight and fight to survive."

—**Sir Richard Branson,** *A Man for All Seasons*

THE GREAT LAMAZOU

Titouan Lamazou

Outside, 1993

"It is good to ride the tempest and feel godlike. I dare to assent that for a finite speck of pulsating jelly to feel godlike is a far more glorious feeling than for a god to feel godlike."

—**Jack London, *The Cruise of the Snark***

At three o'clock on a February morning, deep inside the smoky Haig's Bar in Venice, French sailor Titouan Lamazou is holding court, entertaining a hundred of his best friends and family. To his right at the bar stands Fernando Sena, director of Tencara, Italy's best-known boat-builder. To his left, Christian Veros, president and CEO of the Swiss watchmaker Tag Heuer. Nibbling on the longhaired sailor's ear is a long-limbed movie starlet. The mood of the disparate international contingency packing the joint is joyous fatigue—the night of revelry follows a day of toasting, highlighted by a luncheon at the French Consulate hosted by France's Ministers of Sea and Sport.

No one is higher than Titouan. Just beyond the door of the bar, floating on the moonlit canal, sits a shiny new $18.5 million, ultra-high-tech racing schooner, the boat he hopes will take him around the world in eighty days or less. The French government helped him finance the craft; Tencara built it; Tag Heuer has promised $6 million to support his dream; the blonde, well, she too comes with being one of France's best-known adventurers. Who could fault the guy if he was feeling a tad swellheaded?

Titouan's claim to fame is having sailed around the world faster than anyone: he did it solo in 1990, in 109 days. His next, widely publicized project is to lower his own mark by taking on one of the world's most formidable challenges, a feat dreamed up more than 120 years before by another Frenchman, Jules Verne.

As the blonde whispers into Titouan's ear, I'm in his other, asking him how it is possible to keep ego in check given all this adulation, all this attention, all this, well, nibbling. He pauses, arresting me with crystal-blue eyes, exhales a stream of smoke, and lifts a tumbler of grappa. "You cannot get caught up in ego," he contends. "I have ego, sure, and I know the importance of media and sponsors. But the goal is not to be famous, the goal is not even to have the 'best' boat. What is important is saying you'll do something, then doing it." Okay, I'll go for that. But just for fun I ask him to dig out his business card. We check out the logo together. It is a self-portrait of a handsome, longhaired, seemingly godlike man kissing the moon and sky. Does this self-presentation not evidence signs of a healthy ego? "Okay," he laughs, "maybe I may have a small ego. But I know I can't walk on water."

It is nearly sunrise when the room begins to empty. As we head out the door, someone asks Titouan what he's going to do in the morning, just a few hours away. "I think," he says, "I will go for a sail. By myself. But not until I have a small sleep."

The Venetian night is bathed in fog. I'm not quite ready to retire. Neither is the man from Tag. As we stroll across the brick walk to the Hotel Gritti, he elaborates on why his company believes in Titouan and his dreams. "It's not about selling watches, really. It is about beauty and freedom. It is about image." He pauses, looks skyward. "But we better sell a hell of a lot of watches."

Sailors with logos? Egos bigger than boats? Retail sails versus big dreams? Is this what adventuring has come to? Perhaps. But for Titouan Lamazou—and the other top dozen French sailors, including Bruno Peyron, Florence Arthaud, Philippe Poupon, Olivier de Karsauson, Alain Gualtier, Yves Le Cornec, Gabriel Guilly—big egos, slavering sponsors, and adoring bimbos may be deserved. France produces the best sailors in the world. Twenty-one of the sixty World Sailing Speed Records maintained by the International Yacht Racing Union are held by French—from the 21,000 mile "Round the World Non-Stop Single Handed" to the 355-mile "Plymouth to La Rochelle." It has been this way for decades and their countrymen love their sailors for their successes and panache. (When I asked one sailor about his crew, he said without fanfare that it included a painter to document the adventure. A painter? Only the French.)

When Titouan set his round-the-world mark, he was feted to a ticker tape parade down the Champs-Élysée. Florence Arthaud, the only woman at the top and perhaps the best known of all French sail racers, must change her phone number every six weeks to elude the myriads who want her to christen boats, open stores, send them photographs. After Phillippe Poupon won the 3,700-mile Route de Rhum, every bus stop in Paris featured an ad campaign starring his larger-than-life mug. In other countries such receptions are reserved for returning war heroes, or Michael Jordan. Stop any Frenchman, ask them to name a great sail racer, and they'll rattle off ten.

By comparison, in the U.S. the only time a sail racer gets attention is when he or she dies, preferably tragically (see Mike Plant). This year, for the first time, America's Cup champ Dennis Conner has entered a boat in the quadrennial, nine-month-long, five-stage Whitbread round-the-world race. Yet even as he signed up, Conner confessed there was no way he was going to personally sail the five legs. "This is a young man's deal," said the fat fifty-year-old with a penchant for five-star meals and hotels. "When you get down to the Roaring Forties (40 to 50° S latitude, where winds are notorious for their ferocity), you're cold and wet, and there are no showers. There is no way to get out." A French sailor would never allow such sentiments to cross his lips. They live for such punishments.

There are a few explanations for why France breeds such great sailors and fervent fans. Go into any little village on the country's three thousand miles of coastline and you'll find a sailing club. Everyone from five years old and up is out on dinghies. These are not yacht clubs, available to only the well heeled or aristocracy. They are open to everyone. It's kind of like Little League in the States. Thus the grocer's son has as much chance of becoming an international top sailor as a blue blood.

The French also have a different relationship with summer leisure time than most nations, which can be traced back to 1955 when by law French companies were commanded to give thirty-two days' paid leave to their employees between June 15 and September 15. As a result, the entire country goes on holiday at virtually the same time, most to the coasts. There, they sail. Back in Paris each fall, the annual boat show fills eight buildings and attracts more than 400,000. They don't just come to look; they buy boats. Saltwater is in their blood.

As for the cult surrounding champion sail racers, one man deserves credit for creating the Frenchies' romance with racing. I met Eric Tabarly in the elegant bar of the Hotel Gritti Palace in Venice. He'd come to wish Titouan, one of his protégés, well. Wrapped in a worn leather jacket, his seaworn face a matching hue and texture, the sixty-two-year-old Tabarly made most of the young sailors who are now grabbing records and head-lines. Titouan, Jean-Francois Costa, Yves Le Cornec, Olivier de Kersauson, the Poupon brothers—all learned to race by crewing aboard Tabarly's six *Pen Duick* crafts. During the 1960s and 1970s, he set virtually every speed sailing record and became France's most famous adventurer. When he broke the transatlantic record in 1967, 180,000 people turned out along the Champs-Élysée to welcome him home.

I approached Tabarly hoping he might give me some insight into what makes French sailors tick, what makes them better than the rest. "These are not golfers," he said, looking around the crowded bar and pointing out some of his onetime students. "They risk their lives, they go out there and do something which is the most dangerous sport. When they go off into the Southern Ocean, there is no one on the sidelines who can help them, no helicopter that can save them. They cannot be rescued. If they go over down there, it's over, they're dead. That makes them different from other sportsmen.

"Why are they so popular? The French love somebody who does something unusual. And sailing around the world in eighty days—this would be truly unusual."

Ever since Phineas Fogg's 1872 race by train, boat, and elephant to round the world in eighty days, a variety of adventurers have considered the possibility of its actually being accomplished under their own steam. It's been done by jet, hot air balloon, combination of boat-bus-plane, etc. But when Titouan launched his boat in February, no one had come close by sail alone. If he—or any of his peers—were to break eighty days, it would mean shaving *one month* off his existing record. That would be like lowering the record for the 26-mile marathon from two hours to an hour and a half.

Despite the seeming impossibility of breaking eighty days, a pack of the world's best sailors—most French—actually cooked up a competition, complete with a revolving trophy and prize money. They did it in part because they were bored. They'd sailed across the Atlantic and the Pacific in faster and faster times, around Europe, the UK, Australia, from New York to San Francisco, Marblehead to Halifax, on mono-hulls, catamarans, and trimarans, with crews and solo. What was left? Only to conquer the last of the great romantic adventures: around the world in eighty days.

The organized race traces back to a night in 1985, when Florence Arthaud, Yves Le Cornec, Gabriel Guilly, Yvon Fauconnier, and Philippe Poupon were sitting around a kitchen table after the Whitbread, drinking and talking. It was Le Cornec—veteran of several round-the-world races—who suggested they make a race of eighty days. At the time it seemed unthinkable, even to these guys. The first Vendee Globe Challenge— the single-handed race around the world—had yet to be held. The Whitbread—the crewed, five-stage, round-the-world race—had been run just four times. The record for racing around the world nonstop was 313 days (Britain's Robin Knox-Johnson, in 1968).

Two years later, in 1987, future Whitbread champion Peter Blake—a New Zealander by birth, but an honorary Frenchman given his sail-racing expertise—mentioned he might like to try an eighty-day race. In 1990 he and Arthaud met in Freemantle and the subject was raised again. Later that year—on a barge on the Seine—a half-dozen sailors met with the goal of formalizing "the race."

"While everybody had a lot to say, there wasn't a lot of agreement," says self-confessed sail racing groupie turned promoter/race organizer/ babysitter Jane Redford. "Nobody yet had a boat for such a race, but everybody had an idea of what they wanted to do. Blake and Lamazou envisioned building big, classic monohulls. Arthaud and de Kersauson and Bruno Peyron envisioned huge multihulls."

Over the next year the details were hammered out in Paris, between Arthaud's living room and Lamazou's office. Officially organized as "The Association Tour du Monde en 80 Jours," the "Trophée Jules Verne" was announced on October 20, 1992, by Arthaud, Peter Blake, Jean Francois Coste, Yvon Fauconnier, Gabriel Guilly, Robin Knox-Johnston, Lamazou, Yves Le Cornec, Bernard Moitessier, and Bruno Peyron under the patronage of the French Ministry of Culture and several sailing organizations and with permission from the Société Jules Verne, whose grandson was present at the announcement. They wrangled a $60,000 grant from the Minister of Culture and the Peter Stuyvesant Foundation to have a trophy built. (American sculptor Tom Shannon won the contest to construct it.) A cash prize of $1 million was sought. (French betting organization PMU initially promised the prize, but backed off after being criticized for touting Arthaud and Lamazou's names in advertisements without the sailors' permission.)

The rules were simple: go around the world as fast as you can without stopping, on the boat of your choice, with the crew of your choice, leaving from an imaginary line stretched across the English Channel between the lighthouse Creac'h on Ouessant Island in France and England's Point Lizard. All boats must pass the capes of Good Hope, Leeuwin, and Horn to port and then recross the same imaginary line across the English Channel. Propulsion was to be solely by natural forces of the wind and of the crew. The entry fee was 80,000 FF ($16,000). You didn't necessarily have to join the organization to make an effort, but it was strongly encouraged.

"What made this race different," says Jane Redford, who acted as liaison between the sailors, a necessity since some of them are not on speaking terms, "was that for once sailors got together and organized their own rules, their own association. The Trophée Jules Verne was conceived by sailors, for sailors, to be administered by sailors."

According to Redford, Titouan did most of the organizational work. "He probably did 60 percent of the ground work, while simultaneously financing and building his own boat. It made sense—it was his record that was at stake."

Once the trophy was announced, the hard part began: raising money, building boats, then racing them around the whole damn world. Even Redford, who knows these sailors well, doesn't quite understand the motivation. "It takes a certain amount of courage or folly to do something like this," she admits. "It's not just seamanship—you've got to be half crazy. I wouldn't do it if you paid me $10 million. What's so fantastic about what these guys do is they make our dreams for us. They are our modern-day Shackletons."

Hmmmm.

The February morning after Titouan's big day in Venice, we drift away from the dock in a thick fog, into the Adriatic Sea. He's taking the boat (dubbed the *Tag Heuer*) out for its inaugural sail. He is at the wheel after his "small sleep," shouting out commands as cranks and winches fly and

Sportsmen

the green-coated crew spreads out along the 143-foot-long ship. Curious *batteau taxis* roar up alongside, honking their horns at the spectacle.

Of all the French sailors I have met, Titouan is by far the most intriguing. In part that's because he has interests beyond sailing. A loner, an accomplished painter, he has published a novel and a book of photographs and sketches of Moroccan architecture. He is part-owner of his own boatyard (Capitaine Flint) and is a skilled politician (he played a big part in convincing the French government to allow investors in his new boat to write off their investment).

He did not come from money, or from Brest, where the best sailors in France begin competing as youngsters. His grandparents were farmers in the south of France, his father an engineer in the oil business. His mother, also an engineer, was killed tragically in a car accident just last year. Titouan credits her with encouraging him to be a painter, the career he chose for himself at age eleven. "She was a dreamer and she encouraged me to dream," says Titouan, looking up at the off-yellow sails of his new ship. "Perhaps most importantly she encouraged me to take my heroes from novels—not the writers, but the characters." His favorite fictional heroes? Blackbeard and Tom Sawyer. (His novel, *The Treasure of Atlas*, carried an epigraph drawn from Huck Finn, perfectly matched to a Frenchman's sensibilities: "We did it and we did it elegant, too.")

In the early 1970s an art teacher in Marseille pushed Titouan toward sailing. He made his first crossing of the Caribbean when he was seventeen; his two-year military service was spent aboard Tabarly's legendary *Pen Duick VI*. But when he was twenty-five, he gave up sailing and moved to Morocco, to write and paint. That lasted two years. "I went back to the sea because I realized I didn't finish what I started," he says.

His first big finish was a second in the 1987 Boc Challenge, a solo round-the-world race. He followed that with races across the Atlantic, from Quebec to Malo and from Lorient to St. Barthélemy to Lorient before winning the 1990 Globe Challenge in record time. In 1990 he was named "World Champion of Sea Racing, 1986–1990." His intimates are few and include the designers of his boat, his lawyer, and his meteorologist. ("He and I have been around the world together already many times—on computer," laughs Titouan.) His family members remain his closest confidantes. Brother Josie helps designs the boats and organizes the office;

his father, Jean, is his moneyman. "His biggest advice—after years of being in business and in debt—is keep no debt and don't sign your name too many places," says Titouan. His detractors, including peers like de Kersauson and Bruno Peyron, see Titouan as too serious, a bit of a dilettante. For his record-setting Globe race, Titouan was so obsessed with winning he consulted with doctors and had plastic molds built for his arms and legs: if broken, limbs could be bound in plastic casts so he could continue. During the race he was heard over the radio telling his onshore team, "If I don't win, I'll shoot myself." One result of his obsessiveness was that he took the lead from the first and never lost it. Afterward he admitted, "It's an illusion to think that a boat is a synonym of happiness or dream. A boat is a source of colossal trouble. During a race, happiness is rare. It does not involve being serene or calm or relaxed even for one moment."

Perhaps the greatest testament to his skill and place in the French sailing community is the crew he's assembled to man the *Tag Heuer*. Fifteen men, including some of the best skippers in France, like Yves Le Cornec and Jean-Francois Coste. Why would they sign on with Titouan rather than sail their own boats? "It is an adventure they would never have the energy or the know-how to pull off," says Redford, "but they would hate to miss out on the adventure of a lifetime."

Titouan's lawyer, Marc Frilet, insists Titouan is "a natural leader."

"Many racers turn to Titouan for advice. He is the 'authority' among top sailors because he takes the most responsibility. Florence Arthaud is an employee of her sponsor, same with Bruno Peyron and Olivier de Kersauson. Titouan is a partner. He goes to them with a plan, they arrange a contract, and then all the sponsor worries about is whether he lives up to the services contracted. He gets the ship built, hires the crew, arranges everything. He is very organized, something not all French sailors are."

Right now his biggest responsibility is justifying the $25 million to be spent on his latest dream. There are still many hurdles. The high-tech boat must be fully shaken-down before he takes it on a rigorous sail. And he's still looking for sponsorship money. Then there's the slight challenge of actually sailing the boat more than twenty-one thousand miles around the world. I ask what he expects will be the most difficult part. "On a good boat there is no difficult part. The most immediate one is the Roaring Forties off Antarctica, with their cold, rough seas. But with a good crew, even they should be okay. I am much more afraid of doldrums. "Right now eighty days is quite difficult to do; seventy days is impossible. We are confident it will be possible for us to do it in seventy-four days. By the end of the century, eighty days will be nothing."

As the big boat cuts through six-foot swells, Titouan leans against a four-foot-tall steering wheel. If it takes him eighty-two days, will all his efforts have been for naught? "You cannot say it is a success if you miss your target," he says. "But for me, the adventure must be part of the rest of my life, not the only part. With the boat built, the hard part is finished. Now all I have to do is sail it around the world. No problem.

"THE EVENT IS THE BOAT, THE EVENT IS THE BOAT." This seems to be Titouan's mantra. I wonder if he is saying it because he truly believes it, or if because by repeating it over and over it takes the focus off the eighty-day mark—which many believe impossible aboard a big monohull.

Everyone knows multihulls are faster than monohulls. Thus logic would have it they have a better chance of breaking any record. But few believe a multihull—invariably lighter, flimsier, more susceptible to technical breakdown—can endure the rigors of a super-fast, round-the-world sail. Titouan is convinced the best combination is his lightweight monohull.

Constructed by Tencara, which is best known for building the America's Cups *Il Moro de Venezia* (1–5), the *Tag* is the biggest all-composite boat ever built, from materials previously used primarily for fighter jets and rockets. It weighs fifty-five tons (the bulb alone weighs ten tons) and can put up 1,930 square meters of sail on twin thirty-three-meter masts. Aboard will be the most advanced computer system carried on a private ship. No one doubts the boat will be fast. But is it tough enough? Much of the race will be set in the harsh southern oceans; can this new boat manage the necessary high speeds in fifty-foot seas, while sailing into seventy-and eighty-knot winds? During his 109-day sail, aboard the sixty-foot *Ecureuil d'Aquitaine II*, Titouan averaged 9.48 knots an hour. To make it in eighty days, this boat will have to average 12.8 knots.

The day before we sailed, I spent an hour talking with Frederico Sena, director of Tencara. He was quite open about the boat's experimental construction and about how it had been modified after Mike Plant's high-tech *Coyote* appeared to fail, resulting in tragedy. "This boat is by no means an extreme boat in regard to safety," says the Portuguese-born Sena.

"The technology has been applied to other boats. The America's Cup boats use carbon fiber, Nomax, and other sophisticated products. Many boats built out of composite materials have gone round the world in the Whitbread Race. What makes this boat different is its size.

"We were very, very careful. That's why we are constantly watching smaller boats now racing that are using the same technologies. The issue of the keels in the Globe is one instance. We had three or four weeks of intense recalculation just after Plant's accident, to try and understand why his boat had its problems. It could have been for stupid reasons, or a miscalculation. If it was miscalculation, we didn't want to make the same mistakes. Our designer spoke with virtually everyone in the world who has designed keels to try and understand what had happened."

I ask if they changed anything based on what they learned about Plant's boat. "Yes," he admits, "we built a new keel, of slightly different alloy and shape. We had an aluminum blade that had been cut; now we have an aluminum blade made of sheet, glued together by machines."

Our conversation took place in February, nearly a year before Titouan was scheduled to set off around the world. In a statement that would come back to haunt him, Sena told me, "The fact is, we don't expect the boat having a major problem." Titouan, sitting beside the boat builder, added: "If these boats were totally safe, they would never win."

One subject studiously avoided during those celebratory days in Venice was that even as Titouan's boat was being christened, three others—captained by two Frenchmen and a Kiwi—had the jump on him. Bruno Peyron, Olivier de Kersauson, and New Zealander Peter Blake were attempting to break the 109-day record and making a run at eighty days.

Frenchman de Kersauson—a veteran sailor, perhaps best known for his five years as host of a popular radio show, *The Big Heads*—took off first. An antiestablishmentarian, he purposely ignored the rules of the Trophée Jules Verne and its association. His departure on January 22, aboard an eighty-one-foot catamaran, was kept secret, and was not from the imaginary line at Point Lizard. When he reported back to shore, he gave false positioning.

When two-time Whitbread champ Peter Blake heard de Kersauson was setting out after the record, he hustled to ready one of his old boats, sponsored by the New Zealand apple company Enza. He had hoped to raise money to build a 125-foot monohull for his round-the-world attempt. Instead he refitted a nine-year-old, eighty-five-foot catamaran and invited the first man to sail solo nonstop around the world, Britain's Robin Knox-Johnston, to join him.

Bruno Peyron's reaction to de Kersauson's effort was similar to Blake's. He rushed to the start line aboard an eight-year-old catamaran. The current transatlantic record holder (six days, thirteen hours) and veteran of twenty-seven Atlantic crossings—eleven of them solo—Peyron is a formidable skipper. He and Blake left from Lizard Point within hours of each other, on January 30. The irony to the departure of all three was that despite any pre-launch bragging, none really believed they would break eighty days. To a one, they were attempting to steal some of Titouan's big press, to break his 109-day record.

Twenty-four days after departing, de Kersauson quit just above Cape Town. After twenty-six days at sea, in the middle of the Indian Ocean, Peter Blake gave it up. Only Bruno kept going.

No one, least of all Peyron, thought he'd make it around the world. He left deep in debt, on an aged boat. The best thing in his favor was experience; his four-man crew had more than one hundred transatlantic crossings among them. That counted. In the Southern Ocean, sailing into eighty-two-knot winds, they were making twenty-eight knots per hour—without a sail up. For a full week the boat was readied for capsizing. They almost called it quits off Brazil after hitting two sperm whales, cracking the boat's port hull. Crewman Olivier Despaigne spent two days inside one of the hulls essentially rebuilding the boat from the inside out, with epoxy. Video taken in the Southern Ocean shows Bruno, hands on the computer below deck, asking out loud, "What the fuck are we doing here?"

Ultimately they survived the winds, the whales, fifty-foot swells, and even the doldrums. At 9:18 on the morning of April 20, Peyron's eighty-six-foot *Commodore Explorer* completed the circumnavigation of the globe in 79 days, 6 hours, 15 minutes, 56 seconds. He'd averaged 13.98 knots, and his multihull had not flipped, cracked, or sunk. In somewhat understated fashion, Peyron had accomplished what Jules Verne could have only dreamed: he had sailed around the world in less than eighty days, under his own steam.

A month after his return, I find the thirty-five-year-old Peyron in his hometown of La Baule, on the Atlantic coast. He'd been front-page news since his return; his hometown had swelled with crowds when he sailed into port. He was hardly prepared for the onslaught of media attention and admitted he was having a hard time coming down. "I could never have predicted this," he says, tousling the hair of his ten-year-old daughter, Alexandra. "That's probably why we made it."

The son of a captain in the merchant navy, the Peyron family is hardly foreign to the sea. Bruno is the eldest of three sailing brothers—Loick once held the transatlantic record, Stephane has windsurfed across the Arctic Ocean. As we speak, Bruno is in the midst of writing the inevitable book about his adventure, as well as planning a movie about the feat. When those are complete, he plans to find a sponsor and build a 130-foot catamaran. Then he will try to lower his record.

"I wanted to make the first attempt so I could learn for the second try, the big one," he says. "I was really just trying to beat Blake, and to maybe make a new world record. Unlike some of the others, like Titouan, I refused to say, 'It's easy, we're going to make it, and so on.' We were not so sure."

I ask when he knew he was going to break eighty days. "The last day. That's no joke," he says. "The two or three days before we arrived, there were no winds at all in the Key of Biscayne. We were totally becalmed. So we just waited, and waited." He credits the good humor and skill of his crew—three Frenchmen and American Cameron Lewis—for the successful voyage.

Already Peter Blake, Florence Arthaud, and Titouan are promising to lower the new mark. Does he think his new record will be broken soon? "Of course. Somebody will go faster. But I will tell them it is very dangerous. It is the ultimate challenge on the sea, that's for sure."

Before meeting Peyron, I had spent an afternoon in Paris with Florence Arthaud, who is also trying to raise money ($20 million) to build a 130-foot trimaran so she can take a run at eighty days. Her boat designers and their computer assure her the boat they have planned can round the globe in sixty-nine days. Just how fast does Peyron think his new boat, when built, can make it around? "I should say in about sixty days. I think that will be the maximum."

Back in Paris, Titouan and his team were shocked by Peyron's sail. "No one is more amazed he won than Bruno," says Marc Frilet. He then launches into spin control, French-style. "That Peyron beat eighty days by just a few hours is good; if he had done it in seventy days, that would have been big trouble. Titouan and the designers of his boat think he can do it in seventy-five, seventy-six days. Plus everyone knows multihulls are faster. So if Titouan can beat Peyron's mark aboard a mono-hull . . ."

The new record is heightened by the fact that Titouan and Bruno Peyron are hardly close friends. But in the spirit of the Trophée Jules Verne, he showed up at the finish to congratulate the new record holder.

"It would have been better if he didn't break the record," Titouan tells me afterward. "But now he has set a new standard. It's good for the media. Now there is a real race. For us, it changed not much. For us the most important thing is the creation of the boat."

Titouan's five-room office, early in July: Ornate scroll embroiders the ceiling. Black metal balconies look out over Place de Clichy. Marble fireplaces anchor each end of the main room, which is otherwise dominated by a pair of easels. One holds a work in progress, a painting of a twin-masted red sailboat on black sea. A long table in the conference room holds only models of the *Aquitaine*. and the *Tag Heuer*. The bookshelves are filled with the works of Klee, Hockney, Gauguin.

Titouan is red-eyed. The day before he'd been in Venice, tomorrow it's to Nice for a boat show. Last week it was Japan, lining up a crewmember and publicity, looking for sponsors, arranging for TV coverage.

Much has happened since that glorious weekend in Venice, even worse than Peyron breaking his record. On a Saturday evening, March 27, a storm whipped the Adriatic off the coast of Yugoslavia/Albania. The crew was sailing the *Tag Heuer* back to Venice for a scheduled check-up— Titouan was in Paris—when the boat, sailing into fifty-knot headwinds, hit a still-unidentified floating object, ripping a hole as big as a semi-truck in its port side. It began filling with water.

Quick-minded crewmen rushed below to close the watertight doors, saving the boat from sinking. Instead it floated like a cork, its aft out of the water. A trio of navy ships from the U.S., Italy, and France circled. Due to the high winds ands swells, it was twenty-four hours before crew members could be transferred and towing lines attached. On Monday morning, thirty-six hours after initial impact, the boat was safe in the Italian port of Brindisi.

Three months later Titouan still has no idea what the boat hit. His best guess is a container or a sunken ship. "Whatever it was, it was something strong," he says. "That is the last time I will not be on the boat."

Though the boat is in dry dock at Tencara, he is still hoping for a January departure. Pressures are mounting. Lloyd's of London is threatening not to pay for the boat's estimated $2.5 million repair, contending the damage was due to "faulty design." Tag is threatening to pull its sponsorship if the boat is not back in the water soon. To top it off, the boatyard co-owned by Titouan has had to be closed. "We had to fire everybody," he says. "The economy in France is very bad; nobody is buying big boats."

Jane Redford articulates what others in the French sailing community are saying only to each other. "When Titouan's boat broke up, it demanded a lot of reevaluation. Is it tough enough? The bottom line is, the bigger the boat, the bigger the screwups. A little hole becomes a big hole, a little money becomes a lot of money. But it's too late for him to change now." Meanwhile, others prepare to challenge the eighty-day mark. Specifically, Peter Blake is planning another try, scheduled to depart in December or January. So is de Kersauson.

I see Titouan several times over the next few weeks and he seems to be reevaluating the whole effort, even as he struggles to keep his project moving forward. One night he suggests maybe he'll just re-rig the boat so that he can sail it himself. Another day he laughs that sometimes he doesn't even like sailing that much and imitates a bored crewman pulling in a sail. One day he insists what he really wants to do is paint ("sketches bring me more powerful reward than sailing"); the next he admits right now he would not be wholly satisfied just sitting at a table painting ("I need to go and I need to arrive").

"Nobody has built a boat like this before, so of course it is a risk," he says in July. "Isn't this true: some things have to be unknown, they have to be risky, or it's not adventure."

Titouan Lamazou spent six years wandering the globe, from 2003 to 2008, painting, photographing, and filming his favorite subject: women. A 900-page book, Femmes du Monde, *accompanied a year-long exhibit at the* Musee de l'Homme *in Paris.*

A MAN FOR ALL SEASONS

Sir Richard Branson

National Geographic Adventure, 2007

April 22—It's Earth Day in Clyde River, Nunavut (population 850), one of the northernmost towns in North America, and everything is still in the deep freeze and won't thaw until sometime in late June. Exhaust from a thousand heaters pours out of the trailer homes and one-story official buildings scattered on the short, snowy hill overlooking frozen Baffin Bay. It's nearly ten o'clock at night and, thanks to twenty-four-hour light, it's dusky. My old friend, polar explorer Will Steger, and new friend Sam Branson, walk slowly through town, heading toward the community center.

Steger and team have spent the past three months dog sledding nearly a thousand miles across Baffin Island to explore and draw attention to how the Arctic and its denizens are changing thanks to global warming. It's been a great and somewhat unusual trip for Steger, who's spent many cumulative years traveling across the Arctic, because rather than just plunge through the cold behind the dogs, they've made an effort to stop every couple weeks and spend time in a village. "We wanted a firsthand look at how the ice is changing," says Steger as we trudge, "but also how the Inuit, who have lived in this region for five thousand years, are adapting to the changes."

His team includes three from the U.S. (dog trainer John Stetson and outdoor educators Abby Fenton and Elizabeth Andre), but most importantly a trio of Inuit hunters (Theo Ikummaq, Simon Qamanirq, and sixty-five-year-old elder Luki Airut). "It's traveling with those guys that has made this the most incredible trip we've done," says Steger. "Both to observe their local knowledge, but also hear them talk about the future up here, whether it's changing sea ice, more—or fewer—polar bears, and observing simpler things like how they run their dogs and hunt." For the last leg of the adventure, the 250-mile leg from Clyde River to Iglulik, the team will be joined by mountaineer Ed Viesturs, Sam Branson and—tomorrow—Sam's dad, Sir Richard Branson.

WILDEBEEST IN A RAINSTORM

Steger's hooking up with Branson had come through a friend of a friend; so far they'd only had telephone conversations. Though he's never dog sledded (nor has Viesturs, for that matter), Branson's joining the Baffin Island expedition fits perfectly into his oeuvre. A relatively recent convert to the fight against global warming, Branson has recently announced he'll invest $3 billion in alternative fuel research and he's put up a $25 million prize for anyone who can come up with the best way to remove carbon dioxide from the atmosphere. Plus, he's never been against a good adventure.

"Hey, Sam, one thing," wonders Steger, as we open the door to the giant gymnasium, "At night it's been dropping to -15, -20. Has your dad ever traveled in cold weather like this before?"

The tall and handsome young man pauses. "I'm not sure . . . he did ski down a mountain naked once. . . ."

Inside, the big gym is packed. Hanging out in the community center—with its gym, hockey rink, ping-pong tables—is the only entertainment in this remote, cold place. Benches filled with young mothers and their babies and elders line the walls. The floor is packed with running, screaming kids and teens.

A young Inuit woman greets me, excitedly. "Welcome to Clyde River," she says, with a big smile.

And then another, and another. Friendly place, I'm thinking.

Then smaller kids start coming up, a little bolder. One introduces himself as "Little Man," known around the town as its best hip-hop dancer (a favorite pastime of the youth here, promoted by parents to keep them away from glue sniffing and, far too often, suicide.)

"What's your name? What's your name??" they ask. And then the question they've all been dying to ask.

"Are you the billionaire?""

They have obviously mistaken me for someone else.

Sir Richard Charles Nicholas Branson (SRB to the press, Ricky to his mother) arrives the next day via chartered jet from Chicago, where he'd flown on the inaugural Virgin Atlantic flight between London and Chicago, accompanied by his eighty-five-year-old mother and eighty-nine-year-old father. His friend and personal photographer of twenty years, Thierry Boccon-Gibod, has come north to document the entrepreneur's

186   *A Man For All Seasons*

first day on the ice. Suffering a badly tweaked arm from flipping a quad on recent holiday in Mallorca, where he owns a small luxury hotel, Branson can barely shake hands, extending a pinky instead. "So sorry. I know, it looks *soooo* British, doesn't it?"

Reputation precedes him. *Hippie capitalist.* Man with the Midas touch. *Boy billionaire.* Part Warren Buffett, part P. T. Barnum. Charming and disarming, shy and optimistic, uncomfortable at public speaking and plenty comfortable with a drink in his hand surrounded by pretty girls. ("I'm the first one to make a fool of myself in any way if I think it'll help the party," he told *Esquire*.) Knighted in 1999 for "services to entrepreneurship," during the Thatcher era he was England's official "Litter Tsar." Though a high school dropout, he has been named the number one role model for Britain's young people, as well as No. 85 on a list of "100 Greatest Britons" (and a year later included on a list of "100 Worst Britons").

His first businesses were growing Christmas trees and raising budgerigars (parakeets). Today his Virgin empire of some 350 loosely connected companies includes air and train lines, mobile phone and health care, soda pop, music and bridal shops, nightclubs, hotels, and fashion. It generates more than $8 billion a year in revenues, employs 55,000, and is said to have a stash of $450 million in cash waiting to be invested in new enterprises. The company's expertise is funding and launching companies that benefit from the group's long experience, the almighty Virgin logo, and Sir Richard's flair for promotion. The boss doesn't drive, rarely has cash in his pocket, and often travels carrying only a toothbrush. The man *Forbes* calls "one of the world's most fertile businessmen" has never mastered the computer, has little use for Blackberries or cell phones, and jots down his brainstorms in school notebooks.

He runs his empire from a big, white hammock on Necker Island in the Caribbean, which he bought when he was a twenty-five-year-old music company owner for $300,000. After investing $20 million in hundreds of palm trees, a ten-bedroom house, two guests houses, desalination plant, and generator facilities, he rents it out when he and his family (wife Joan, daughter Holly, and son Sam) aren't there—for $40,000 a night.

The idea for his best-known and most profitable company—Virgin Atlantic—came during the same 1975 trip on which he discovered Necker for the first time. His flight to Puerto Rico was canceled. Rather than huff and puff, he chartered a plane for $2,000 and walked around the airport carrying a blackboard that read "Virgin Airways, $39 single flight to Puerto Rico."

"Sometimes I wake up in the mornings and feel like I've just had the most incredible dream," he says. "I've just dreamt my life."

A few hours after arriving in Clyde River, SRB's been fitted in his dog-mushing gear, a one-piece red suit with fur-ruff hood, bearing a shoulder patch promoting his Earth Challenge Prize. During the gear sort, he laughs when handed a piss bottle, recounting how during one of his cross-ocean balloon flights they'd run out of toilet paper and resorted to fax paper instead.

Outside on a cold, clear night, we're again walking to the community center for a send-off feast of raw caribou and char, which the local hunting committee has spent the afternoon chain sawing and heaping onto blue tarps in the middle of the gymnasium floor. Early tomorrow morning Steger, et al, are off for two weeks, across Baffin Bay and past the Barnes Ice Cap, hopefully before late spring temperatures begin to melt the ice.

As we walk, I ask Branson if he'd done any research on Arctic travel before arriving. "Not really," he admits, "but I have been reading about my relative, Captain Robert Scott. He was my grandfather's cousin? Of course everyone knows him for being the second to arrive at the South Pole, but did you know he was the first to fly a balloon in Antarctica?"

Inside the gym, kids swarm. "What's your name?" they're asking Branson. "Are *you* the billionaire?"

SRB laughs and responds sheepishly, pulling out his empty pants pockets. "My name is Rich, that's true," he jokes. "But I have a big family— more than 50,000 people working for me—so I have a lot to take care of I'm afraid."

In the midst of the crowded gym, at six foot one, 205 pounds, and blond, with that movie-star smile, Branson *looks* like an adventurer, especially compared to Steger's European soccer star compactness and Viesturs's all-American look. Despite—or perhaps because of—the crush of people swarming around him, he comes off as shy . . . which may be hard to square with the image of the guy who recently hung from a crane in Times Square dressed in a nude suit, a cell phone covering his privates, to introduce Virgin Mobile to the U.S.

Sportsmen

Before the mad dash to the still mostly frozen caribou and char, speeches are made. Steger and Simon talk about the expedition, and the mayor of Clyde River thanks everyone for coming and asks those from south of the border to carry back to Washington a message that they don't want polar bears put on the Endangered Species list. Branson follows. "I just wanted to come and see first-hand the impact of global warming on this part of the world. And traveling with the Inuit will help. I'm especially excited to see all these happy, smiling kids."

Virgin has already invested in conventional ideas like ethanol plants and solar power, but he's also developing a formula for a new ultra-clean fuel that can power his jets as well as cars and trucks. Last September he announced the creation of Virgin Fuels, a company that would invest up to $400 million over the next three years in biofuels. His motives are various; of course cheaper fuels will be good for his company's energy-dependent bottom line. He's the first to admit he can't believe his business conversations have turned from the Sex Pistols to cellulosic butanol.

The next morning the sun is shining brightly for the first time in two weeks and the whole town has turned out at ice's edge for the send-off. Branson, decked out in his red suit, leather mitts, and brand-new muk-luks, wades through the circuslike atmosphere. He approaches the dog teams and sleds looking a bit . . . well . . . lost, which is probably unusual for him.

He's no stranger to adventure having raced speedboats across the Atlantic Ocean and co-piloted hot air balloons more than halfway around the world. His nickname could easily be "Lucky." In 1972, marlin fishing off Cozumel, he swam two miles from the storm-swamped boat through ten-foot waves to shore. In 1977 he was the first to try flying a kind of tricycle with wings and managed to land it after soaring hundreds of feet above the ground; its inventor was killed a week later doing the same thing. Prior to his first hot-air balloon adventure, he took skydiving lessons and nearly killed himself by inadvertently unhooking his own parachute; a jump instructor rescued him in mid-air. He's been plucked from the ocean by rescue helicopters on five different occasions.

Young Ricky was not adventurous by nature and he credits his mother with giving him the adventuring bug. Eve, a former flight attendant, flew gliders at a time when few women drove cars and was trained by the RAF for duty during World War II. One day when he was four she left him in the countryside with a sack lunch and told him to find his way home. Neighbors eventually found him chasing butterflies. A few years later she dropped him fifty miles from home with his bike. "I'm sure you'll find water along the way," she said, waving goodbye.

His twin interests in adventure and promoting the Virgin brand began in 1985, with the *Virgin Atlantic Challenger* speedboat attempt to set a record for racing from Canada to the U.K. He was rescued off the coast of Ireland after the boat sank near Ireland. (The following year the *Virgin Atlantic Challenger II* set the record.)

In 1987 Branson joined balloonist Per Lindstrand in an effort to cross the Atlantic by hot air balloon, another would-be record. It also crashed into the Irish Sea, both pilots jumping out of the balloon into the cold ocean. A year later, they set the record.

In 1991, again with Lindstrand, they made the first successful transpacific hot-air balloon crossing, traveling nearly seven thousand miles from Japan to Canada at speeds up to 240 miles an hour. They set a record, but missed their target by two thousand miles. In 1997 and 1998 he made four attempts to be the first to balloon around the world, with Lindstrand and American Steve Fossett. During the last try they made it from Morocco to Hawaii . . . but crashed into the Pacific Ocean.

Today, as the four dog teams race away from Clyde River, excited to be back on the trail, Lucky Ricky is momentarily left standing alone, silhouetted against the Arctic horizon, a man without a sled. Running to catch up, he jumps on with Theo and Simon.

It's a spectacular day, especially for a first dogsled, as the well-rested dogs run fast over the flat ice, paralleling majestic, five-hundred-foot tall rock-and-ice cliffs.

Ten miles out of Clyde, we stop to untangle dogs and slurp warm soup. Despite his bad arm, Branson wants to get off the sled and ski alongside. We talk about the coldest place he's ever been. "Right here, maybe. But after crossing the Pacific, we crashed the balloon four hundred miles north of Yellowknife. We called on the radio and told the guy who responded that we were on a frozen lake surrounded by fir trees. He paused a minute before saying, 'Well, this is Canada . . . you could be in any of ten thousand places.'" They were picked up by rescue helicopter eight hours later, suffering from minor frostbite.

It's a relatively warm, fifteen-degree day. The sky couldn't be more blue, the surroundings more spectacular. Talking with SRB, watching him interact lovingly with his son, I find myself thinking, "Who wouldn't want to be this guy? Handsome. Very, very rich (he could liquidate today and retire to his tax-free island haven with some $7 billion). Great family. Men admire him. Women love him. He loves adventure and seems to be doing the right thing for the environment. And he gets to play himself in James Bond movies."

He'll spend the first days tenting with Steger, and I ask if he's inquired about Will's culinary likes and dislikes, which I happen to know tend in cold climates toward blocks of cheese and sticks of butter. "I'm sure it will all be great," he laughs. "Nothing could possibly taste bad out here, on a day like this!"

Three weeks later, I catch up with Branson for a post-expedition debriefing. He's calling from his hammock, on Necker Island. He has just finalized the deal allowing Virgin America to fly routes in the U.S., starting with New York/L.A., New York/San Francisco, potentially a $500 million investment. He sounds ebullient.

Today you have your feet in the Caribbean rather than on the ice. Any preference?

Well . . . it was a wonderful trip. Cold, but brilliant.

In the end I was with the team for seven, eight days, and for the first five or six we were sledding along flat ice, under sunshine, in one of the most beautiful places on the planet. Spectacular scenery, surrounded by glaciers, everything white, incredible light everywhere. Seals popping up through the ice, polar bears wandering into camp at night. We were actually blessed by the weather, and sunburn was often more of a concern than the cold. Though it was cold at night. Inside the tent my face and beard froze, even the two pair of pants I was using as a pillow were frozen in the morning.

I clearly got the sense from the Inuit guys that despite the beauty of the place, things are changing up there fast. Everything is melting faster, receding. They pointed out things we would never have noticed, have a knowledge outsiders can't have. Theo showed us seal holes that were much more shallow due to less ice, new birds in the far north, like gannets and robins, which they'd never seen before. And told us that killer whales are coming much further north since there is less ice, threatening seals and polar bears. Just little signs in some ways, but clear evidence that things are changing.

And in their villages the permafrost is melting, leading to buildings collapsing, something happening all over the north. Unlike our lives, they are truly being impacted right now by the changing climate.

The Inuits—Theo, Simon, and Luki—were good travel companions?

Quite. At the edge of the glacier, the Barnes Ice Cap, which has been around since the last ice age, Theo showed us how the warmer winds and temperatures are changing the ice formations that Inuit hunters have used as landmarks for hundreds of years. The big ice cap—sixty miles wide, one hundred miles deep—is shrinking. Theo said they used to be able to see it from the village at Foxe Basin, but now they cannot.

So joining the expedition worked out as a combination of adventure and a kind of ramped-up learning experience?

Yes, absolutely, and great training for the next generation. My son Sam, I may very well lose him to the Arctic. (Steger dubbed him a "real expeditioner.") Will's invited him to do a three-month trip to Greenland next year, which would be great. He's a young man who can do just about anything he wants with his life and learning about that part of the world would not be a bad thing to start with. He tented with Ed Viesturs for a while, and I think Ed was encouraging him to climb Everest . . .

In the end, how was Will's cooking?

Dreadful! You know he's very comfortable eating bloody, raw caribou meat every night. The good thing was I lost ten pounds . . . . But it was an honor to travel with him.

Do you have a next adventure planned? Or is it all business in the near future?

Well . . . the space flights are coming up, which I guess could be considered both adventure and business. We expect the first test flights early next year and the first commercial flights by 2009. We're currently building the rocket ship—that sounds funny, doesn't it?—and working on a landing strip in New Mexico, which probably won't be finished in time, so we'll land initially in the Mojave Desert.

Among its various businesses, Virgin Galactic is the company's most visionary, and potentially risky, attempting to be the first airline company to carry passengers into space. In 1995 Virgin quietly registered with the British government to use the company name for a space tourism business; in 1999 they trademarked the name; and in September 2004 they licensed the technology behind SpaceShipOne, designed by aerospace pioneer Burt Rutan, to build their own craft.

Virgin has ordered five, which are under construction, and has already collected full fares—$195,000 per ticket—from more than 175 passengers. The Philippe Starck-designed Virgin Galactic Space Port America in Truth or Consequences, New Mexico, is in design. The initial trips will last two hours and take a half-dozen customers sixty-eight miles into space— for ten minutes—serenaded by David Bowie's "Space Odyssey."

How did you first get interested in space?

Well, it's a story I tell quite often, and involves Jane Fonda in *Barbarella*. I was twenty-one years old, in hospital recovering from having just been circumcised, when the movie came on, and let's just say my stitches ripped open thanks to the movie.

Ten years ago I thought, "How can Virgin be the first company to send people into space commercially?" We went out and talked to every single person in the field so that we'd learn the ins and outs of space travel. By the time Burt Rutan had his breakthrough (winning the X Prize for building and flying a spaceworthy craft), we were the first on the scene.

The spaceship will have a few test runs before you take paying passengers?

Yes, and then I'll take Sam, my daughter Holly, and hopefully both my parents on the maiden commercial trip.

Sounds like risky business. And quite expensive?

Any venture like that is risky, of course. But I think this one is worth it. Could it sink the Virgin companies? I don't think so. If you ask a thousand people if they would like to go to space if they could, 950 will say yes.

Won't you quickly run out of people who can afford a $200,000 ticket?

True. But in our lifetime, that ticket will be affordable by the average American and others around the world.

But is this really a business opportunity, or anotherr way to promote the Virgin brand?

I believe that in our lifetime we'll be able to fly from New York to Australia in half an hour to an hour. My thinking is that if we can make space fun . . . the rest will follow. And I hope we'll get to the moon in my lifetime. Maybe we can put a Virgin bank in space, or maybe a Virgin tax haven.

What do you learn from your adventures about risk taking? Or maybe vice versa, what have you learned from taking risks in business that apply to your adventures?

I think the adventurer and the entrepreneur have lots in common. Similar skill sets. Both are taking risks, but often after years of practice and experience, so they become more calculated risks. The more you are out there adventuring, the more adventures you survive. If something does go wrong, you have developed some instinct about how to survive, how to deal with whatever comes up. It's exactly the same with business.

There is a very, very thin dividing line between survival and failure in both. You've just got to fight and fight and fight and fight to survive.

Is there anything you wouldn't do, adventure-wise?

I'm afraid the days of big-mountain climbing have passed for me.

Your investments in biofuels and alternative energy, interest in global warming and environmental issues . . . are those new interests?

Only in the last four or five years have I come to the realization that global warming is real. Before that, I subscribed to the theory of the Danish academic Bjorn Lomborg. His book *The Skeptical Environmentalist* challenges the idea that man is responsible for global warming, which provides a kind of balm for big business, maybe especially airline owners. He basically said technology could cure anything, that things are not so bad . . . And then I read Tim Flannery's *The Weather Maker* and some other books and met with Al Gore, and realized what was really happening. The truth is that we—man—are having an impact and it has to be slowed.

I'm absolutely convinced that the world is spiraling out of control. CO_2 is like a bushfire that gets bigger and bigger every year. All of us who are in a position to do something about it must do something about it. Because Virgin is involved with planes and trains, we have even more responsibility. So we've put aside quite a lot of money to invest in alternative fuels. Over the next four years, we'll invest something like $1 billion in alternative fuels. The money is going into a whole series of different things, like building ethanol plants. We're looking into wind and solar power, we're also actually working on developing a new kind of fuel, which I can't say much about (but) is quite exciting.

Virgin fuel?

Yes!

When I plug my own travel and lifestyle figures into the zero-carbon template, I score horribly, mostly becausee of all the flying I do.

I know, it's a hard one to overcome. Which is why we're working hard with GE on new jet fuel, and other alternative fuels. Virgin Atlantic is now using tugs to move our airplanes from the gate to the runway, which saves two tons of fuel per flight, hopefully setting an example for the rest of the industry.

You have to weigh the good gained by air travel versus the pollution. There are good things to come from our ability to fly around the world. Going to the Arctic to see it firsthand, for example, and come back energized to make changes is one example. In a couple weeks, I'm flying to Africa for an unpublicized, unprompted meeting of some of the most interesting minds in Africa—Sir Desmond Tutu, Nelson Mandela, Kofi Annan, Jimmy Carter, and more—to talk about how we can really make a difference in Africa, environmentally, economically. I wouldn't want to have to walk to that meeting.

You seem to be having a pretty good run. Business is good. You're out there having fun, new adventures all the time. Does Richard Branson have anything to complain about?

It's funny. Last week *Time* magazine wrote, "If Richard Branson died today he'd want to come back as . . . Richard Branson." Which is absolutely true!! I'm very lucky. Business is good, a loving family surrounds me, and the sun seems to be shining on us. So no, no complaints!

Sir Richard Branson continues to grow businesses and adventure. In late 2008 he and a crew, accompanied by his son and daughter, attempted to break the speed record for sailing across the Atlantic Ocean from west to east. Heavy seas stopped the attempt after just two days. On his return to New York, Branson — no surprise — said he would try again.

RAISING THE STAKES

Will Steger

Outside, 1989

A crowd of Greenlandic locals—Inuit men, women, and children—are scattered on couches and chairs in the lobby of the Arctic Hotel. Although it is midnight, they sit hypnotized by the flickering light of the television that hangs from the ceiling. *Dynasty* is a Friday-night tradition here in Narssarssuaq, and much of the town of 130 has turned out for the event. They suck on bottles of Jolly Cola and twenty-ounce beers, and fill ashtrays the size of hubcaps with nonstop smokes. Deep in the haze, slouched in an overstuffed chair, sits America's soon-to-be best-known adventurer, Will Steger. It is the first time he's seen the show, and he, too, is entranced.

In twelve hours, Steger and five other veteran polar explorers will set off for two months on the ice cap. Their goal is to traverse Greenland by dog and ski, sixteen hundred miles from south to north. But tonight—as on the eve of each of his fifteen thousand miles' worth of Arctic expeditions—Steger refuses to go to sleep. While his mates are snoring on the floor of a nearby deserted building—the last roof they will sleep under for weeks—Steger, co-leader in 1986 of the first confirmed, unsupported team to reach the North Pole by dogsled, cracks open another beer. "This is my last night before two months of visual monotony," he says, "and I don't want to waste it."

Dynasty ends and Steger's efforts to stay vertical are richly rewarded. Onto the screen, in living, writhing color, roars Tina Turner, live from Rio de Janeiro. Steger squirms upright. The Narssarssuaq gang, who only know this scrawny guy in their midst as the fellow who flew into town with a pack of wild dogs, do not recognize the importance of this moment. Unbeknownst to them, one of this would-be American hero's heroes—if he has any—has just appeared on the screen before them. Steger is so crazy about Ms. Turner, in fact, that when he retires to his Ely, Minnesota, privy, he is greeted by a three-foot-tall cutout of the woman herself.

Steger sits enraptured through the hour-long concert, then slips into the hotel's crowded bar and tries, unsuccessfully, to down one last warm beer. Finally, he gives in to his weariness and trudges off across the hard-packed snow toward his sleeping bag. The sky is filled with stars, the horizon rimmed by glaciers. Steger hums Tina Turner's encore under his breath, and it is fitting. "We Don't Need Another Hero" sputters through his lips and floats into the frigid night air. It is a concern that Steger wrestles with privately every day.

Since the North Pole trip, demands on his time have grown exponentially. His energies are split a hundred different ways. He is courted by sponsors, revered by staff, and deified by volunteers. As he trudges through the Greenland night, he is looking forward to two months on the ice, if only so that he can be more himself and less a "hero."

Steger, his teammates, thirty-two Huskies, and five tons of equipment had flown into this little pit stop of a town two days before, on April 13. For most, skiing across sixteen hundred miles of ice would be the adventure of a lifetime. But for this crew, it's a mere training exercise, a dress rehearsal for an August 1989–March 1990 assault across Antarctica on an unprecedented four-thousand-mile west-to-east traverse. At a time when some are claiming that there are no more grand "firsts" and others are moving toward smaller, back-to-basics expeditions, this latest Steger project boggles the imagination of veteran and novice explorers alike. And not simply because of the adventure itself. By the time the six-man team—from the United States, France, China, Japan, Great Britain, and the Soviet Union—sets foot on the Antarctic Peninsula in August, it will have raised close to $10 million to support the effort—$3.5 million of it for a computer-designed research ship that will serve as a floating communications base during the traverse. Sponsors may well spend another $10 million trumpeting the adventure. If all goes according to plan, licensing agreements will bring in millions over the next few years to the "Trans-Antarctica Expedition," as well as to its co-leaders, Steger and Frenchman Jean-Louis Etienne. Steger is planning to write several books based on the adventure.

The expedition has employed ten full-time people at the Homestead (Steger's base camp outside of Ely), one part-time and two full-time assistants at the St. Paul headquarters, and four others in Paris. Moreover, the team's success, or lack of same, will be followed by a worldwide audience—forty-three countries have signed on to use film and video footage to be provided by a French film crew that will drop in periodically. And, in an expedition first, ABC Sports will reportedly spend more than a million dollars producing five one-hour documentaries. It won't be surprising to hear Peter Jennings weighing in weekly on the team's fate, nor to see a "Steger Watch" column in *USA Today*. A relatively shy, unassuming guy only five years ago, Steger has warmed to his new role as spokesman and fundraiser with seeming ease. With coaching from a New York publicist, he says he's "ready for those run-ins with Koppel." But the enormity of their Antarctica traverse has not really sunk into the minds of the men as they prepare in Greenland. For now, their mission is to jam-pack sleds with gear and food. *Everything* will be tested in Greenland: clothing, tents, skis, bindings, poles, sunglasses, cook stoves, sleds, food, and dogs. All six men are experienced polar explorers. Two— Geoff Somers (Great Britain) and Victor Boyarsky (U.S.S.R) —have spent many months in Antarctica. Steger and Etienne will live long into history for their past accomplishments. But each man has his own system for surviving out on the ice, based on years of experiment, and now they must come up with one system that will work for all. Some like to cook on white gas, some prefer kerosene. Some enjoy a stick of butter with their evening meal, others like leaner cuisine. Some like domed tents, others prefer pyramids. The hope is that by the end of the Greenland trip, they will have tried one another's methods and agreed on a centralized approach, a single Trans-Antarctic way.

It's also assumed that this sixteen-hundred-mile tune-up will test the chemistry of the group, and that any tensions on the ice will be fleshed out long before reaching the seventh continent. Steger and Etienne emphatically agree that a $10 million personal adventure is far too extravagant. (By comparison, a well-funded Everest assault, minus the media hype, costs less than $200,000.) But they insist their impetus is much broader than simply "because it's there": With the treaty that governs Antarctica due to be renewed in 1991, they hope to focus the world's attention, for at least eight months, on the continent's uncertain environmental future. Despite the team's best publicity efforts, however, only time will tell whether the world will care. If, as even some of the expedition staff and sponsors fear, it doesn't—if Steger, Etienne, and friends come off the ice in March of 1990 and six months later are doing American Express commercials (Hi, remember me? I skied across Antarctica . . .")—all this hullabaloo may live on only in their quickly remaindered memoirs.

So what does Will Steger want? "It's simple, really," he says. "Getting to the North Pole was a kind of personal best for me. The spirit of the Antarctica trip is much different—hopefully it will draw attention to the need for international cooperation. If we can exhibit that cooperation in even our small way, by six men from different backgrounds and origins surviving a rugged test of mind and body, it'll serve as a fine example to the world. Face it, if we all don't learn to cooperate better, the future looks grim."

Face it, too: Mount Steger has a nice ring to it. So does a bank account filled with post-expedition royalty and endorsement money. At nine Steger traded his hockey skates for a stack of *National Geographic*s, at fifteen he boated the length of the Mississippi with his brother—and he's lived a kind of Huckleberry Finn existence ever since. He's climbed twenty-thousand-foot peaks in Peru and kayaked a total of ten thousand miles. He once spent eighteen consecutive months in the far reaches of the Arctic, traveling seven thousand miles by dogsled. And though his intentions are sincere, he'd be the last to deny a newfound pleasure in some things only money can buy. He figures he's eaten enough seal meat and scrounged by long enough on two thousand dollars a year to be reaping some rewards for his addiction to the cold and lonely places.

Just last winter he was still hauling supplies to the Homestead by foot, canoe, or dogsled. Today he hops to the Twin Cities and beyond—fulfilling the duties of a seven-day-a-week schedule—by chartered floatplane. There is a part of him that is anxious and ready to shoulder the attention—and the responsibility—that accompanies his newfound recognition. But Will Steger hasn't changed that much. He still mooches phone and beer money, likes his life in the woods, and prefers the Arctic wastes to the cement canyons.

"My goal, believe it or not, was never to be seen as a conquering hero or anything like that," says Steger. "Some days I don't like that that's how some people see me. In fact, always being on my best behavior and putting on a good face in public can be a pain. But I think I'm getting better at facing people's expectations of me.

"I don't think that people have to think or be like me," he continues. "But people have a natural curiosity about nature and the world, and a lot of people live vicariously through adventure, and thus through me. In everyone there's a fascination with the world around us, and I guess my place is just to try to give people a better glimpse of it."

Dr. Jean-Louis Etienne, dressed in bulky red parka and bibs, stands in a back room of the abandoned administration building that the folks in Narssarssuaq have loaned the team for their three-day stay. It is the night before departure, and he is testing the radio that will be their only link to civilization once on the ice cap. Etienne has strung an antenna to a ski he's planted in the snow ten feet out from the window, and now he is purring in a thick French accent, over and over and over: "Greenland Expedition to Frobisher, come in. Greenland Expedition to Bradley Air, come in." After an hour with no reply, he gives up. "Maybe tomorrow," he smiles weakly.

While Steger is the on-ice leader, Etienne is his business partner in the Trans-Antarctica venture, in part due to the support of Etienne's longtime sponsor, UAP, the giant Paris-based insurance company. UAP's contribution is sizable—its $3.5 million is building the research ship that will trace the explorers' steps from the sea. The twin-engine, twin-masted, 120-foot-long, 120-ton ship is shaped like a walnut so that it will pop out of the frozen sea instead of freezing into it. It is named, of course, the *UAP*. The company's logo will also adorn team members' caps and parkas. "I'd wear it on my underwear if I thought anyone would see it," smiles Etienne. (When the trek is over, Etienne will keep the *UAP*, fulfilling a dream of his to captain a research ship. In return, Steger will have rights to the sale of all photos from the expedition, as well as improvements to his Homestead.)

In France, the jovial Etienne is a national hero. Since 1975 he has successfully completed nine major expeditions, including a sailing-and-climbing foray along the northwest coast of Greenland, two trips to Patagonia, and three Himalayan adventures—one an ascent of the northwest ridge of Mount Everest. A physician in Paris, he once hosted a national talk show and has written two books—one on his successful solo ski to the North Pole in 1986, another on sports medicine. If Steger represents the wound-up, ambitious American, Etienne is indeed the Frenchman: he favors sugar-laden coffee before starting his day on the ice, and he's requested caviar and champagne to be waiting for him at the end of the Greenland trip. In the middle of a fitful sleep the night before departing, he rolled over and Magic Markered on the window a reminder to himself to throw in some extra salt and pepper.

Etienne and Steger first met in a scene direct from Ripley's, a chance encounter on the ice en route to the North Pole in the spring of 1986. Steger was leading his eight-person team by dogsled and ski; Etienne was attempting to become the first to ski to the Pole alone. "I'd heard of him," says Steger. "But I wrote him off like everyone else. I lumped him in with all those wackos who gather in March to go to the Pole. I didn't think he'd ever make it."

Two hundred miles out, the Steger crew ran across a think set of tracks. Five hours later, paralleling a monstrous ridge, Steger's dogs veered hard to the right. Ahead stood a man in a thin blue parka. "Jean-Louis, I imagine?" malapropped Steger. The pair spent the night in Etienne's tent, talking of Antarctica. The next morning they exchanged phone numbers, and now they're riding herd on perhaps the most ambitious—and soon most publicized—expedition yet concocted.

At forty-two and forty-four respectively, Etienne and Steger represent "perfect" ages for taking the Antarctica trip, as defined by the two of them. "We needed mature people," stays Steger, "not guys who were still striving to find out who they are. People who were not self-centered, but self-sacrificing."

Steger and Etienne also knew they wanted to involve a Russian—not only to hit the global cooperation theme, but because the Soviets have two bases east of the South Pole, and the only base in the eastern interior. Initially they requested a renowned Soviet explorer, Dmitry Shparo, but were told he was "busy." Instead, Victor Boyarsky was "recommended"— a thirty-eight-year-old scientist and member of the Soviet Arctic and Antarctic Research Institute. When Boyarsky learned of his "appointment," and that he'd first be spending a lot of time in a place called Me-nee-sotuh, he was both overjoyed and concerned. Certainly he was qualified— he'd been on four research trips to the Antarctic—but in school he had studied German, not English. (He arrived in Ely accompanied by a trans-lator and rumored KGB man.) In Greenland, while his English improved, he often was given tasks that didn't involve too much interpersonal communication, jobs like fetching the dogs. The other team members are also well versed in polar living, and they, too, have their areas of expertise. Geoff Somers, thirty-nine, once spent thirty-three consecutive months, from 1978 to 1981, as a guide and dog handler with the British Antarctica Survey. He arrived in Ely in January 1988 to start working with the dogs. He was to train and weed out the best thirty to thirty-six dogs from the ninety that live at the Homestead, and Keizo Funatsu was named his partner. A dog trainer from Osaka, Japan, and a friend and student of the late Naomi Uemura, the only other explorer to traverse Greenland top to bottom, Funatsu had spent most of the previous four years working at an Outward Bound camp near Ely. He didn't meet Steger's and Etienne's age requirement—he's thirty-two—but his Zen-like devotion to the most mundane task and his ability with the dogs convinced the co-leaders to bring him on.

The final member of the team was to have been Martyn Williams, a Canadian explorer with vast experience in the Yukon and Antarctica. But he bowed out, citing business pressures—he runs a flight and guide service in Antarctica called Adventure Network, which will provide logistical support for the expedition at a rumored $1 million-plus. (His place was filled in Greenland by Bernard "Le Huge" Prud'homme, an experienced, six-foot-seven mountain climber, a pal of Jean-Louis's, and the sound man on the French film crew that is documenting the Trans-Antarctica venture.) The sixth teammate in Antarctica will be Qin Dahe, a forty-two-year-old Chinese glaciologist who has spent two winters in Antarctica, one as a base manager for the Great Wall Station. And then, of course, there are the most critical members of the expedition: the dogs. Most are a Steger blend of Siberian Husky and Canadian Eskimo that he has bred over two decades. Handfuls are direct descendants of early polar explorer Richard E. Byrd's teams that Steger recently acquired via New Zealand. Since January of 1988 the dogs have been munching daily on bricks of a customized chow with twice the calories of commercial dog food. No matter how much they worked during the training in Ely, they kept gaining weight. In Antarctica they'll consume more than ten tons of the stuff.

Saturday dawned gray and cloudy, especially inauspicious considering that the chopper pilots who would deliver the team to the Greenland ice cap had never set their big twenty-two-seat Sikorsky down in the snow.

No one knew for sure if they would be sinking their rubber wheels into two or twenty feet of powder.

Nor did anyone know how the team would fare once left to itself on the ice. Etienne and Funatsu were worn from nagging fevers, and tension was high, especially between Somers and Steger. The former was used to the British way of expeditioning: if you're going out for ten days, you take the equipment stacked under the red tarp; if you're going out for two, you go with what's under the blue tarp. A quiet, meticulous man, Somers was put off by Steger's more random, seemingly chaotic approach (and piqued that Steger had been "sneaking off" to the hotel for lunch while the rest of the crew ate pemmican, noodles, and rice). Several in attendance during the three days in town had guessed that the pair's relationship would soon dissolve totally. Officially, both Somers and Funatsu were called "candidates" on the Greenland trek—just in case there was a clash of personalities. Moreover, while Steger and Etienne are well versed in dealing with media and sponsors—and well aware of the value of both—Somers, Funatsu, and Boyarsky weren't inclined to much candor with outsiders. Although polite, even friendly on occasion, Somers compared the press he's met on past expeditions to "vultures just waiting for a dead body."

When the first helicopter finally went up, a different sort of apprehension filled the cabin. The men flew forty miles toward the heart of the island, rising four thousand feet in fifteen minutes, soaring over deep fjords and ice that would never, ever melt. Then, suddenly, there was nothing but whiteness spread out ahead for sixteen hundred miles. Steger and Etienne, peering out of the same tiny porthole, smiled and mugged for the film, video, and still cameras. But one could see that the view had caused their blood to roil, like hunting dogs on the chase. After two long, slow circles around what appeared to be a safe place, the helicopter bounced once, twice, and settled. Steger, dressed in torn and muddy blue jeans and black, buckled rain boots, opened the side door, shielded his eyes from the now-bright sun, and scanned the immense expanse before him. Then, as the steps went down, he graciously allowed the chopper's engineer to take the first step into the snow. Who knew, he might have plummeted out of sight. But the snow turned out to be only a foot deep, and the chopper was unloaded and sent back with Steger for two more loads. When the chopper set down for the third and final time, its whirring blades sending dog food and ski poles flying, Steger emerged in full adventure dress: pink Rossignol sunglasses and a black Marmot suit with his name stitched across the breast. On his back he wore a foot-wide American flag; the others bore their own flags.

As the helicopter lifted, leaving the team behind, Jean-Louis toasted with a tin cup of coffee and yelled out, "Have a safe trip." His teammates, looking like neon ants in a very large bowl of sugar, waved. The dogs barked. Borne away on the helicopter were Steger's muddy jeans and black rubber boots, which were gratefully accepted by one of the airport workers back in Narssarssuaq. "They are very courageous men," he pondered out loud. "Aren't they?"

To those who know him best, Will Steger is both a hero and a recovering party animal. His forty-four years have been filled with contrast. A member of the 1986 North Pole team calls him a "dreamer." A current staffer prefers "visionary." He has, mistakenly, been labeled a recluse and a loner. A friend of twenty years insists, laughingly, that Steger is "an incorrigible womanizer and beer drinker—and he'll never change." Recently a volunteer in the expedition's St. Paul office wondered if she could just "touch him." A stunned Steger shook her hand.

Since his success at the North Pole, he's had to make adjustments, to learn how to ease his way from the backwoods to the boardrooms and back again. As the demands soar, he juggles his many roles—boss, colleague, buddy, hero. He does it smoothly, but it isn't easy. "I'd kill for a week off," he sighs. "Going to Antarctica will be like a vacation." One recent two-week stretch took him from a design session at The North Face in Berkeley to a sports show in Dallas to a positive-thinking seminar in Tampa to an expedition meeting in New York and back to Ely. Another foray took him to seven cities in nine days at the behest of a sponsor. So while the juggernaut he's created roars onward, he sometimes longs for the days when it was just him and his dogs.

"When I was young, I didn't invest much power in heroes," he says. "I don't think I really had any, and I don't really understand hero-worship. The simple truth is that all the young boys I hung around with had adventuresome dreams; I was no different than my peers. The difference is that I kept up my adventures. That's what was important to me.

"At my twenty-fifth high-school class reunion," he continues, "everybody came up to me and told me how proud they were to have gone to school with me. But I reminded them that they all have jobs and families. . . . They'd say, 'Oh, but that's common.' Well, to me, that's quite an accomplishment. I could never have done that."

Steger's Homestead has changed quite a bit since the day five years ago when he called Du Pont about sponsorship for his North Pole trip, just another guy looking to be bankrolled. Last summer a road was finally cut through two miles of dense woods. At least ten friends and low-paid employees—cooks and seamstresses, carpenters and dog trainers—have spent the winter preparing for the coming months of training and the inevitable influx of sponsors and press. A half-dozen new huts have been built, the wood-fired sauna was expanded. And a slab has been laid for Steger's dream house—still mostly in the explorer's head, it is now envisioned as a multistory building complete with a meeting room, a conservatory, and a windowless, all-white room where he'll sleep. (He insists he's never slept better than he does on the ice.)

But for the moment, home is still the two-room cabin he built twenty-five years ago. The walls are cluttered—a photograph of him and his favorite dog, Zap, leading a parade in downtown Minneapolis; a painting of a dog musher running a team through falling snow; a "think South" poster. Bookshelves rim the room—Peary and Shackleton, Scott and Amundsen are his favorite authors. On the penguin-patterned sheets of his loft bed are a flashlight and an open book, Knud Rasmussen's *Across Arctic America*. In a corner is a porcelain piss pot, and a coyote skin covers a chair. Beneath a window is a shrine of sorts—a shelf holds a woodblock of Jesus, a small cross, candles, incense, and a "Prayer for a Safe Journey": "O Lord, we humbly ask you to give your almighty protection to all travelers."

On July 15, a Soviet plane will pick up Steger and his men in Minneapolis and deposit them on King Georges Island off the Antarctic Peninsula. On July 30, the six men and thirty-some dogs will depart from the Argentine camp at Seal Nunataks on the peninsula and begin traveling east in the shadow of the Ellsworth Mountains, stopping every four hundred miles to collect caches of food and sundries, and occasionally to hook up with one or more film crews. "The first 2,500 miles to the Pole are really to get ourselves in top shape," says Steger. Physically, the traverse is not likely to match the grueling North Pole trip. Some days, as they sledged north, hauling heavily laden sleds up and down pressure ridges and over ice floes, Steger and his teammates advanced only a mile or two. In Antarctica, though the men will face winds of more than a hundred miles per hour, temperatures down to fifty below, and elevations as high as ten thousand feet, the demands will be more mental than physical. They will be on the ice for eight months, skiing an average of twenty-five to thirty miles per day. Monotony may well be their worst enemy.

By early December, they expect to have reached the South Pole, where they'll be met by the film crews. Then the real test: to the east of the Pole lies the aptly named Area of Inaccessibility—a five-hundred-mile stretch of remote ice where rescue will be difficult. No one has ever crossed this stretch of the continent on foot. It is truly an unknown place. For most of a month, between the South Pole and the Soviet station at Vostok (called the Coldest Place in the World), they will be essentially on their own.

Their final destination is the Soviet base at Mirnyy on the Queen Mary Coast, which they hope to reach by March 1. There they will be met by the *UAP*. If successful, they will have crossed Antarctica via the longest path imaginable. The only expedition thus far to traverse it took much shorter routes along the Greenwich meridian. In 1981, Sir Ranulph Fiennes's Transglobe Expedition rode 2,254 miles in snowmobiles. And in 1957–58, Sir Vivian Fuchs led a British juggernaut that traveled 2,158 miles in half-ton, Day-Glo-orange snowcats.

On June 16, sixty-two days and sixteen hundred miles after they left Narssarssuaq, Steger and company reached the Humboldt Glacier, at the northern peak of Greenland. They had traveled the last 1,450 miles without resupply—shattering Steger's own thousand-mile North Pole record. Temperatures had dropped to twenty-seven below, winds had gusted to eighty mph. They'd suffered frostbite, severe sunburn and windburn, and god-awful boredom. But when they flew off the world's largest island and back to New York for a press conference, they returned as something they weren't when they left—a real team. In fact, parading outside the United Nations for photographers and cameramen, the teammates, dressed in brand-new, ill-fitting jeans, thongs, and Trans-Antarctica T-shirts, looked like locked-arm international Monkees ("Here we come, walking down the street . . .").

"Before we left, I was concerned about how we'd get along—especially Geoff, because he's real set in his ways," Steger admitted after the press conference. "But he was very open to experimenting, too. I cook in Teflon, Geoff likes aluminum. He uses a pyramid tent, I prefer a domed tent. Keizo likes spices, I don't. Jean-Louis is allergic to fat. I like fat. Victor— well, Victor will eat anything. But I think by the end—after switching off tent mates throughout—we perfected a traveling system that will work in Antarctica. It was like six nations trying to work something out, building up open lines of communication."

For his part, Somers appeared ecstatic about the success of the trip, even while chiding Steger for exaggerating at the press conference. "I know *I* certainly didn't eat a pound of butter a day," he laughed.

Since the return from Greenland, Chevrolet has taken an interest in the Trans-Antarctica venture, and W. L. Gore has added $2 million to the pot. Gore joins Eastman-Kodak, which will provide all film and processing, and DuPont's Fiberfill division (Steger's primary North Pole sponsor), which has kicked in $250,000. Hill's Pet Products values its contribution of Science Diet dog food at more than $1 million. A Minnesota company is minting gold coins in honor of the Antarctica trek; Target stores has licensed the expedition name and will spend millions promoting a nationwide back-to-school Antarctica theme, including appropriately labeled Thermoses, crayons, lunch boxes, sleds, mittens, and toys; another licensing agreement with Dayton's department stores will produce a Trans-Antarctica line of clothes and linens. Next winter's line from The North Face will feature a "Trans-Antarctica Collection." Even the dogs are getting in on the act: a calendar will feature a dozen of the studs, and W. L. Gore will produce full-size models of the beasts for use in stores. Gore has also had life-size mannequins of Etienne and Steger made, an enterprise that gives blush to the reluctant heroes.

The expedition's one major disappointment, though nobody's willing to detail it, is the lack of support from the National Science Foundation, which oversees the American presence in Antarctica. The team has enlisted support and cooperation from the Soviets (planes, fuel, ships, and bases), the French (technological assistance in building the *UAP*), the Chinese (base support), and the Japanese (funds through a complicated kickback from Sony-sponsored documentaries on state-owned television). But so far the NSF has refused to recognize the expedition and insists it will not be allowed to use American bases. Says NSF spokesman Guy Guthridge: "Our mission is research, not aiding expeditions."

It is now late last December, and Steger is sitting in the coffee shop at Manhattan's Barbizon Hotel. Two octogenarian matrons eavesdrop open-mouthed as he relates bawdy tales of high Arctic adventures.

"This is going to be much different than the trip to the North Pole," he says between bites of salad. "We were under extreme tension and stress during that entire trip. While I never saw it as life threatening, there were a lot of dreams on the line. There was one point, about three weeks from the Pole, where I thought the team was going to split. I was convinced that we didn't have enough food to make it, and we took a day off to talk it over. At that point, success was beyond mathematics; the only thing that would get us there was our collective spirit. It was really the optimism and youth of some of the others that forced me to reconsider my calculations and proceed.

"Well, I think the spirit and optimism of this team is even stronger. We developed a real brotherly affection for each other in Greenland, and when we parted I missed them, I was heartsick. I know Jean-Louis felt the same way. I've never experienced that with an expedition before." Only time will tell if those feelings will last. While Steger remains on polite terms with most of the North Pole team, he rarely sees or speaks with them. "I'm 90 percent sure we can make it across Antarctica," he says. "I wouldn't attempt it if the percentage was any less. I'm willing to take on risks, but only calculated risks. That's one reason I'm alive at forty-four. If I was a risk taker, I'm sure I would have died in my twenties climbing. It would have been very easy."

This will be Steger's last big expedition. While he tries to stay in shape, his back is fading, and he has recently been tormented by unexplained eyestrain that makes wearing much-needed contacts or glasses painful and causes severe headaches. He has taken to wearing a black patch to rest his eyes during the day. He says he hopes his next adventure is as a fund-raiser, spokesman, and environmentalist. But there's always that solo kayak trip through the Northwest Passage lurking in the back of his mind. And if the Antarctica trip is as monetarily rewarding as he thinks it will be, he plans to build an observatory at the Homestead, buy expensive astrophotography equipment, and turn the place into a haven for atmospheric scientists and visionaries.

"I don't really know what's next," he admits, doodling his fork in his salad. "I'm in a different league now. I have more choices, more expert advice. It's not just the dogs and me anymore. But every time I go out now, the stakes are higher. We may have more tools down the road to raise money with, but we need more money. And, too, the risks keep getting bigger."

As he pauses, I notice that his left thumb is purple and swollen to twice its normal size. He smirks the smirk of a kid caught in a cookie jar as he explains. A couple days after arriving back at the Homestead from Greenland, right around the Fourth of July, he managed to blow off part of his thumb while trying to light an M-80 firecracker. His friends packed the thumb in ice, wrapped up his other broken and bleeding fingers, and paddled, portaged, and drove to the hospital in Ely for a quick patch-up. The next day Steger flew to Duluth, where surgeons corrected his miscalculation as best they could. The thumb still turns blue in air-conditioned rooms.

"OK, that was an example of an uncalculated risk," he says. "But believe me, they're few and far between these days."

The crossing of Antarctica was a success and Steger followed it with a crossing of the Arctic in 1995, from Russia to Canada via the North Pole. In 2008, accompanied by a team of six young explorers, Steger traversed Ellesmere Island by dogsled. He continues to speak out about climate change issues, from his base in Minnesota.

MURDER IN THE KARAKORAM

Ned Gillette

Outside, 1998

Death occasionally crossed the mind of Edward "Ned" Gillette, though he didn't dwell on it, wasn't scared of dying. But like anyone who makes a career out of adventuring, he wondered how he might die. Perhaps the penultimate late-twentieth-century adventurer—renowned for the variety of his expeditions as well as a singular skill at convincing corporate sponsors to finance them, whether they are around mountains, across oceans, or through deserts—Gillette, fifty-three, had dared the gods in a variety of treacherous settings. When his time was up, he had to assume it might come beneath the coldest part of the Atlantic, or deep inside some mountain crevasse.

In his darkest moments he could never have expected to be shotgunned to death through the wall of his tent.

On August 5, 1998, a beautiful, blue-sky summer day, he and his wife, Susie Patterson, forty-two, were camped at the base of the sixty-eight-hundred-meter Laila Peak, beneath Chogolumga Glacier in the Northern District of Pakistan. They had left the U.S. in early July for two months of exploring, climbing, photographing, and writing. It was almost a holiday compared to some of the more arduous trips Gillette had made over the past thirty years.

That afternoon they had completed a tough, five-day trek across the glacier; they jeeped from Gilgit to begin their climb from the small village of Daku. They had attempted the route—though in reverse—last September, but were turned back by deep snows. They returned early in July to spend two months, finishing this trek as well as the circling of Nanga Parvit, which they had finished just weeks before.

It was rugged, remote country. The Haramosh Valley is one of forty that carve east and west from the Karakoram Highway and the Indus River gorge dead-ending at the glacier. Angular, jagged peaks rose all around their camp spot—the very same place they'd camped last September—to twenty-three thousand feet. Three small villages hung precariously along the ridges of the narrow, fifteen-mile-long valley.

From their tent they were three kilometers from the nearest small village, and six hours walking from the road that led to the Karakoram. It was another three hours by jeep to Gilgit, eighty miles away. The Karakoram Highway is frequented by buses, trucks, and military vehicles. In fact the highway is littered with police checkpoints (where, ironically, Ned had filled in false names as they passed by). "This trip was a goal for Ned that was much more important for him than it was for me," says Patterson from their home in Sun Valley. "I really loved the Nanga Parvit part, the beauty of it, the goal. This thing Ned really wanted to do. We didn't know if we could get up and over the pass.

"The day before it happened was such a cool day. We had just a beautiful day, photographing. Cloudless, blue sky. The pass was at sixteen thousand feet—which for Ned was no problem. Easy enough where we could go fast. But beautiful and fun and carefree. We were on the glacier, but going up the pass, so the crevasses were open enough at this time of year that we could see them. They weren't big. Fairly easy travel, beautiful country.

"The top of the pass was good and fun; coming down was nothing but hideous loose rock. There was a faint trail. We actually ran into one local person coming the opposite way over the pass, so we knew it was doable. We didn't know if it was, though Ned never thought anything was impossible. He always thought he could make something work, without it being death-defiable.

"The descent of this was really scary, slightly out of control, lots of loose rock. It wasn't like crampons and ice axes would work on all these slick rocks; another real problem that I always feared, that even if Ned and I were roped, that I'm so small I didn't have the confidence I could do a good belay.

"We didn't see any other tourists. In the past three years people just don't go to Pakistan unless they're going to climb the high mountains. Or travel along the Karakoram Highway. So what Ned and I wanted to do was something in the middle. Which is why it was cool. We would be in really remote areas, wouldn't see any Westerners. And we always liked that, especially Ned. He was always asking, "Have any Westerners been here before?" I'm pretty sure no one had done this trip before.

"It took us four hours to get down the pass; Ned especially was really beat. We camped in the exact same spot we'd camped when we'd come up the valley last fall, in these shepherd areas. Green grass. We also wanted to camp there so we could look back up at the pass we'd just crossed. It was cool.

"We got down in early evening, put up camp, had tea, made a dinner. We put up our little green two-man tent, which blended in with the grass. Ned especially was really psyched that we'd accomplished this crossing. Exhausted, but really psyched. It was a real goal of his. With night came a moon that was not quite full, kind of eerie. It was pretty bright. We could see the moon's craters and it felt really close. We had a really beautiful dinner together, literally said 'I love you,' and went to sleep.

"The next thing I heard was a gunshot." It was between 10 p.m. and midnight.

"The sound was piercing, loud. I woke up and Ned was wild-eyed. All he could say was 'It's my insides. . . . I think I'm dying . . . my insides are whacked out . . . I think I'm dying. . . .' Then he passed out.

"I thought he'd gone deaf, because he had ear problems, or that he was having a bad dream. I was just waking up and I didn't understand the seriousness of it right away.

"There were more shots. I'm yelling at him to wake up. I wasn't hysterical, I just didn't know what was going on. I think I never, ever wanted to admit to myself the seriousness of what was happening. I got him back to consciousness by shaking him and yelling at him, slapping his face. His eyes were glazed (starts to cry) . . . with such a wild look on his face . . . it was so scary. Then he came to, and seemed almost normal.

"I kept saying 'I've got to get help,' and he kept saying to me, like a little boy, 'Don't leave.' But he was coherent enough to say, 'We've got to get out of the tent, it's dangerous.'

"Ned was in shock. That's the only way he was physically able to get up, because he was in such pain. We started putting our boots on . . . and then I got shot. Ned said, 'Oh, God, they got you, too.' It felt like a sledge-hammer slamming into my back—it didn't knock the wind out of me—I just felt so nauseous. I think Ned realized what was happening to us, better than I, and I think maybe then he felt better somehow, that maybe I was with him now, that we were going to die together. . . .

"We were just able to get out of the tent, to hide behind our packs, which were up against the side of the tent. We couldn't stand up, couldn't walk, couldn't travel. We couldn't see anyone.

"I just got so cold, I said to Ned, 'We can't go anywhere, I've got to get back in my sleeping bag.' I was starting to crawl back into the tent when we saw a man, or a kid, coming out of the darkness with a big rock over his head. Somehow Ned managed to get a rock and lunge at this guy and the guy just disappeared back into the dark. . . .

"We got back in the tent. We didn't have any energy to do anything else. We couldn't really talk. Then another gunshot went off—I don't think it hit anything. Both of us were yelling now, 'Please stop, we're dying, you've done enough, please stop. . . .' " She thinks about a half hour passed between the first and last gunshot.

"Ned held my hand, but he never said he was in pain. At one point he said, 'I'm worried,' at another point he said, 'I'm losing a lot of blood.' I'm sure he was in shock, and acute pain, but I was the one saying, 'Please, Ned, please help me.' I kept having to crawl across his head because I felt like I had to throw up, but I couldn't throw up, it was too painful.

"We just focused in on getting through the night, and on being together. We both really had a lot of hope.

"Dawn came and we were both still alive. Neither of us could move, we just lay there. We knew that at some point someone would come up to the meadow. Ned was still able to get his head up and look out both sides of the tent to see if anyone was coming.

"We didn't have enough energy to yell any louder than we're talking now. Finally someone came and one guy spoke some basic English. Ned kept saying 'We got shot.' He was really clear. "Six shots, two men. Go to a phone, get a helicopter up here, go now." Then two more men came.

"Eventually one guy went down, but an hour later a kid came back up and said no one had gone to phone for help. So Ned got a bunch of rupees—he zeroed in, he was really coherent—and said 'Get somebody down there, get a helicopter up here . . .' After that Ned started losing consciousness (she starts to cry again) . . . at this point I think he knew it was only a matter of time. His breathing started getting labored. I felt his stomach, I could feel the gunshots, his heart was erratic . . . during the course of the morning all he really said to me was 'I love you, I love you,' that's all he said (stops talking, crying softly). . . .

". . . I propped him up, cut his T-shirt off him . . . and he just closed his eyes. . . . It was peaceful for him . . . but for me, I just didn't care anymore (crying, crying). . . . I didn't care, nothing mattered anymore. . . . I'm really sorry, I thought I could get through this. . . .

"After that I just laid in the tent all that day . . . I had to plead with the villagers not to leave me alone because I was terrified. They asked me if they wanted me to leave Ned in the tent . . . and I said yes, because I thought maybe he'd say something, or move (crying, crying, crying) . . . and finally I realized this was awful, and I had them take him out and the whole tent floor was full of blood . . . there were down feathers everywhere. That was the first time I really saw the blood, and the degree of the gunshot wounds, and just how brutal and horrible it was . . . .

"I was in a lot of pain, but I just didn't care about anything. I laid there all that day and all that night, waiting for help, but I can't tell you what I did. I was like an insane zombie. There were ten villagers around the tent now and they did everything they could for me, encouraging me to be strong, to have courage.

"Finally the next morning—almost thirty-six hours since the shootings—I agreed to let them take me down in a stretcher. It was the most incredibly painful ride down on this stretcher, but these villagers were incredible. It took four hours to get down, over really rough terrain. They used our climbing rope to strap me in; I couldn't breath I was tied so tight. But they didn't want me to fall out. I could only lay on my side; I was shot on one side and my back. So they slammed me between two big posts, a rudimentary/homemade stretcher, and tied me in.

"Halfway down the police were finally coming up. There was a doctor in the car. . . . They got me into what they called an ambulance, a busted-up jeep." She was kept in the hospital in Gilgit for five days, one lung filled with blood, sixty to seventy buckshot in her back and side, before being allowed to fly to Islamabad, where her brother, Pete—a good friend of Ned's, who had introduced the two—was waiting.

Two days later, on Saturday August 8, two suspects, Abid Hussain and Naun Heshel were arrested, turned in by local villagers. A shotgun was recovered, the pair charged with murder and assault. A trial was to be held quickly; if found guilty, the pair will be hung within a matter of weeks.

"Just a couple dimwitted kids doing a stupid robbery of the rich Americans," says Bob Law, Gillette's brother-in-law. According to local police, Gillette was the first foreigner ever murdered in this region of Pakistan.

"The pair were turned over after 'prompting' from police," says U.S. Embassy Counsel General Bernie Alter, from his office in Islamabad. "I suspect that the police heard rumors of who might have done it, went to that village, and said they would make things nasty for the whole village if they didn't help."

(Patterson does not believe robbery was the motive. "I think this Muslim stuff just makes these kids crazy. Think of it—nothing was stolen. Why not?")

The sad irony is that at the time of his death, Gillette had moved away from the big, corporate-financed, riskier expeditions and back to simple, more pure individual trips. "Ned had evolved into this incredibly beautiful person," Susie wrote in a note to Ned's family. "He got back to why this adventure stuff intrigued him in the first place. The beauty, the simplicity, the purity, yet still maintaining that desire to find a goal to explore and do incredible things in a new place, country. . . ."

His sister, Debby Law of San Francisco, confirms Gillette's evolution back to more simple trips. "He'd come around to doing small, independent, self-reliant, creative, fun trips—with Susie. Their relationship meant everything to him."

Gillette's death has fallen particularly hard on his eighty-five-year-old mother, Janet, of Quisset, Massachusetts, who lost her husband just five months before.

Ned Gillette was one of the most successful of a breed of modern-day "career adventurers." His greatest love was doing things no one had done and perhaps not even imagined. He didn't specialize in any particular region, was the first to admit he was not the most gifted athlete. What propelled him were an incredible wanderlust and a kind of patrician/New England sense of hard work. He succeeded where so many others failed, because he knew how to work the system—how to attract sponsors, coax dollars out of their pockets, and keep them happy during and after his expeditions, by never hesitating, in his writings or lectures, to thank out loud the corporations that made his chosen lifestyle possible. "You've got to differentiate yourself from others in the field, and you've got to always remember to say thank you to the guys who sent you," he told *Outside* in a 1986 cover story. "I'm selling a product really," he admitted. "There's the adventure itself, which is why I'm in it. But it's at least half promotion. It's a funny business."

His jack-of-all-trades love for adventure and sport began early. Father Bob was chairman of the National Life Insurance Company of Vermont, and his mother, Janet, took Ned and his sister, Debby, to Quissett Harbor on Cape Cod, where Ned learned to sail. He first skied at age five at Stowe and spent summers with his family sailing off New England. Holderness School, a prep school, led to being an NCAA cross country ski champion for Dartmouth in 1967, then an alternate member of the 1968 U.S. Nordic ski team at the Grenoble Olympics in 1968. Briefly flirted with business school; worked for a year-and-a-half in the management training program of International Paper. Entered business school at the University of Colorado in Boulder. Lasted twenty-four hours.

His first jobs were working as director of skiing at Yosemite, then running the ski touring center at the Trapp Family Lodge near his birthplace in Vermont. Jan Reynolds eventually did five big expeditions with Gillette, and met him when he hired her to teach skiing at the lodge. "Ned loved bizarre characters, and they were drawn to him.

"He had run the ski school at Yosemite, until the Von Trapp family lured him back to Vermont to do the same job. When he came, all these wacky California characters came along with him, just to be around Ned."

He began to climb seriously in Yosemite. "I was an eastern preppie Ivy Leaguer, but at Yosemite I ricocheted off in another direction," he told *Sports Illustrated* in 1990. "I started doing things, saying things, smoking things, thinking things that were totally new to me. I opened my eyes to life as an adventure. I've always thought, if you have a solid upbringing, it allows you to be crazy by election thereafter."

In 1978 he (along with Galen Rowell) made the first one-day ascent of Mt. McKinley; in 1980 he was among the first Americans to climb in China, summiting 24,757-foot Muztagata and skiing off; in 1982 he climbed Mt. Everest; in 1984 he made the first Nordic ski descent of Argentina's Mount Aconcagua; in 1985 he was the first American to climb the Himalayan Peak Pumori. He led several long-distance ski trips in a wide variety of frozen places—across the Robson Channel and Ellesmere Island in Canada, and, in 1981, a first circumnavigation of Mt. Everest. He considered a 1980, three-hundred-mile winter traverse of four Karakoram Himalayas, the highest mountain range on earth, the most physically challenging trip he'd undertaken. "We live in a time where you can no longer climb the highest peak, or no longer explore blank spots on a map," he told *Outside*. "Adventure is looking at old subjects in new ways. None of us are explorers anymore. We're guys who dream up things that might be fun to do."

His 1988 voyage via the self-dubbed *Sea Tomato*—an enclosed rowing boat that resembled a bright-red pickle—was perhaps his most publicized, most wacky, most death-defying adventure. During the crossing of the Drake Passage, from Cape Brecknock, Chile, sixty miles northwest of Cape Horn, to a landfill near King George Island, Antarctica, the twenty-eight-foot aluminum craft, designed by Gillette, capsized three times.

The first day out, gusts were up to fifty knots. "We were shot out of there like a rocket," he said afterward. "We capsized three different times and one of us went overboard each time." They covered ninety nautical miles the first two days, without touching the oars. Squalls tossed the fifteen-hundred-pound boat around like a . . . tomato. They had expected to be at sea for twenty days, but completed the 720-mile crossing in a wind-assisted thirteen days.

Soon after, he met Susie Patterson, then thirty-five, introduced in Sun Valley by one of her brothers. A ski phenom—she made the U.S. National Ski Team for the first time at age thirteen—Patterson was the U.S. women's slalom champion in 1974, and downhill champ in 1976. After the 1976 Olympics, where she placed fourteenth in the downhill, she skied the World Cup circuit. A self-confessed "ski princess" for the first twenty-five years of her life, she says, "I'd been up high mountains all over the world—on chairlifts. I was good and I loved what I did." She'd spent maybe one night in a tent; today she jokes she wasn't even sure where Asia was.

"I didn't know who he was or what he did: I only knew he was the one. . . . We met a little more than ten years ago—shortly after he did his *Sea Tomato* trip—and we fell in love in a weekend. He and my brother Pete had done a trip; they did the first ski descent down Aconcagua. He came up to visit Pete, and it was the first time he had introduced me to any of his friends. Ned kept asking him, 'Hey, what's the deal with your sister?' and Pete would say, 'Oh, she's trouble.'"

They were married at Sun Valley's Roundhouse Restaurant on Bald Mountain August 18, 1990. Ned now had a full-time partner in crime: "Now I can bring my home life with me," he quipped.

"What I said to Ned was, 'I'd like to climb a mountain someday, a big one. Do you have any ideas?'

"Soon I was listening to a madcap scheme to sneak across a Chinese border closed to Westerners, climb a peak illegally, and then escape. Because I didn't say no—I guess I said yes.

"In short, we agreed to climb Tibet's 25,355-foot-high Gurla Mandhata, the Mountain of Black Herbal Medicine." It was an adventure in the tradition of a time past, when mountain climbers were romantically inclined explorers.

"'So what happens if we get caught?' I asked.

"'Oh, we might have to spend a few nights in jail or, worst case, get tossed out of the country,' Ned answered vaguely.

"'Guerrilla mountaineering,' Ned called it, and I liked it."

After an oxygen-starved, stormbound honeymoon in a tent at twenty-one thousand feet while climbing the Tibetan peak of Gurla Mandhata, in 1994 the pair traced five thousand miles of the Silk Road, through China and Central Asia, by camel caravan. That was Gillette's last heavily financed, heavily publicized trip.

In retrospect, what made Gillette special was his great sense of himself, his own limitations, his place. He was first in a growing breed of modern adventurers who recognized that what mattered for the contemporary adventurer was not just skill and intrepidity, but style, flair, finesse.

"Ned was very strong in an endurance sense," says Jan Reynolds. "Alan Bard, who was big and strong, used to say he'd never traveled with anyone as strong as Ned. When Galen (Rowell) and Ned climbed McKinley in one day, it was Ned who broke the trail all the way to the end.

"He always admired the good, hardcore climbers; he was more bold than fancy. Strong mentally and physically, but what made him special was that he was also such a regular guy, with insecurities like the rest of us. Always concerned that he was dressing like a dork. He really was 'Everyman's' friend."

"I don't undertake these things to please my fellow skiers or my fellow climbers or my fellow rowers," Gillette said in 1986. "I do them to please myself and, I like to think, to give something back to the man in the street, the guy who sits at a desk and maybe isn't doing what he wants with his life.

"If anything, I'd just like to think I remind people that it's possible to do what you want. If adventuring is about anything, that's what it's about."

Their next trip was to be to the Dolbo region of Nepal. The tickets for it are still on Gillette's desk.

"Ned's famous last words were, 'I've always wanted to do this,'" remembers Susie. "And I'd say, 'But Ned, you've always wanted to do everything.'"

Jan Reynolds, who accompanied Gillette on the Southern Cross expedition in New Zealand, then climbed in China, Mutagada, and then the Everest Circle, "what made him special was his way of inspiring people. If he'd had a motto, it would have been 'Dream, then do.'"

The senseless and seeming randomness of the killing sent shockwaves through the adventuring community. The only controversy centered on just how dangerous was this region of Pakistan. Could—or should—the pair of experienced adventurers have known the area was unsafe? In March the U.S. Embassy in Islamabad had warned of threats against Americans in Pakistan, after gunmen in the southern port city of Karachi shot dead four American oil company employees apparently because a Pakistani was convicted in the U.S. of murdering two CIA agents. Greg

Mortenson, director of the Central Asia Institute, a private agency providing schooling and aid to poor people of the region, assures me that Gillette's killing was not political. "The cold-blooded nature of it is a freak thing. It was an isolated thing, not a specific act against Americans."

How dangerous depends on whom you ask. A State Department spokesman in Islamabad, Richard Hoagland, said by phone after the killings, "Though very remote, the Northern District is not especially dangerous. But it is a very traditional area, very tribal, steeped in Soviet-era wars, still imbued with what is known as the 'Kalashnikov culture.' Many people there carry guns."

Mortenson goes further: "This area is totally wild. Everybody carries an AK-47. The people are very isolated, and notoriously violent and dangerous. I would never go there myself, especially not without a local porter or a guard." He suggests that maybe this time Gillette ventured too far off the beaten path. "The foreigners who go in there are usually large groups of mountaineers, with hired local porters. You rarely see individual backpackers traveling there. (Gillette) was a worldwide traveler, and knew what he was doing, but I would never have gone up there without hiring a local, somebody who at least spoke the language." (Mortenson worked in the region for six years and had his own near-disastrous experience: in 1996 he was abducted and held hostage for eight days. "I got lucky, because I can speak the language and they knew who I was.")

The State Department's Bernie Alter, on his second tour in Islamabad, says that this northern region is not as dangerous as the North-West Frontier, a hundred miles away. "The area doesn't get thousands of tourists, but hundreds of trekkers each season; the only reports of violence are occasional assault and rape of woman travelers."

Patterson, recuperating at her home in Sun Valley, is adamant that the image of the area as dangerous is overblown, that it's not true that everyone has guns.

"Whenever you're in a border area of China, India, or Pakistan it's dangerous. But we weren't near a border area. Some people said we were in Kashmir, which is not true. A lot of Pakistan along the Indian border is restricted, but we weren't near any of that.

"The only thing I'm bitter about is that it appears the police stood in the way of the military, the only people who could have dispatched a helicopter. The police were really tedious, unwilling to work with the military and others trying to help us.

"The only thing that's really saving me right now is that I've been told that even if Ned had been shot like that in his backyard, there was enough damage that he wouldn't have lived.

"It was awful and brutal. But neither of us made a mistake. Ned would never have forgiven himself if he had gotten us in this situation by having made a bad decision. This was totally out of our control. Ned took only calculated risks. There was nothing he could have done about this."

Gillette's body was cremated, in Pakistan, on August 12 and carried back to the States by Patterson. By his request, there was no burial, no ceremony, though a private memorial was held at the Von Trapp Lodge in Vermont.

Susie Patterson lives in Sun Valley, Idaho.

UPHILL RACER

A. J. Kitt

The New York Times Magazine, 1992

A.J. Kitt—the American alpine skier with the best chance of winning a medal in Albertville, France, next week—stands with his arms crossed in a blowing whiteout, staring up into the Austrian Alps. Atop the mountain the snow is deep and shifting, the winds are fierce and the visibility is near zero.

It is four days before Christmas, and the five-hundred-year-old town of St. Anton is filled with holiday vacationers, many of whom have come to watch the prestigious, sixty-three-year-old Arlberg-Kandahar races. But snow has been falling on the picturesque ski village at the rate of a foot a day for several days in a row, and racing is doubtful.

With practice runs out of the question, the twenty-three-year-old Kitt, a Rochester, New York, native who shocked the ski-racing world in December by winning a World Cup downhill at Val d'Isere, France, and then grabbing fourth a week later at Val Gardena, Italy, is reduced to training in his head, envisioning the top of the piste and the start of his run.

Helmeted, sealed in a skin-tight purple-and-green Lycra racing suit with the American team's distinctive spider-web motif, he envisions himself waiting as the imaginary countdown reaches "One" and then skates madly away from the starting gate, folding into the tuck that will carry him down the thirteen-hundred-meter course. His immediate goal is to become as aerodynamic as humanly possible: hunched forward, eyes and buttocks up, knees bent, poles tucked tightly under his armpits, his calves bearing most of the extraordinary force generated as his skis pick up speed.

He is so compressed by pressures external and internal he doesn't dare take a breath, and couldn't if he wanted to—the breaths he does take come almost accidentally, in response to jarring bumps. Within seconds of the start, his entire body is threatening to come loose at the joints as he takes the first of several long turns at sixty miles per hour. His skis shudder wildly as he tops ninety on the straightaway. On the first of several jumps, he fights desperately to stay compact, close to the snow, bulletlike. The most famous ski racer of all time, Jean-Claude Killy, has compared this two-minute blast to riding a brakeless bicycle down a mountainside.

Kitt speaks out of his reverie, addressing the storm: "You know, I never get scared. I can't allow that," he says, brushing heavy flakes from his eyes. "I won't race if I'm scared. I won't even go to the start gate."

Has he ever, in seventeen years of ski racing, turned away from the gate at the last minute? "Never. Never."

Alva Ross Kitt IV (his parents called him A. J. from day one, to distinguish him from all the other Alva Rosses around the house) is the men's best hope for Olympic glory, and he is perfect for the role. With the downhill race at St. Anton officially canceled, Kitt pulls up a chair in the oak-paneled bar of the Hotel Post for a talk before a team dinner. Throughout the conversation he has a difficult time not being distracted by the attractive waitress, who pays him inordinate attention. Such are the rewards of winning a World Cup race. Along the circuit, which begins in November and ends in April, everyone in Val d'Isere, Val Gardena, St. Anton, Garmisch-Partenkirchen, Kitzbühel, and Wengen wants to meet this new phenom.

A stand-tall, no-excuses competitor, only the second American to win a World Cup downhill race (Bill Johnson was the first), Kitt is exceedingly polite when necessary, cocky when it fits. Built like a college wrestler (five feet eleven inches tall, 192 pounds), he is freshly showered after an afternoon workout and dressed in T-shirt, Levi's, black cowboy boots, and a silver-buckled belt. With his hair cropped military-short, he could easily pass for a marine out of uniform. His left wrist sports a hefty Rolex (the watchmaker is one of his sponsors); as he talks his muscular biceps twitch.

Like most racers, Kitt was raised a ski brat. His parents worked part time as ski instructors at a rope-tow hill outside Rochester called Frost Ridge, and A. J. first skied at the age of two. By the time he was six, he was racing, at what would become his home hill, Swain Ski Center (vertical drop: 650 feet). He distinctly remembers his first race, because he argued with an official who claimed he had missed a gate. The pint-size Kitt won the argument and the trophy.

Alpine ski racing breaks down into four disciplines: downhill, giant slalom, slalom, and super G, which is a hybrid of downhill and giant slalom that became an Olympic event in 1988. Skiers normally specialize in one or two, usually either the speed events of downhill and super G or the finesse events of slalom and giant slalom. By age twelve, however, Kitt wasn't worried about specializing, only winning, which he says he did in more than half the races he entered.

At thirteen he enrolled in the Mountain House School, a ski academy in Lake Placid, New York; two years later he transferred to Green Mountain Valley School in Waitsfield, Vermont, one of the best ski academies in the country. He graduated in 1986 and spent a year competing across Europe and North America under the guidance of his prep-school coach, Kirk Dwyer. His parents—Alva III (everyone calls him Ross) runs the family business, which publishes law books—picked up the tab. In 1987 he joined the United States ski team as a backup to the then-stars—Bill Johnson, Doug Lewis, Tiger Shaw, Felix McGrath—and raced in the downhill at the Calgary Olympics at age nineteen, finishing twenty-sixth.

When the older skiers retired after Calgary, Kitt quickly emerged as the team's most promising member, winning back-to-back national championships in the super G in 1990 and 1991 and the 1991 downhill crown. He also had early success on the World Cup circuit, ranking fifteenth in the downhill in 1990 and eighteenth last year. His major goal now is to win the overall World Cup downhill championship.

Before this season, Kitt's biggest fear was never winning a World Cup race. He resolved that quickly by beating the world's best at Val d'Isere, including the current leader in the downhill, Franz Heinzer of Switzerland. One week later at Val Gardena, Kitt had the fastest time trials, then took fourth in the race, even though he lost his grip on a ski pole two-thirds of the way down. He missed third by two one-hundredths of a second. "If you can make a mistake in a World Cup race and still finish in the top five, you're doing well," he admits, pausing to glance around the room to see if his teammates are eavesdropping. In January he placed eighth at Garmisch-Partenkirchen, second at Kitzbuhel, and fifteenth in the St. Anton makeup, also held in Kitzbühel. In the Kitzbühel downhill, one of the toughest in the world, both Kitt and the winner, Heinzer, bettered the old course record. With only four downhills remaining in the World Cup season, Kitt still ranked second.

His win at Val d'Isere did more than attract fans; it earned him fifteen thousand dollars in prize money, plus an estimated sixty thousand to eighty thousand from his sponsors, who pay him extra for victories and—depending on the sponsor—finishing in the top ten or fifteen. This year his income will reach the mid-six-figure range.

Though he is not willing to boycott races that pay no prize money—as some veterans have threatened—he welcomes the cash. "We deserve it," Kitt says. "Look at tennis and golf stars. If they're winning they make a lot of money. For me the risk of injury is a lot greater than that of a golfer. How's he going to hurt himself unless he trips on a sprinkler and cracks his head? I'm going ninety miles an hour on skinny boards, down an icy hill. I may not have that long a career, so I can't wait until after the Olympics to turn professional and earn some money. I've got to get it now, when I can."

With some of his earnings he moved to Boulder, Colorado, last August, where he bought a three-bedroom condominium. He plans on taking courses at the University of Colorado. While he once wanted to study physical therapy or sports medicine, he now says he will concentrate on business. His agent is convinced that if Kitt has a respectable season, he will need a better understanding of high finance.

"A few more victories, a good result in the Olympics, and anybody who follows any type of media at all will know who A. J. Kitt is," says his agent, Jon Franklin, of the International Management Group. "When Americans win in individual sports, when they are truly world champions, they are followed in America. Take Mary Lou Retton, Chris Evert, Andre Agassi, Arnold Palmer. Those are all individual athletes who have become household names. I think the potential is there for a skier if he can go out and win. But you have to win to attract the attention of the American public, and thus to be of value to American corporations."

Kitt's coaches trot him out as representative of the "new" men's team, a hopeful emblem of a rebuilt, winning program.

It is, in fact, a program desperately in need of a winner or two. While American men have never exactly dominated ski racing, since the 1960s the ski program could be counted on to field reasonable teams and produce a handful of individual stars, people like Tom Corcoran, Billy Kidd, and Spider Sabich. But lately, even that modest level of accomplishment has seemed out of reach. The team peaked in 1982, when the men's and women's teams combined to place third in the competition for the Nations

Cup, which is awarded to the team amassing the most World Cup points over a full season. The men then won two gold medals and a silver at Sarajevo.

But after the 1984 season, the team imploded. Bill Johnson, who in 1984 became the first American man to win an Olympic downhill, won only two more international competitions. Brothers Phil and Steve Mahre, who between them won twenty-three World Cup races, retired, as did many coaches and administrators. They left behind a program in disarray: nearly broke, with little effort made to line up corporate support and virtually no grass roots training and development. As a result, the team that went to Calgary in 1988 was made up of a couple of has-beens and a bunch of nobodies, overwhelmed by injuries and marred by dissension and demoralization. No medals were won; no one even placed in the top ten.

Though the ski team had a long reputation for burning out skiers, coaches, and administrators, Calgary was truly rock bottom. Since 1988 there has been a wholesale changing of the guard: new skiers, new coaches, new morale, new conditioning techniques, and the introduction of cash prizes for World Cup winners. The members of today's Olympic team grew up racing together in this new and steadier environment, and are just beginning to make their mark on the World Cup circuit.

In the lobby of the Hotel Post in St. Anton, Austria, as the snow swirls outside, Tommy Moe, a twenty-one-year-old from Palmer, Alaska ("He can beat A. J. on a good day," says the team's downhill coach, Bill Egan), swings one leg over the arm of an overstuffed chair as he talks with the two-time national downhill champ, Jeff Olson, of Bozeman, Montana, at twenty-six one of the team's veterans. Across the room Reggie Crist, twenty-three, of Ketchum, Idaho, Todd Kelly, twenty-two, of Squaw Valley, California, Kyle Rasmussen, twenty-three, of Angels Camp, California, Joe Levins, twenty-three, of White Bear Lake, Minnesota, and Steve Porino, twenty-five, of Edwards, Colorado, sit around a table sipping coffee, soft drinks, and beer.

All are competing in their first full season of World Cup competition. (Two promising slalom specialists, Matt Grosjean, twenty-one, of Steamboat Springs, Colorado, and Jeremy Nobis, twenty-one, of Park City, Utah, are injured; Nobis will be out until next season.) After Kitt, one of the most promising skiers on the team is Paul Casey Puckett, a nineteen-year-old from Wheat Ridge, Colorado, who dominated the junior circuit last year.

What the American team lacks most is depth. "When Jeremy Nobis blows his knee out, it is devastating to us," says Dennis Agee, director of the alpine program. "An Italian of similar talent blows his knee out, he's shipped home and there are five guys immediately fighting for his spot."

Officials are hoping that a new emphasis on regional development will build that sort of depth. A computer in the ski team's Park City headquarters tracks the race results of twenty thousand young alpine skiers as well as more detailed profiles of about eight hundred elite athletes. Three regional ski teams have been established and their coaches promised job security, because keeping coaches has been as hard as keeping athletes. Since 1984 more than seventy coaches have worked on the alpine side; the team that will guide the skiers at Albertville has been together less than two years, and its coaches have relatively little international experience.

Perhaps the biggest change this season, however, is the introduction of cash prizes for top finishers in all World Cup races. This American innovation has drawn the wrath of many Europeans, who fear that skiing will go the way of tennis, where the emphasis is on individual stars rather than team accomplishments.

Howard Peterson, the president and chief executive officer of U.S. Skiing, the parent of the United States Ski Association, which administers and finances all the American ski teams, has been the driving force behind the cash prizes. In addition to moving skiing away from the sham amateurism of the past, he sees cash prizes as a way to give the sport a higher profile and to attract and keep racers.

The insistence on prize money may have earned Peterson the enmity of the Europeans and traditionalists, but it is already paying dividends. In the first World Cup race of the 1991–92 season, held in Park City, Utah, the Italian superstar, Alberto Tomba, won two races and forty-five thousand dollars: fifteen thousand for each win and a bonus of fifteen thousand for accumulating the most World Cup points over the weekend. The response of other top racers was, "If they're going to offer prize money like they did in Park City, then let's have more races in the U.S.." As Americans see it, the more races that are held in the United States, the greater visibility for the sport and the easier it will be to attract more ski racers.

These rebuilding efforts will be on display at Albertville and at the next Winter Olympics, in Lillehammer, Norway, in 1994. (To avoid having both the Winter and Summer Olympics in the same year, as they have been, the International Olympic Committee decided to move up the next Winter Olympics.) The hope is that this young group will at least do well enough to restore some respect for the program.

Will it? It isn't fair to prejudge, but the coaches' subtle shift of emphasis from Albertville to Lillehammer is a tip-off that the men's team is probably not ready for prime time. Other than Kitt there is not a consistent top ten competitor among them. Even the team's media guide is brutally frank about the chances for Olympic medals in '92: "Once a U.S. stronghold, the U.S. men will go into Albertville with few medal hopes in slalom." The book also says the American men "are a long shot, at best, in Super G."

Next Sunday, just before the Olympic downhill, try to catch a glimpse of the skiers milling around the starting gate. You will see as many as ninety racers with similar skills, physiques, and flexibility. Each will be wearing a Lycra racing suit and stepping into the latest in ski technology. Each trains virtually year round, and has the rippling muscles to prove it. They have all been racing since they were about six years old, but among them are five to ten truly great racers who know they can beat the rest.

What separates the great downhillers from the merely good, in a sport in which milliseconds separate millionaires from also-rans? The answers most often supplied by skiers and coaches are intelligence and mental preparation. The importance of mental discipline and psychological preparation becomes clear when you consider what it is like to race at speeds of ninety miles an hour.

In the days before the race, after walking the course and skiing two time trials, you will have run the race in your head dozens if not hundreds of times. Memorizing the course is crucial, since at speeds averaging seventy miles an hour there is little opportunity for adjustment, and you need every precious instant to react to the unknown and unforeseeable, primarily imperfections in the skiing surface. At the top of the mountain, before the race, you rehearse your run again and again, imagining every gate, drop, flat, and turn.

When you finally burst out of the starter shack for your one and only run, you skate hard to gain speed. No coasting, no gliding. You then drop into your tuck and within ten seconds you're making the first turn, then leaping for your life down a steep drop-off.

Officials will have watered down the course the night before with a hose, so it's as hard as a rock, which is the way you like it; an icy surface is more consistent. Nevertheless, you are always looking ahead for ruts and soft snow, which might grab your skis and upset your run, whether in subtle ways like throwing you off the ideal line or less subtle ways, like sending you crashing headlong into the hay bales that line the edge of the run.

The biggest test is your first jump. You try to avoid "taking air," because you go slower in the air than on the snow, and the longer you remain airborne, the greater the chance you will make the fatal mistake of coming out of your tuck. If that happens, ski tips come up, arms go out, you go higher and higher—and the race is lost.

Once over the jump, you go immediately back into your tuck and on to a flat. If you haven't hit the flat at maximum velocity, you will soon find your speed flagging badly—and once again, you will know you have lost the race.

Above seventy miles per hour, all you can hear is the clacking of skis on ice and the whistling of the wind in your helmet. Everything's bouncing and rattling, and you're seeing double and triple because of the constant jarring. That's when you're glad you've memorized the course. Despite all this, if you have trained properly, you are so concentrated that everything seems remarkably clear.

The ultimate disaster, of course, is a fall. At such velocities, and with the racers' ski boots virtually locked into their bindings to withstand the enormous force generated in high-speed turns, serious injury is always a possibility. For example, one promising American downhiller, Bill Hudson, who skied in the 1988 Olympics, injured his back, broke his shoulder and wrist, bruised a kidney, punctured a lung, and suffered a concussion and double vision in a training-run spill a year ago. Kitt himself was disabled part of the 1987 season with a sprained knee ligament and again, in 1988, with a broken arm.

In Kitt's eyes, the key to being a great racer is just being smart. "We're not meatheads," he says. "You have to be smart to ski downhill. There's not just one course to follow, there are no tracks. You have to know where you can let it hang out and where you have to be conservative. You have to be able to adjust in a millisecond, and you have to be in great shape."

John Atkins was the head trainer and conditioning coach from 1978 through the 1984 Olympics, then served as conditioning coach from 1987 to 1990. With Topper Hagerman, director of sports medicine from 1987 to 1990, he now runs a sports-medicine clinic in Vail, Colorado. In the last couple of years they've worked with such diverse athletes as Dan Marino, the quarterback of the Miami Dolphins, and Martina Navratilova, as well as an abundance of the world's best ski racers, including Marc Girardelli of Luxembourg, Armin Bittner of Germany, and the Mahre brothers.

"What separates the best from the also-rans is intensity, concentration, and commitment," says Atkins. "It's mental more than physical." It's more than lifting weights and constantly engaging in strenuous aerobic and anaerobic exercise, although all that is essential. To Bill Egan, the team's current conditioning coach, it's the ability to "focus" and "set goals" that distinguishes Kitt and other winners from their peers.

"People think skiers just get up in the morning, slap on the boards, and race," Kitt says in his mildly irreverent fashion. "But it's a job. Mental preparation is twenty-four hours a day."

In working with the United States team, Atkins tries to build the skiers' confidence first by making them stronger. After that, he says, "You can get them to do things they didn't think they could ever do. That transfers over into confidence." On the current team, he says, only Kitt and Grosjean have the mental attributes of champions. "As A. J. has gotten stronger, he has gotten more confident on his skis. Now he looks around at his competitors and says, 'Hey, I can beat these guys.' Most kids are not willing to pay the price to make that true commitment. Great ski racers are committed to the sport 365 days."

Atkins insists that primarily cultural reasons account for the European dominance of alpine skiing. "The Europeans see ski racing as an avenue out of their little farm town, like a kid in Harlem might see the NBA as his ticket. That gives them a mental edge over Americans, who come from a country where ski racing is not quite as accepted or rewarded." In America skiing is mostly a sport of the upper classes. The words "ski racer" are often synonymous with "ski bum," and American children have plenty of other options in life.

And Americans, by and large, just don't pay much attention to ski racing—except once every four years, when they run the Olympic downhill—condemning the sport and its stars to second-tier status. Kitt's recent success clearly illustrates the difference for European and American skiers.

In mid-January, halfway through the World Cup season, Kitt ranked second in the downhill behind veteran and Olympic favorite Franz Heinzer. No American has ever won an overall World Cup downhill championship, and Kitt is close; his performance this season is easily as remarkable as a twenty-three-year-old Swede quarterbacking a Super Bowl champion. Nevertheless, he is far better known in Europe than at home.

It will take an Olympic medal to turn Kitt into a household name here, and an Olympic medal to restore some respect in the ski program. That's a lot of pressure to put on one kid, and on one race—especially since Kitt has been loudly critical of the Olympic course. It is highly technical, full of steep drop-offs and sharp turns, better suited to super G specialists like Marc Girardelli and Kitt's teammate Tommy Moe.

And even if Kitt should win, that probably won't mean much for the team. Franklin, Kitt's agent, puts it bluntly: "A. J. is a great ski racer, like Steve and Phil Mahre were great ski racers. But I'm not sure how much credit a team can take and how much is simply the fact that they are great athletes." As one Swiss coach put it in St. Anton: "Okay, they have improved. We all see that. But as a team, where do they stand? Still near the bottom." Midway through the World Cup season, the men ranked eighth in the Nations Cup, just thirteen points ahead of Luxembourg, which has only one racer, Girardelli. "That's really lousy," admits Bill Egan. So, when Kitt skates to the starting gate next Sunday, the weight on his young, broad shoulders will be enormous. "The Olympics are a huge deal in the U.S., maybe the only time people watch skiing," admits the young athlete, rolling a glass of red wine between thick fingers. "But for skiers, it's still just one race. The difference is, if you do well on that one day, it means money, it may mean a career, it may mean a lifetime's security. So it's a catch-22. You want to take it in stride, treat it like just another race, but there is a lot of pressure."

A four-time Olympian, A.J. Kitt works with the ski program at Swain Ski Center where he began his career.

WARREN MILLER
REELS 'EM IN

Warren Miller

Outside, 1988

Dave "Hollywood" Anderson must have been doing forty miles per hour when his skis lifted off the crescent-shaped jump, sending him skying high over Vail's China Bowl. A bright morning sun glinted off the Wayfarers lodged on his movie-handsome face. Thirty of his ski patrol cohorts watched from beneath the jump they had shaped and packed the night before. The only sound in the empty valley was the fading drone of the snowmobile that had towed him, fast, to the precipice.

Hollywood cleared a nine-foot-high snowcat, parked beneath the jump, by mere inches, and dropped fifty feet into the pristine, waist-deep powder. He made three long, graceful turns and stopped. Raising his shades, he turned and looked back up the hill, his eyes searching for the man in red. Warren Miller, his movie camera tucked tightly under one arm, looked down upon the daredevil and gave him the thumbs-up. A grin as wide as the entire bowl cracked the skier's face, and a long "yeeehaah" echoed through the valley. "Am I going to be in the movie?" he shouted through cupped hands. Warren Miller, the "Godfather of Skiing," gave him a second, baptismal, thumbs-up. For Hollywood Anderson, who bought his first pair of skis after seeing a Warren Miller ski film twenty years ago, that gesture confirmed the jump as the biggest of his life.

Now it may have been Hollywood's biggest jump, Miller is saying on the way back down the mountain—and it was a good one, technically speaking—but it was hardly the most daring he's filmed. And that is because over the years Miller has coaxed skiers into jumping out of gondolas and helicopters, off seventy-degree vertical drops, and down into crevasses. Once he even talked to Jean Claude Killy into paralleling down the side of a bubbling volcano in New Zealand. But the be-all and end-all of lunatic jumps staged for Miller had to be the one by the guy who doused himself with gasoline, set himself on fire, and schussed down the hill a dozen years ago. Dangerous? Sure, admits the filmmaker. Foolish? Definitely. And all for thirty seconds of film that Miller knew would elicit whoops and hollers in auditoriums across the country.

You see, Miller has this theory that the reason people keep coming out to see his ninety-minute, vignette-packed skiologues—and they've been coming out for nearly four decades now—is because they love to watch risk. That simple four-letter word, insists Miller, is what lures people to the mountains, though many resort operators wish he'd keep his idea to himself. They'd prefer he *not* show skiers running into trees (invariably accompanied by the sound of brakes screeching and metal crunching) or sliding the length of a run on their fannies. What, Miller counters, do you think people ski for, if not risk? Below-zero weather and snow down their parkas? If they wanted to be safe and comfy, they'd go lie in the sun at Club Med. People ski, says Miller, because it adds a little danger, a little exhilaration, a sense of freedom and independence to an otherwise drab day. And if there is one thing Miller hates, it's a drab day.

It's lunchtime on the afternoon following Hollywood's jump, and the newly renovated Mid-Vail restaurant is packed with skiers. Robert Redford and Dick Bass, both in town to speak to the Young Presidents' Organization, are tucked in a corner slurping hot soup. Rose Gillett, wife of meat packer, media mogul, and Vail resort owner George Gillett, sits nearby, watching the crowd and flipping through a newspaper. At a round table in the center of the room, Miller hosts a half-dozen old friends and a CBS camera crew. The crew is spending the day with the filmmaker, shooting a segment for Dan Rather's nightly broadcast. As Miller entertains, he is approached by a handful of skiers seeking autographs on their ski gloves and down vests.

Like Redford and Bass, Miller is at Vail to address the YPO (a not-so-casual group of young millionaires), and also to scout out locations for a promotional film he's making at the request of his good friend George Gillett. This day, Miller doesn't look like he belongs with the monied crowd. He looks more like a ski bum in his worn, mustard-stained ski sweater, suit pants over cotton long johns, two pairs of navy socks, and a pair of shiny black brogues. Despite the fact that he has more than four hundred films under his belt, a production company that keeps seventeen employees scurrying from project to project year-round, and annual grosses in the neighborhood of $3.5 million, the Godfather of Skiing is renowned for his tight way with a dollar. To save money on airfare, he drove to Vail from his California home in his beat-up Ford van with a plywood bed in the back.

He mentioned that one of his idols, author John D. MacDonald, passed away a couple of weeks earlier. Like the writer, Miller is saying, he likes to use his profession as a forum for his own opinions on a world spinning slightly off center. Whereas MacDonald used his eighty-plus books, including the best-selling Travis McGee series, to rail against the drug smugglers, the crooked politicians, and the developers that swarmed his adopted home state of Florida, Miller loves to gently chide greedy resort operators and unskilled hotdogging skiers. This comparison might seem a bit far-fetched to other MacDonald fans, but it's hard to argue with Warren Miller.

Miller is a big guy, bald and jowly and leather-skinned. His legs aren't what they used to be, and it's getting tough for him to lug that fifty-pound pack crammed with camera gear up and down the mountains. But at sixty-three, he still skis faster, windsurfs longer, and sails better than most men half his age. He is a confirmed ski bum, has been since that day back in 1937 when he traded two dollars and a pair of roller skates for a pair of Northland pine skis at a Hollywood, California, garage sale. Significantly, four years earlier, he paid thirty-five cents for his first camera.

Miller shot his first ski film, *Deep and Light*, at Squaw Valley, California, in 1949. Over the past thirty-nine years he's outlasted dozens of competitors and has established his Hermosa Beach production company as a premier sports filmmaking outfit. For most of that time the staunchly independent filmmaker ran a paternal, one-man shop. He picked the twenty to thirty sites he and his crews would film each year, did the bulk of the shooting, wrote and narrated each film, chose the needle-drop music, sold advertising for the accompanying programs, and in his spare time hustled short movie projects for resorts and corporations. Between October and December he would hand-deliver the featured ski film to one hundred auditoriums around the country. The fringe benefit was that he was skiing or sailing or windsurfing almost every day of the year.

In 1984, Miller was introduced to California's most successful rock concert promoter, Terry Bassett. Within two weeks they were partners. The combination of Bassett's management and promotional expertise and Miller's creativity and ski industry connections has since turned Warren Miller Enterprises into a gold mine. Miller's 1986 film, *Beyond the Edge*, was seen by 500,000 theatergoers, and is now available on videocassette. In 1987 he appeared on the morning talk shows, the *CBS Evening News*, *The Late Show* (where he shared a couch with Pee Wee Herman), and *Lifestyles of the Rich and Famous*. He keeps a powerboat in the San Juan Islands, a Hobie 33 in California, and owns three windsurfers and a dozen sails. He skis ninety days a year. Last season, tired of motel rooms, he bought his first ski house, at Vail. He's constantly telling his audiences and friends that he has "the best job in the world."

Indeed, Warren Miller, who refers to his films as "the jockstraps of Walt Disney movies," is finally hot. "There's an old showbiz cliché: 'You've got to work hard all your life to become an overnight success.' I haven't worked all my life, yet, but I think we've turned the corner on success."

The beginning of that road to success was hardly auspicious. Miller was raised in Hollywood, the youngest of three, in a home where he quickly learned about independence. "I don't think I ever had a full paragraph of advice from my father and only one or two from my mother," he remembers. He sold magazines when he was nine, got his first paper route when he was eleven.

Remember that thirty-five-cent camera? He would take it on Boy Scout trips and organize showings of his pictures when he came home. Even as a kid during the Depression, spurred by a bunch of James A. Fitzpatrick's travelogues—popular documentaries that featured a different country or city each month—Miller dreamed of someday producing films. He attended the University of Southern California for a couple of years, quit to join the Navy, and found himself on a submarine-chaser in the Pacific. When he got out of the service in 1945, he paid a hundred dollars for an 8 mm movie camera and started filming California surfers.

By the winter of that same year, Miller had discovered a way to combine his passions for sports and filmmaking. He started showing his amateurishly edited surfing movies to small crowds at Sun Valley, where he was becoming a regular, and established a pattern that would last a lifetime: surf in the summer, ski in the winter, film year-round, and live the best he could by his wits. During his second season at Sun Valley, he and a surfing buddy, Ward Baker, lived in a tiny trailer home in the parking lot. Miller earned a season pass by painting a mural in the employee's cafeteria, and the pair got by on rabbits they shot, and oyster crackers with catsup. An aspiring cartoonist as well, Miller painted caricatures on cocktail glasses and sold them at the resort. He'd visit the local hospital and draw cartoons on the newly injured's casts in return for his and Baker's dinners. "In those days you could rent a room for a dollar a day," he remembers, "but we didn't even want to spend that. We wanted the freedom of getting up in the morning, thawing out the milk, cooking oatmeal, and skiing our brains out until the lifts closed. I didn't want to work, not even at night, because then I'd be too tired to ski the next day." By 1947, Miller had become an instructor at the resort and no longer had to sneak onto the lifts. But he was still in a hurry not to grow up.

Then, in the spring of 1949, he got some unexpected help in deciding his career. He had given ski lessons to a couple of guys one day, and that night had accompanied them to a party where somebody showed a film supposedly about Sun Valley. "But the whole movie was about getting from Calgary to Sun Valley," Miller recalls, "and by the time they got there, they'd run out of film." Riding home later, Miller criticized the film and talked about his desire to get into the travel/lecture business. His new friends asked why he wasn't doing it already. "Well," he explained, "I make $125 a month and the camera I need costs $227." It turned out the pair worked at Bell & Howell in Chicago, and the next day Hal Geneen (who later became CEO of the corporate giant ITT) arranged for a 16 mm camera to be delivered to Miller. Charles Percy (who went on to become president of Bell & Howell and a U.S. senator) invoiced him. It took Miller two years to pay for the camera, but he knew exactly what to do with it.

So began thirty-nine years of annual films that still serve as an indication that ski season is about to begin. Miller Time. The music for his first effort was played by the organist of a Hollywood church. The two would sneak into the church, where he'd set up the projector, and she'd make up some music to go with the action. Armed with prints of the finished film, Miller would hop in his car and drive around showing them at ski clubs and resorts. He'd charge the clubs a hundred dollars or 40 percent of the gate, whichever was higher. The local sponsor would rent a high school gym for twenty-five dollars and spend twenty-five dollars on announcements; Miller would provide the posters that went up in the ski shops.

But where was the profit? "Say eight hundred people showed up at a buck a head," says Miller. "That's $320 in one night for me. The ski club got $480 and was ecstatic." The Cascade Ski Club in Portland, Oregon, was so happy with the setup that it has sponsored every one of Miller's annual films. The club made seventy-five dollars on his first movie; Miller took home thirty dollars, and drove round-trip from Los Angeles to show it. Today the club shows the newest film for three days at a local auditorium, and fifteen thousand people attend. Ski retailers who want to set up exhibition booths in the auditorium lobby face a three-year waiting list. "The concept hasn't changed much," says Miller, "except that now the split is 50/50."

But it hasn't all been so simple. When Miller was at work on his second film, he fell in love, got married, and he and his wife had a child. In the fall of 1953 he was exhibiting that film at resorts and starting to film the third when his wife complained of a backache. It was diagnosed as cancer and she died six months later, leaving Miller to raise their one-and-a half-year-old son. To make ends meet, Miller worked as a carpenter during the day in Torrance, California, and assembled that third film at night. "But I never thought about quitting," he insists. He hung in through the fifties and sixties, and slowly built a reputation for his honesty, humor, reliability, and slope smarts. He lurched through the seventies besieged by financial headaches, but his business and celebrity grew. He claims he's gone broke four or five times during his career. He's put three kids through college, paid for one very expensive divorce in 1973, and rebounded into another marriage that ended quickly. Sometimes he wonders why he's stuck it out. "I know why, though," he reminds himself. "When you're hanging out that helicopter door, shooting a skier at top form, it's the same exhilaration an athlete gets. That's why I've always hung in there, just for that feeling."

Miller's filmmaking formula hasn't changed much over the years. His detractors say it hasn't changed a whit, which they claim makes his movies tedious and repetitive. "Hey, Bob Hope didn't say, 'Oh, God, we've got to do *Othello* this year because we've done this same old road show a thousand times,' " counters Miller's production manager, Don Brolin, who has worked with him for twenty-three years. Evidently, the two men live by the "if it ain't broke, don't fix it" school of filmmaking.

Each year, Miller and Brolin map out an elaborate strategy. They contact the resorts they want to visit, then plot a hectic schedule for the half-dozen cameramen they dispatch around the world. Miller's first film cost less than five hundred dollars; 1988's *White Winter Heat* came in just under a million dollars. Each features the same four elements of razzle-dazzle excitement; heart-tugging sentiment evoked by, say, a blind skier or a child overcoming multiple sclerosis; a celebrity (recent films have included Martina Navratilova, Dr. Ruth, and Robert Redford); and Miller's own warped dumb-funny sense of humor. Whether it's people falling off chairlifts, skiing into ponds, or plowing into snowdrifts, the humor is sticky glue that holds the films together. All are narrated by Miller and star his, er, wit. ("While I was watching the races somebody stole my wife's credit cards. I haven't reported it, though, because (the thief is) spending less than she did." "You know why jumpers wear helmets? To keep the stitches from their lobotomies in place." "If God had believed in permissiveness, He would have given us the Ten Suggestions.")

Miller often compares the success of his films to that of X-rated movies. "It's like showing a porno flick on an aircraft carrier when you're still three weeks of out of port," he says. "People just go bonkers." A few critics have even dubbed him the Russ Meyer of skiing, and some take it a step further. "His stuff is a lot like porn," says one Los Angeles filmmaker. "You'd rather be doing it than watching it." An editor chimes in "Yeah, and after fifteen minutes of either, you've seen it all."

Technically, Miller's films are superb, the cinematography seldom matched in sports films. But the mountains are the real stars; most of the skiers work anonymously and for free. ("How much do you pay a guy to jump off a cliff?" poses Don Brolin.) The combination of a rock music track and a heady dose of high-energy risk skiing guarantees that viewers will come to their feet, whether they're skinheads in untied high-tops or monied young Republicans. For ninety minutes, Miller takes them all to the mountains. "That's why we keep the audiences year after year," says Brolin. "It may not snow this year, you may not get the big raise so you can afford the condo at Mammoth, but you know come fall, at your favorite auditorium, you can go see Warren's film. He's more dependable than snow."

WILDEBEEST IN A RAINSTORM

Warren Miller Enterprises lies behind a nondescript gray storefront wedged between a coin-operated laundry and a dentist's office on the main drag of sleepy Hermosa Beach. On the street corners old codgers in red vests direct traffic with handheld signs. The ocean is a few blocks away, and smoggy L.A. is a full forty-five minutes to the north. Miller's facility is being renovated to accommodate a growing staff, a larger screening room, and burgeoning videotape and film libraries. The walls of his wood-paneled office are crammed with plaques, awards, and trophies from film societies, ski resorts, and races. Two pairs of old wooden skis stand in one corner, a gumball machine in another. On his desk a simple reminder is taped to a penholder: WARREN MILLER IS A LUCKY MAN.

Terry Bassett is sitting at a round table in a corner of the office. Dressed mostly by Armani, he looks like the millionaire he is. Tanned, carefully coiffed, all California cool. He started in the concert-promotion business with the Beatles, Jimi Hendrix, and Cream (in the late sixties he took Hendrix to Birmingham, Alabama, where folks had never seen whites and blacks onstage together), and went on to promote Elvis, Neil Diamond, and Paul McCartney. He doesn't like to ski; too cold, he says. But when his son took him to see one of Miller's films in Santa Monica, he saw gold and quickly set out to mine some. Two weeks after they met, Miller and Bassett struck up a 50/50 partnership. "He was one guy trying to do it all," says Bassett. "He'd oversee the tickets, the promotion, the movie, the filming, the planning. It was physically impossible to do it all. So he gave us the opportunity and we never looked back. To me, it's as exciting as doing Neil Diamond in concert. This is a sixty-some-year-old guy who is a phenomenon."

Bassett, who promotes 250 concerts a year and operates the Irvine Meadows Amphitheater, has brought a flare for show biz to Miller's homegrown operation. "We want people to think, 'This is not a movie, this is an event,'" he says. Over the past three years, Bassett has applied that "events" strategy by pulling Miller's films from high school auditoriums and booking them at ballrooms and convention centers. He then contacts resorts, manufacturers, and ski shops to set up booths in the lobbies. The film is shown five or six times over a weekend for eight to ten dollars a head per show.

Since Bassett has come on the scene, Miller's company has expanded to work all the angles. There are the hundred events each fall, about 150 additional one-night stands, plus two hundred showings in Canada, Germany, Austria, New Zealand, Australia, Spain, and Great Britain. While marketing the current film is still the biggest job, there are plenty of other profit centers. The company rents short sport films to resorts to show over closed-cable networks, and leases them to bars and restaurants; sells stock footage of skiers, windsurfers, and sailors to other production companies; sells foreign distribution rights; and charges a few manufacturers and resorts for the privilege of being included in the annual film. But the most profitable vein tapped by the new team is videotape. The company claims it sells a hundred tapes a day through a toll-free number. In the last two years, Lorimar, the mammoth videotape distribution company, has sold more than fifty thousand tapes of Miller's old ski, sailing, windsurfing, and off-road racing movies. An instructional tape, "Learn to Ski Better," has been lodged on the *Billboard* charts for months. The company also publishes two ski magazines, *First Tracks* and *Ski World*—with combined circulations of 800,000—which are distributed free at resorts and retail shops. Last year it produced promotional sports films for Nissan (featuring Paul Newman), New Zealand, and Quebec.

Comptroller Gary Goldman says the revitalized company is "the greatest avenue to the ski industry marching down one side of the aisle and us down the other. We've become the catalyst of the industry." For the first time, this year's film boasts two major corporate sponsors, Audi of America and American Airlines. And last but not least, the company has half of a first annual beach film in the can, and reports that as of next summer two Warren Miller movies will be making the rounds each year. Since Miller and Bassett have joined forces, the company's annual gross has mushroomed 300 percent. "It's a love affair," says Bassett. "That guy sure knows how to make money," says Miller.

When Miller first got into the ski-film business, there were only twelve chairlifts in the country. Since then he's witnessed the introduction of metal skis, snowmakers, and snow compactors. He's also been roundly rewarded for his efforts. Last month he became the eighth member of the Ski Business Hall of Fame. He's already a member of the National Ski Hall of Fame and has been honored by sports-film societies around the globe. But more importantly, he has become a kind of pipeline of information. "I've been milling around this industry for over forty years," he says, "just making movies, not competing with any of the resorts. So inevitably, I'll go skiing somewhere and end up with some of the investors or the owner of the resort. I've become a kind of 'Father Confessor' figure. I have all this inside, privileged information and everybody wants to know what everybody else is doing." Someday, he says, he may try to sell his services as a consultant. Don Brolin, who has been to every resort in the world that Miller hasn't, confirms his friend's business acumen. "We were together at Copper Mountain the first year it opened and they were showing us around the cafeteria. That was decades ago. They asked Warren, 'What do you think?' 'It's a neat cafeteria,' he told them, 'but what you guys need is a nonsmoking section.' Nobody had ever heard of such a thing. Now they're everywhere."

In a currently flat industry, where the number of ski resorts has dropped from 882 in 1979 to 650 in 1987, Miller's films and opinions do carry some weight. (A couple of years ago he praised a certain British Columbia helicopter service in his film and today it's so busy he can't get a seat with it.) But resort owners are mixed about the effects. Some don't like Miller's "tell it like it is" approach to the risk and expense of the sport and worry that the films scare off, rather than attract, potential customers. Others, such as George Gillett, who snapped up Vail for $125 million two years ago, see Miller as the king of the skiing business. "If somebody takes offense to someone who tells them the truth about the business, it means they're not paying enough attention to the industry," Gillett insists. "I think a lot of people in the industry don't understand Warren, or the tremendous affection and following of his constituents. He has a better feel for the pulse of the American skiers, what they're interested in, what their problems are, than anyone I've ever met."

Jack Brendlinger, who ran the Aspen Ski Corporation's marketing department for ten years, concedes that Miller is enjoying phenomenal popularity, but voices a concern other resort operators only hint at. Aspen, for example, hasn't been in a Warren Miller film for more than a dozen years. Why? Because the resort refuses to pay the $5,000 to $10,000 fee that Miller demands, says Brendlinger. Brolin sidesteps this issue, but admits that most smaller resorts do foot the bill for filming on their slopes. "With that in mind," says Brendlinger, "the films have pure advertising, pure promotion." Bassett ignores such criticisms. "Warren makes people laugh and gives them some excitement, two of the elements there aren't enough of in this world. That's really what matters."

"I don't care what his critics say," adds Brolin. "Warren Miller is an incredibly successful guy, and his influence on the industry has been nothing but good. He's worked hard all his life. People don't realize how much security you have to sacrifice if you're going to play all your life. It's easy to do when you're a postgrad for a year or two; it's almost expected. But it's not expected when you're thirty, forty, fifty, sixty. And to be a success and play that hard is very difficult. A lot of people are just jealous of Warren's lifestyle . . . and his success."

It's noon on a drab day in Manhattan and this time Warren Miller looks like a million bucks. He's wearing a nice tan and an expensive suit, and it's ensconced in a gray-and-burgundy hotel suite. He is ebullient, despite that fact that he's been up since 5:30 a.m. plotting production schedules for next year's film. He has come to the city to premiere his new film.

"A lot of people ask me, 'How do you get successful?'" he says over orange juice. "I always tell them the same thing. Buy three alarm clocks. Set one for 4:30 and put it near the bed. Set the second for 4:45 and put it in the bathroom, with the light on. Set the third for five and put it in the shower. With luck your workday should be done by ten at night. Follow that recipe a minimum of five days a week, and if you really want to get ahead do it seven. Theoretically the world works forty hours a week. If you work sixty, within two weeks you're a week ahead of your friends."

The Godfather of Skiing, the king of ski bums, pauses and fingers a bran muffin. He may have the best job in the world, but he still has some unfinished business. "You know," he says, "all this success is a relative thing. I may have made some money, won some awards, but I still can't do a decent duck jibe on a windsurfer."

Warren Miller Entertainment, based in Boulder, continues to pump out ski and adventure films; Warren Miller sold the company in the late 1980s and it is currently owned by Time Inc. Miller, 84, lives in Seattle with his wife, Laurie.

HAPPINESS IS BEING SINGLE

Jake Burton Carpenter

Outside, 1988

The skies are blue and still, the mountains white and crowded, the parking lots full and muddy. Just another perfect late-winter Saturday here at Stratton Mountain in Vermont. But there seems to be an exorbitant mount of commotion on the slopes, and an excess of snowboarders this day. Midway up Tinks Link trail, a thousand people have congregated along the sides of a quarter-mile-long half-pipe that has been bulldozed out of the snow.

After shaking the mud off my boots and trudging up the slope, I introduce myself to a handful of the professional snowboarders who are all the object of all this attention. They have come to the Green Mountains from nearby towns and as far away as France and West Germany to compete in snowboarding's U.S. Open. The first competitor I say hello to, young and handsome, gives me a fold-out, four-color business card. (PROFESSIONAL SNOWBOARDER, it reads.) The second, dark eyes hidden behind recently dyed matte-black bangs, gives me the finger. The third, a former elementary school teacher from Queens, wears feathers in her hair, fringed chaps, and a bikini top, and wonders if I want to party later. The tone for the day, and maybe for the whole youthful and restless snowboarding industry, is summed up in those few quick encounters: the Good, the Rad, the Flaky.

From a rickety wooden shack at the base of the half-pipe, beneath a temporary judging stand, emanates the raucous blathering of the event's announcer. His running commentary can at times barely be heard over the rock and roll shaking from a half-dozen slopeside speakers. The sides of the half-pipe are rimmed with competitors and wannabes—punks, skinheads, teen queens, suburban jokesters, and even some moms and dads. Snowball fights break out at the first hint of calm.

The riders swoosh down the half pipe, carving from side to side, up and down the ten-foot walls of snow. This is the third of four World Cup events (the first two were in Zürs, Austria, and Bormio, Italy; the last will follow in two weeks at Breckenridge), and today is the third of four days of competition. Individual championships have already been awarded in the moguls and slalom. Tomorrow is the downhill. Despite the laidback feel of this sunshiny day, all the swooshing and careening is done with serious intent. There is a total of twenty-five thousand dollars on the line, and the week's overall winners, man and woman, will each take home a Suzuki Samurai, plus bonuses from their sponsors.

The announcer tries to do justice to the riders' stunts as they slide through the half-pipe. "Whooa!!! Heeere's Bert, folks. Bert LaMar. Watch for his patented look-back-lay-back. Hey, great outside air . . . somebody check the radar screens. There he goes . . . a hand plant to wind up a superb run . . . let's hear it for the reigning half-pipe champ, Bert LaMar; this guy's been ripping it up!"

The announcer segues into yet another bravo for the event's sponsors—Burton Snowboards and Suzuki—as he traces the second run of Shaun Palmer, of the matte-black dye-job. The nineteen-year-old bad boy finishes a "super" run, and, after spraying the judging stand with wet snow, turns to the half-pipe, sneers, and gives it the finger. The crowd roars. "What a finish," screams the announcer. "What a far-out, flipped-out finish!"

The state of the snowboarding industry looks good from where Jake Burton Carpenter stands, just in front of the announcer's shack. A golden retriever at his side, Jake shades his eyes and looks up the hill, gazing at the success, and future, of the sport he helped wrought. Many of today's top racers are riding his Burton boards and wearing his team's colors. He started this event six years ago, calling it the national championships. On this very hill, in fact, he tested the boards that were to become the standard for the sport.

In 1977, at age twenty-three, the Long Island native moved to Stratton to make the perfect snowboard. That winter he turned out a hundred experimental models. He layered and glued thin plywood sheets together, hung paint cans off their tips to curve them. He experimented with ash and fiberglass. He visited a surfboard maker in California, ending up, for a time, with snowboards shaped like blimps. He spent a winter in Austria testing a handful of his experimental boards. That first season, the winter of 1979–80, he sold only three hundred boards. Today Burton Snowboards operates out of a sixteen-thousand-foot warehouse in Manchester Center, Vermont, and runs a second plant in Innsbruck, Austria. Burton has produced more than 60 percent of the 250,000 snowboards sold worldwide in the past decade. Last year, the company moved into clothing and accessories, and grossed close to $10 million.

The lift lines at Stratton this day exhibit sure signs of success: there's a snowboarder for nearly every skier. Across the country, ask the people who sell snowboards or allow snowboarders to shred their mountains, and they'll tell you business has tripled, quadrupled, or some-such-multiplied in the past couple years. "Fad" is no longer a word used to describe the sport. From the giveaway Suzukis at the base of the hill to the multitude of sponsors' logos emblazoned on the uniforms of these pro riders, indications are that the sport is here to stay. And Jake Burton is far from alone in angling for all those snowboarding bucks. Sims, his West Coast-based chief competitor (headed by skateboard impresario Tom Sims), is heavily represented at the Stratton races. So are companies as small as Hooger Booger, Gnu, and Avalanche, and as big as K2 and Rossignol. In fact, R&D men from several of the big companies are here today, talking to riders and assessing the future.

Arguments against snowboarding—focusing on safety concerns, not to mention the hot-dogging image—have finally caved in to the sport's growing popularity. Early problems with the cautious mountain managers and wary skiers are almost things of the past. Although the median age of a snowboarder is still in the teens, the number of thirty-year-olds buying boards is increasing. The skateboarders and surfers who came to snowboarding early have been joined by a broad range of experimenters, from preteens to yuppies, demographically rounding out the audience in a way that sits well with event sponsors. More than three-quarters of the ski resorts in America, many facing an otherwise stagnant business, now welcome snowboarders with open arms—especially the thirty bucks they plunk down for a lift ticket. This season, for the first time, the Professional Ski Instructors of America will take responsibility for teaching the tens of thousands of new boarders coming into the sport each year. And in the glide-oriented countries of Western Europe, the sport is growing even faster.

The mood at the Stratton event is festive, if a little unsteady, the way common to new events operating more on adrenaline than on experience. The truth is, behind the scenes, things are reeling. During the first two days of competition, there have been protests, delays, bad calls, and near fist-fights. Too many contestants, too many inexperienced judges, and too many new rules are confusing organizers and racers alike. One day the French contingency is said to be ready to walk, the next it's all the Europeans. The men's overall leader, Craig Kelly, is threatening a lawsuit and/or physical violence over a particularly bad call in the mogul event. None of which, of course, is known by the crowd, nor should they care. They've come to watch these guys grab air, jar through four-foot moguls, and tear down the hill at sixty miles an hour.

At a cheese-dip-and-booze schmooze following day three of the Open, the organizers wrangle most of the top riders into presenting themselves for the gathered press (which isn't as sizable a group as had been expected). In one corner sits a gaggle of Sims riders—Eveline Wirth, twenty-nine, from Switzerland, and Petra Müssig, twenty-three, from Orange County, California. The two women are vying for the overall World Cup championship and LaMar, who is wearing almost a dozen Swatch watches (guess who his other sponsor is?), is the defending World Cup half-pipe champ. Across the room, Amy Howat of Bellingham, Washington, talks with her chaperone/sister. Only fifteen, Howat is sponsored by Gnu and is hot on the tail of Wirth and Müssig. Burton's team is represented by Kerri Hannon, twenty-six, a former champion in the moguls; Jean Nerva, twenty-nine, from France; American Mike Jacoby, eighteen; and Andy Coghlan, twenty-five, one of Jake Burton's early board testers and a former national champ. Laurie Asperas, twenty-five, the former Queens schoolteacher, who rides for Burton and is best known on the tour for her eclectic on-mountain attire—from full-length furs to bikinis—is telling anyone who will listen that snowboarding "saved my peace of mind."

They munch on meatballs, drink free beers, and look slightly uncomfortable away from the snow. But press gatherings are the sort of inconveniences a rider can put up with. For the first time, the best riders are paying the rent with their snowboarding winnings. Most are off to Europe soon, where they will spend the summer teaching at snowboarding camps on the glaciers of eastern France. Although just eighty thousand dollars in prize money was awarded last season, that figure is expected to double this year when the World Cup is expanded to five races, with a finale in Avoriaz, France. The combination of salaries, prize money (the individual winners at Stratton got fifteen hundred dollars per event), matched winnings from sponsors, and new sponsors crawling out of the woodwork makes the future look bright. Peter Bauer, a handsome, ponytailed West German, enters the room wearing a white turtleneck, black jeans, and loafers. (It is his four-color business card I have in my pocket.) He is not in the best mood, even though he looks to have a shot at the overall World Cup title. He has circulated a petition over the past couple of days seeking to disallow a ruling in the moguls that cost him valuable points to Craig Kelly. Despite his threats of walking out on the tour if he doesn't get some kind of satisfaction, he is polite and soft-spoken. (His appeal would not be recognized, and the call would effectively cost him the World Cup title to Craig Kelly. Kelly himself is at the center of yet another controversy: Before last season he walked out on his contract with Sims for a better offer from Burton. Sims sued, and while the matter is in the courts, he must ride an unmarked snowboard.)

Ask these boarders why they have devoted themselves to the sport, and there seems to be one simple answer: skiing got boring. Even many ski patrolmen, often the most traditional skiers on the mountains, agree that once you've tried a snowboard, and gotten over the initial out-of-control feeling, it's hard to go back to two skis. More than one of the pros said they gave up skiing simply because "it sucked."

That sentiment is repeated often at Stratton, in varying degrees of articulateness, as is a scene involving noncompetitors: dad and son (or daughter) arriving at the foot of the hill, the old man with two slats on his shoulder, his kid with a board nearly as big as he is hugged under his arm. And despite the number of older people coming to the sport, it is snowboarding's very youthfulness that is propelling the industry. It's hot, it's cool, it's sexy. It has the same old draw as surfing, skateboarding, and sailboarding—it's a challenge, something to experiment with and master. Something parents don't understand.

Bauer, twenty, grew up thirty miles south of Munich and has skied since the age of three. Two years ago he tried a borrowed snowboard, a Burton Cruiser, and "went totally bonkers. "I love skiing," he says, "but after a while, it just sucked. It was always the same. Very boring." Last year was his first full season of competition, and he won the German and European championships and finished third in the Worlds. Like most of the Europeans, he grew up on skis, and because of that he excels at the downhill and slalom. (The Americans, many of whom come from skateboarding backgrounds, dominate the moguls and half-pipe.)

Last year, Burton paid Bauer's travel expenses, matched his winnings, and threw in occasional bonuses. He hopes to get a small salary this season. Bauer also represents Scott goggles, Raichle Snowboard boots (which sell for $350 a pair), and Windsurfing Hawaii clothes. "I am used to winning," the German says, "and when I got fourth in the slalom, I was really pissed off. But I hate all this protesting; it's so American. In Europe everything's much freer, much cooler. Here it seems like such a business. "

Bert LaMar stands off to one side, eavesdropping. Two clip-on Swatch watches pinned to his label, LaMar is representative of the kind of entrepreneurial boardheads who dominate this pro circuit. Since picking up the sport just a year before, and winning the World Championship half-pipe competition three months after first riding a snowboard, LaMar has become one of the most visible, and best paid, snowboarders on the tour. Part of that success comes from his background in skateboarding, a sport he dominated in his early teens. Ironically, although he has switched sports, his major sponsor has stayed the same—Sims.

"I dropped out of skateboarding when I was sixteen," LaMar says. "It was getting to be a real hard-core scene—I was going to clubs, seeing Black Flag, there were drugs everywhere. I just didn't see a future in it, for making money or a career. So I quit and went to beauty school."

He was working as an LA hairdresser when he first tried a snowboard (although he remembers fooling around with a plastic Sims prototype, in the early eighties, and being convinced it would never catch on.) After trying a new model in January 1987, he became hooked, and began driving four hours round-trip each day to Big Bear or Snow Summit to board. Two months later he entered the World Championships at Breckenridge. Sims gave him a board, but he paid his own airfare. "I went straight for the half-pipe, where I could apply my skateboard-type maneuvers," he remembers with a laugh. "I beat everyone, including the guys who had been winning the event for years—Craig Kelly, Terry Kidwell, and Shaun Palmer. Everyone else was at least a year behind us."

Since then LaMar has helped organize events in Europe and the United States, has taught "Bert LaMar" courses in France, and is pushing Sims for his own model. He hints that his take from snowboarding next year will approach six figures. "At least at first, I was really worried that snowboarding would go the same route as skateboarding—guys cussing and throwing boards, riding with skulls on their hats, that kind of stuff," he says. "But that image doesn't help the sport—I mean, throwing your board at a skier when he cuts you off isn't going to endear you to the guys who run the mountains."

LaMar differs with those Europeans who accuse Americans of protesting too much. "Bullshit," he says. "It's the Europeans who seem to get so upset. I think they take all this a little more seriously than we do. I mean, when we raced in Europe, it was like first you were racing against Peter Bauer, and second against a German. It was like the Olympics or something." He also takes mild offense when I show him Bauer's four-color business card. "Yeah," sneers the model-handsome LaMar, "well, I've got a six-color card."

The competition resumes bright and early the next day, and so does the controversy. The final event is the downhill, and although the North American Snowboard Association rules call for ten gates, this course has only five. It is also only two-thirds the required length. The result is a short, frighteningly fast course. To top things off, at the last minute the running order for the men and women is switched, and several of the women must hustle to the top of the mountain to warm up. At the bottom of the hill, a group of European riders threatens to skip the upcoming Breckenridge races if the organization doesn't improve.

I stand behind a snow fence and watch as the racers, in Lycra suites and crash helmets, blaze down the mountain at sixty miles an hour. The wailings of the same hippy-dippy announcer become more reserved as the first couple of boarders crash at the bottom and tumble head-over-heels into the fence.

Snowboarding competitions are a cross between skateboarding and skiing. The slalom and downhill are races against the clock—the former through breakaway gates, the latter straight shots, such as the one in front of me this morning, down hard-packed slopes. But it is the freestyle events that draw the biggest crowds at Stratton. The mogul hill—riddled with knee- and chest-deep humps—demands the same flexibility, rhythm, and balance as freestyle skiing. As in the half-pipe, the winners are crowned by a panel of judges. And the pipe remains the most subjective of the competitions, with judges comparing the fakes, method airs, rocket airs, lean airs, and hand plants racer by racer. New tricks are dreamed up every week;

style is as important as skill. And it is in these subjective events that the competitors are getting worked up about this weekend, because a new sport draws relatively inexperienced judges, too. So far, most of the racers do reasonably well in each of the four competitions. But as more and more competitors join the ranks, their ability to excel in all four will dwindle, and racers will begin to specialize.

LaMar, dressed in white, helmet under his arm, comes over after his second run. "This is not my favorite race," he admits. But he hadn't appeared to be skittering out of control any more than the rest, though the jump just prior to the timing gate—taken at more than sixty-three miles an hour—had left him obviously shaken. The winner of the men's race is Andy Coghlan, a three-time overall U.S. Open Champ.

LaMar checks the time on one of his three wristwatches and leads the way into the lodge, where he will pick up a crystal bowl for winning the half-pipe. Craig Kelly and Petra Müssig will collect keys to new Suzukis. The event's sponsors are all smiles. Jim Driver, national advertising manager for Suzuki, accepts thanks from Kelly, then steps to the side of the raucous crowd and explains his company's season-long sponsorship to me. "Anybody can sponsor a ski team," he says, "but that's pretty boring, isn't it? Snowboarding is hot, new fun—and the kids are coming to it like flies to shit."

Jake Burton Carpenter dispenses the crystal trophies. Outside the window swirl hordes of snowboarders. While the pros accept their awards, the half-pipe is filled with enthusiastic kids imitating their moves. Burton stares out the window, and his grin is broad enough to erase the little squabbles that dogged his event.

Shaun Palmer, of the matte-black mop, finished out of the top three in all four events. Still, seated in the center of the lodge, a rack of empty beer bottles in front of him, he remains a crowd favorite. Responding to a rising cry of "Shaun, Shaun, Shaun," he stands—and gives his fans the finger. They love it.

Postscript: Two months later, at a crowded Swatch promotional party in midtown Manhattan, I run into LaMar, recently returned from France. He takes my arm and leads me to a corner of the room. "You've gotta see this, man, gotta see this." Reaching into his billfold, he pulls out his *new* business card. It's made of metal. "Can you believe it?" he wonders. I ask if I can keep it. "Oh, no," he says, shouting to be heard above the band. "They're too expensive to just give away."

Jake Burton Carpenter, 54, continues to run the Burton Company, now one of the world's largest snowboard and snowboard-equipment manufacturers with annual sales of $40 million.

JON BOWERMASTER

Writer and filmmaker Jon Bowermaster is a six-time grantee of the National Geographic Expeditions Council. His recent 'Antarctica 2008' was the final expedition in his OCEANS 8 project that over the past decade has taken him and his teams around the world by sea kayak, including expeditions to the Aleutian Islands, Vietnam, French Polynesia, Chile/ Argentina/Bolivia, Gabon, Croatia, Tasmania, and Antarctica. Seeing the world from sea-level over the past decade has given Bowermaster a one-of-a-kind look at both the health of the world's oceans and the lives of the nearly three billion people around the globe who depend on them.

During the past twenty years Bowermaster has written for a variety of national and international publications about the state of the world's environmental health, its most remote corners, and most intriguing conservationists and adventurers. Author of nine books and producer of a dozen documentary films, he lives in Stone Ridge, New York. Check out daily dispatches from sea level at www.jonbowermaster.com.

DEAR CUSTOMERS AND FRIENDS,

SUPPORTING YOUR INTEREST IN OUTDOOR ADVENTURE, travel, and an active lifestyle is central to our operations, from the authors we choose to the locations we detail to the way we design our books. Menasha Ridge Press was incorporated in 1982 by a group of veteran outdoorsmen and professional outfitters. For more than 25 years now, we've specialized in creating books that benefit the outdoors enthusiast.

Almost immediately, Menasha Ridge Press earned a reputation for revolutionizing outdoors- and travel-guidebook publishing. For such activities as canoeing, kayaking, hiking, backpacking, and mountain biking, we established new standards of quality that transformed the whole genre, resulting in outdoor-recreation guides of great sophistication and solid content. Menasha Ridge continues to be outdoor publishing's greatest innovator.

The folks at Menasha Ridge Press are as at home on a white-water river or mountain trail as they are editing a manuscript. The books we build for you are the best they can be, because we're responding to your needs. Plus, we use and depend on them ourselves.

We look forward to seeing you on the river or the trail. If you'd like to contact us directly, join in at www.trekalong.com or visit us at www.menasharidge.com. We thank you for your interest in our books and the natural world around us all.

SAFE TRAVELS,

Bob Sehlinger

BOB SEHLINGER
PUBLISHER